Mike
SCAPEROTIA

·THE·
SHORT
PROSE
READER

·THE·
SHORT
PROSE
READER

THIRD
EDITION

Gilbert H. Muller
Harvey S. Wiener

*The City University of New York,
LaGuardia*

McGraw-Hill Book Company
*New York   St. Louis   San Francisco   Auckland
Bogotá   Hamburg   Johannesburg   London   Madrid
Mexico   Montreal   New Delhi   Panama   Paris
São Paulo   Singapore   Sydney   Tokyo   Toronto*

THE SHORT PROSE READER

1 2 3 4 5 6 7 8 9 0 BKPBKP 8 9 8 7 6 5 4

ISBN 0-07-044012-3

See Acknowledgments on pages 379–382.
Copyrights included on this page by reference.

This book was set in Century Schoolbook by Monotype Composition
Company, Inc. The editors were Phillip A. Butcher and David Dunham;
the production supervisor was Leroy A. Young.
The cover was designed by Robin Hessel;
the cover illustration was done by Vicky Maggio.
The Book Press, Inc., was printer and binder.

Library of Congress Cataloging in Publication Data
Main entry under title:

The Short prose reader.

    1. College readers. I. Muller, Gilbert H., date
II. Wiener, Harvey S.
PE1417.S446 1985   808'.0427   84-12551
ISBN 0-07-044012-3

CONTENTS

ALTERNATE THEMATIC CONTENTS

Childhood and Family

Social Problems and Issues

Men and Women Today

The Minority Experience

City and Country

Sports, Travel, and Leisure

Psychology and Behavior

Science, Technology, and Medicine

PREFACE

Now in its third edition, *The Short Prose Reader* continues
to offer lively reading selections for college composition
courses. Its ten chapters cover all important patterns of
writing, offering students concise and lively prose models
for analysis, discussion, and imitation. Designed as a practical text, it addresses the challenge that faces today's college
students in reading and writing short essays.

The organization of *The Short Prose Reader* is one
of its major strengths. Each of the first nine chapters contains
four short essays that illustrate clearly a specific pattern or
technique—description, narration, illustration, comparison
and contrast, definition, classification, process analysis, causal
analysis, or argumentation. For this edition we offer new
selections in every chapter. We organize the text by starting
with the forms of prose mastered most readily by college
students, and by then moving carefully to more difficult
types of analytical and argumentative writing. Students
learn to build upon earlier techniques and patterns as they
progress through the book. The last chapter, consisting of
ten essays, offers students the opportunity to read and to
discuss short prose pieces that reflect the various rhetorical
strategies.

Teachers and students will discover that the essays
appeal to a broad audience. Readers will be excited by
William Least Heat Moon's "Arizona 87," Langston Hughes's
"Salvation," Linda Bird Francke's "The Ambivalence of

Abortion," Ernest Hemingway's "Camping Out," Judy Syfer's "I Want a Wife," E. B. White's "The Three New Yorks," and the many other timely or controversial pieces included in the text. This is a readable text, and one that has ample representation by many different types of writers. Moreover, the essays, which range typically between 300 and 1,200 words, achieve their goals succinctly and clearly and are easy to read and to understand. The essays will alert students both to the *types* of college writing expected of them and to the *length* of essay required frequently by teachers.

Finally, the exercises we have included for each essay are comprehensive and integrated—designed to develop and reinforce the key skills required in college writing. We have included two vocabulary exercises for each selection; the Words to Watch exercise alerts students to words they will read in context, and the Building Vocabulary exercise uses other effective methods (prefix/suffix, context clues, synonym/antonym, abstract/concrete) of teaching vocabulary. A section called Understanding the Writer's Ideas reinforces reading comprehension. Sections entitled Understanding the Writer's Techniques and Exploring the Writer's Ideas provide an excellent basis for class discussion and independent reading and analysis. The last exercise for each essay involves a dynamic approach to writing projects. Guided writing activities—a novel feature of *The Short Prose Reader*—tie the writing projects to the reading selections. Instead of simply being told to write an essay on a certain topic, students through Guided Writing will be able to move from step to step in the process of composition.

The Short Prose Reader can be used flexibly and effectively by students and teachers alike. The text is simple yet sophisticated, presenting essays and exercises that are easy to follow but never are condescending. Weighing the needs and expectations of today's college freshmen, we have designed a rhetoric-reader that can serve as the major text for the composition course.

We wish to thank our colleagues for support and are especially grateful to those who read the manuscript for this and previous editions and offered helpful suggestions:

Professors Harry Crosby, Boston University; Robert Esch, University of Texas, El Paso; Owen W. Gilman, Jr., St. Joseph's University; Wilma H. Hasse, Mitchell College; Roland Holmes, University of Illinois, Champaign-Urbana; Sharon Katz, Iona College; Robert Reising, Pembroke State University; Michael H. Riley, West Virginia Northern Community College; and J. C. Searles, Pennsylvania State University; Rowena Flanagan, Kansas City Kansas Community College; Albert Geritz, Ft. Hays State College; Isabel Kidder, Holyoke Community College; Elizabeth Latosi-Sawin, Missouri Western State College; and Ann N. Weisner, New York Institute of Technology.

Gilbert H. Muller
Harvey S. Wiener

·THE·
SHORT
PROSE
READER

1

Description

Since a writer's main purpose is to explain things clearly, description is an important aid to good writing. To add liveliness to an essay, descriptive details are necessary to create a visual impression of an object or a scene. As a technique in writing, description matches the sort of details we see in vivid and effective photographs. Good descriptive writers help the reader to "see" objects, scenes, and even moods by means of language.

The essays in this section reflect key qualities in all good descriptive writing. First, description relies on a basic talent that we all have—the ability to see, touch, taste, hear, or smell various elements in the world. Talented descriptive writers refine the power of their five senses in order to recreate people, places, things, emotions, and ideas. Second, in descriptive writing, the author must select details carefully. There might be thousands of details in any given scene, but clearly a writer cannot present all of them. Instead, the writer must choose only those details most useful in painting a picture for the reader. Third, writers must organize their descriptions carefully. With description, the writer must decide on a perspective (for instance, top to bottom, left to right, front to back) and then move carefully from detail to detail. The descriptive writer has a "camera eye" that ranges over its subject in a careful, consistent way. Fourth, descriptive writing creates a "dominant impression" of its subject. This main impression arises from the author's focus on a single subject, and from the feelings that the writer brings to that subject. Finally, descriptive writing offers a thesis or main idea concerning its subject, as does all sound writing. In short, description makes a point.

Writing good descriptive papers is a challenge, because we (like the authors in this section) have to look at our world anew, to remember, to search for meaningful details, to recreate the images around us. As we write descriptive paragraphs and essays, we should keep a basic goal in mind—to permit the reader to see the world that we describe in a fresh, vivid, and concrete way. As descriptive writers, we have to be willing to look at the world, perhaps for the first time, close up.

Jade Snow Wong

UNCLE KWOK

In this selection from *Fifth Chinese Daughter,* an autobiography of her childhood in San Francisco's Chinatown, Jade Snow Wong creates a unique portrait of her Uncle Kwok. As you read this short essay, try to picture Uncle Kwok—his dress, features, and behavior. How does the description the author provides show that, from the moment that he enters the Wong Factory (which also serves as the family's home), Uncle Kwok is a decidedly unusual man?

Words to Watch

ambled (par. 1): walked in a leisurely manner
satchel (par. 1): a small bag for carrying clothes, books, or articles
deviation (par. 3): a turning aside from a normal pattern of behavior
sauntered (par. 4): walked carelessly or idly
meticulousness (par. 4): extreme care about details
fastidious (par. 5): not easy to please; excessively refined

Among the workers in Daddy's factory, Uncle Kwok 1 was one of the strangest—a large-framed, awkward, unshaven man whose worn clothes hung on him as if they did not belong to him. Each afternoon around three-thirty, as some of the workers were about to go home to prepare their early dinners, Uncle Kwok slowly and deliberately ambled in through the Wong front door, dragging his feet heavily, and gripping in one hand the small black satchel from which he was never separated.

Going to his own place at the sewing machine, he 2 took off his battered hat and ragged coat, hung both up carefully, and then sat down. At first Jade Snow was rather afraid of this extraordinary person, and unseen, watched his actions from a safe distance. After Uncle Kwok was settled in his chair, he took off his black, slipperlike shoes. Then, taking a piece of stout cardboard from a miscellaneous pile which he kept in a box near his sewing machine, he traced the outline of his shoes on the cardboard. Having closely examined the blades of his scissors and tested their sharpness, he would cut out a pair of cardboard soles, squinting critically through his inaccurate glasses. Next he removed from both shoes the cardboard soles he had made the day before and inserted the new pair. Satisfied with his inspection of his renewed footwear, he got up, went to the waste can some seventy-five feet away, disposed of the old soles, and returned to his machine. He had not yet said a word to anyone.

Daily this process was repeated without deviation. 3

The next thing Uncle Kwok always did was to put 4 on his own special apron, homemade from double thicknesses of heavy burlap and fastened at the waist by strong denim ties. This long apron covered his thin, patched trousers and protected him from dirt and draft. After a half hour had been consumed by these chores, Uncle Kwok was ready to wash his hands. He sauntered into the Wong kitchen, stationed himself at the one sink which served both family and factory, and with characteristic meticulousness, now proceeded to clean his hands and fingernails.

It was Mama's custom to begin cooking the evening 5 meal at this hour so that the children could have their dinner before they went to the Chinese school, but every day she had to delay her preparations at the sink until slow-moving Uncle Kwok's last clean fingernail passed his fastidious inspection. One day, however, the inconvenience tried her patience to its final limit.

Trying to sound pleasantly persuasive, she said, 6 "Uncle Kwok, please don't be so slow and awkward. Why don't you wash your hands at a different time, or else wash them faster?"

Uncle Kwok loudly protested the injustice of her 7 comment. "Mama, I am not awkward. The only awkward thing about my life is that it has not yet prospered!" And he strode off, too hurt even to dry his hands finger by finger, as was his custom.

BUILDING VOCABULARY

1. You can sometimes determine what words mean if you look at smaller words which make them up. What are definitions for the words below? First write down words within them, or based on them, that you may be able to recognize; then write your definition.

     a. deliberately (par. 1)
     b. ragged (par. 2)
     c. inaccurate (par. 2)
     d. thicknesses (par. 4)
     e. characteristic (par. 4)

2. In several of her sentences, Jade Snow Wong uses two or three descriptive words in a series. For example, in the first sentence she describes Uncle Kwok as a "large-framed, awkward, unshaven man." Write similar sentences, using a series of descriptive words for the following subjects.

     a. woman
     b. factory
     c. subway
     d. storm
     e. highway

UNDERSTANDING THE WRITER'S IDEAS

1. What is the main point that Jade Snow Wong wants to make about Uncle Kwok? In which sentence in the selection is the point clearly established?

2. Describe in your own words the specific details we learn about Uncle Kwok.

3. Describe Uncle Kwok's daily routine.

4. What do we learn about Jade Snow Wong's attitude toward Uncle Kwok and about her mother's attitude toward him?

UNDERSTANDING THE WRITER'S TECHNIQUES

1. Descriptive writing relies on words that create pictures (images) that the reader can see. These words create images because they appeal to our sense of sight (through color and action), sound, smell, touch, and taste. In this essay, the writer concentrates on the sense of sight because she wants to create a visual impression of her uncle. What are some details about Uncle Kwok's features and his clothing? How do these descriptive details help to create a dominant impression of him?

2. We also see Uncle Kwok in motion. Describe the way he moves. Find five words in the essay that capture the quality of his motion.

3. Writers often provide a *thesis sentence* to express the main idea of a composition. The thesis sentence establishes the subject, limits it, expresses the writer's attitude toward it, and when well expressed, captures the reader's interest. Is there a thesis sentence in this essay? Which one is it?

4. Why does the thesis sentence appear in the place that it does? Which functions of a good thesis sentence does it reflect? Does it capture your interest?

5. Wong arranges details carefully; the essay progresses from one stage in the description to another until we have a sound impression of Uncle Kwok. At what point do we meet Uncle Kwok? What are the stages in his

activities? How do these stages correspond to the paragraphs in the essay? How do the individual paragraphs help us understand the pattern of Uncle Kwok's activity?

6. What is the purpose in selecting a short one-sentence paragraph (par. 3)?

EXPLORING THE WRITER'S IDEAS

1. The author suggests that people (like Jade Snow's mother) become upset by those who follow set routines. Do you agree? Describe someone you know who annoys you because he or she follows set patterns.

2. Why do we fall back on set routines or repeat the same pattern of behavior from day to day?

3. What makes an individual "strange"? Is the word ever misleading? Should we fear "strange" individuals?

4. What does Uncle Kwok's statement in paragraph 7 explain about his behavior?

IDEAS FOR WRITING

Guided Writing

Write an extended paragraph or a short essay describing someone you found strange, frightening, delightful, amusing, or eccentric when you were a child.

1. Establish a strong thesis sentence and place it near the start of your composition.

2. Concentrate on images of sight (color, outline, appearance, and action) to describe the individual.

3. Try to use a series of descriptive terms in several sentences. See paragraph 4 in Wong's essay, for example.

4. Fill in the details of your character in a carefully organized manner. Place the character in a particular setting at a given point in time. Try to use a "camera eye" movement that follows the character from detail to detail in the description.

5. Try to create a "dominant impression" of the character, one that conforms to the main idea expressed in your thesis sentence.

More Writing Projects

1. Write a vivid description of one of your teachers or of someone in your class.

2. Cut out a photograph of someone from a newspaper or magazine and then write a clear description of that individual.

3. Describe one of your favorite television or movie personalities.

Patricia Cayo Sexton

BACKDROP OF POVERTY

In this selection from *Spanish Harlem,* Patricia Cayo Sexton uses description selectively in order to support her analysis of the subject. Her commentary never becomes dull or lengthy, because it is balanced by the clarity of her description. Sexton has long been involved in social causes, and the thesis that she offers in this selection reflects her concerns.

Words to Watch

silk-stocking (par. 1): upper class
bustle (par. 1): to be active and noisy
affluent (par. 4): rich
kibitz (par. 5): to gossip
disdain (par. 6): to consider unworthy; to scorn
estranged (par. 6): alienated; cut off

At 6:30 A.M., while silk-stocking Manhattan is 1 asleep, East Harlem is starting to bustle. The poor are early risers. They have the jobs others don't want: the early-hour jobs, the late-hour jobs. Many rise early because it is a rural habit.

Along about 7:30 the streets are filled with fast- 2 moving people: men, women, and swarms of children of all sizes. The parochial school children can be seen in clusters, with their togetherness identity tag—a school hat, a blouse, a uniform.

You may be able to buy a *New York Times* at the 3 corner newsstand in the morning, but you probably will not be able to buy a cup of coffee. The poor drink their coffee and eat their breakfasts, such as they are, at home. Few eat out.

Some will stand at the bus stops, but most will crowd 4 into the downtown subways that speed them to jobs in commercial or silk-stocking areas: to serve the affluent, or work in their stores or small industrial shops. Many of the Negro women will go to domestic service; and the Puerto Rican women, to their sewing machines in the garment shops.

Later in the day, if it is warm, the men who have 5 no jobs will come out and stand on the sidewalks and talk together. They will watch the street and the passers-by and kibitz with one another. The old people, and from time to time the housewives, will sit at the window and join the watchers. And those with leisure may call them idle. Later, when the children return from school, the sidewalks and streets will jump with activity. Clusters of men, sitting on orange crates on the sidewalks, will play checkers or cards. The women will sit on the stoop, arms folded, and watch the young at play; and the young men, flexing their muscles, will look for some adventure. Vendors, ringing their bells, will hawk hot dogs, orange drinks, ice cream; and the caressing but often jarring noise of honking horns, music, children's games, and casual quarrels, whistles, singing, will go on late into the night. When you are in it you don't notice the noise, but when you stand away and listen to a taped conversation, the sound suddenly appears as a background roar. This loud stimulation of the senses may produce some of the emotionalism of the poor.

East Harlem is a busy place, night and day, filled 6 with the joyous and troubled lives of residents—rather than the heavy commercial traffic of mid-Manhattan. New York's street life is unique. So much action, so much togetherness. The critics who lament its passing have a point. The middle class who disdain life conducted so openly in the streets might compare its satisfactions to the sometimes parched and estranged quality of their own backyards.

BUILDING VOCABULARY

1. In her attempt to capture the noise and rhythms of life in East Harlem, Patricia Cayo Sexton employs many words that suggest action. For instance, in the first sentence of the essay she writes that at an early hour East Harlem "is starting to bustle." Find five action words in the essay, and explain why you think the writer chose them and whether you think they are effective.

2. Write original sentences in which you use the five action words you selected above.

UNDERSTANDING THE WRITER'S IDEAS

1. What is the tone of this essay? (*Tone* means the writer's attitude toward her materials). In other words, what is Sexton's attitude toward the people of East Harlem? Is she critical, supportive, angry, humorous, impartial? Give examples to support your idea.

2. Why are the poor "early risers"? What are some other traits of the poor that Sexton mentions?

3. What contrasts are established between the poor and the rich, between upper and lower Manhattan, between the city and the suburbs?

4. Describe the activities that take place on the streets of East Harlem.

5. Clarify Sexton's statement in paragraph 5 that "those with leisure may call them idle."

UNDERSTANDING THE WRITER'S TECHNIQUES

1. Is there a thesis sentence in this essay? If not, why not?

2. In what sense does *time* serve as an important structuring principle for this selection? How much time passes in the essay? Does Sexton concentrate on particular times of the day? Which words in paragraph 5 indicate the passing of time?

3. The first four paragraphs in this essay are short. Are they effective? Why? Could they have been combined into one longer paragraph without hurting the impact of the message?

4. The fifth paragraph has the most description in it. What is the quality of this description? What senses are appealed to by the description? What is the dominant impression that emerges from the paragraph? What single sentence in this paragraph ties all of the thoughts together?

5. Of what value is Sexton's use of the future tense in many of the paragraphs in this selection (for example, "Some will stand at the bus stops")?

6. Which two paragraphs have the least amount of description? Why?

7. How effective is the conclusion of the essay? How does Sexton suggest a contrast between the poor and the middle class in paragraph 6?

8. What do the words "So much action, so much togetherness" mean? This is not a complete sentence; it is a fragment. Do you think it effective or ineffective in the conclusion? Why?

EXPLORING THE WRITER'S IDEAS

1. Judging from what you have seen or read, why might you agree or disagree with Sexton's thesis that middle-class life is not necessarily more satisfying than the lives of the poor?

2. Why do many people have misconceptions about poverty and about poor people in America?

3. Do you agree or disagree with the assertion that the poor frequently "serve the affluent"? Why do they?

IDEAS FOR WRITING

Guided Writing

Select a neighborhood (either your own or one that you know
well), and write a description of a typical street, its residents
and their activities.

1.   Establish an early morning scene that incorpo-
rates description and commentary. Name the street.

2.   Identify clearly whether you are describing a
poor, rich, middle-class, or possibly mixed neighborhood.

3.   Try to capture the various rhythms and activities
of the people. Use colors, sounds, smells, actions to make
the scene alive.

4.   If possible, compare and contrast this street with
other sections of the town, city, or region.

5.   Be certain that your own attitude toward the
neighborhood and its people is clear. Emphasize your opinion
in the concluding paragraph.

More Writing Projects

1.   Using both description and commentary, analyze
the people you observed in one of the following situations:

   a. a bus during rush hour
   b. breakfast at a diner
   c. a highway during a storm
   d. a park at dusk
   e. a concert or a game on a summer evening

2.   Bring to class photographs from newspapers or
magazines that capture the lives of people in a particular
surrounding. Be prepared to analyze the descriptive details
in these photographs.

William Least Heat Moon

ARIZONA 87

In this chapter from his 1982 book, *Blue Highways*, William Least Heat Moon presents us with a bittersweet, richly detailed description of the landscape he sees while driving his truck called *Ghost Dancing* through the Southwestern United States. As he drives through central Arizona, his careful eye photographs both the natural and the human landscape around him. In converting these snapshots to language, Least Heat Moon relies upon rich sensory detail and especially vivid and original comparisons.

Words to Watch

friable (par. 1): easily crushed or pulverized
persnickety (par. 1): fussy about small details
pollinate (par. 3): to carry pollen to fertilize plant seeds
kamikaze (par. 3): a member of a corps of Japanese pilots assigned to make a suicidal crash at a target
aerial (par. 3): occurring in the air
cache (par. 4): something hidden
marauding (par. 6): roaming about in search of plunder
Apaches (par. 6): a tribe of Native Americans of the southwestern United States
rodeo (par. 4): a performance featuring cowboy stunts
badger (par. 7): a burrowing animal with long claws
diabolic (par. 7): devilish
unobtrusively (par. 9): not very obviously
escarpment (par. 9): a long cliff
coalesced (par. 12): came together

I don't suppose that saguaros mean to give comic 1
relief to the otherwise solemn face of the desert, but they
do. Standing on the friable slopes they are quite persnickety
about, saguaros mimic men as they salute, bow, dance, raise
arms to wave, and grin with faces carved in by woodpeckers.
Older plants, having survived odds against their reaching
maturity of sixty million to one, have every right to smile.

The saguaro is ninety percent water, and a big, two- 2
hundred-year-old cactus may hold a ton of it—a two-year
supply. With this weight, a plant that begins to lean is soon
on the ground; one theory now says that the arms, which
begin sprouting only after forty or fifty years when the
cactus has some height, are counterweights to keep the
plant erect.

The Monday I drove northeast out of Phoenix, sa- 3
guaros were in bloom—comparatively small, greenish-white
blossoms perched on top of the trunks like undersized Easter
bonnets; at night, long-nosed bats came to pollinate them.
But by day, cactus wrens, birds of daring aerial skill, put
on the show as they made kamikaze dives between toothpick-
size thorns into nest cavities, where they were safe from
everything except the incredible ascents over the spines by
black racers in search of eggs the snakes would swallow
whole.

It was hot. The only shade along Arizona 87 lay 4
under the bottomsides of rocks; the desert gives space then
closes it up with heat. To the east, in profile, rose the
Superstition Mountains, an evil place, Pima and Maricopa
Indians say, which brings on diabolic possession to those
who enter. Somewhere among the granite and greasewood
was the Lost Dutchman gold mine, important not for whatever cache it might hide as for providing a white dream.

North of the Sycamore River, saguaro, ocotillo, 5
paloverde, and cholla surrendered the hills to pads of prickly
pear the size of a man's head. The road climbed and the
temperature dropped. At Payson, a mile high on the northern
slope of the Mazatzal Mountains, I had to pull on a jacket.

Settlers once ran into Payson for protection from 6
marauding Apaches; after the Apache let things calm down,

citizens tried to liven them up again by holding rodeos in the main street. Now, streets paved, Payson lay quiet but for the whine of sawmills releasing the sweet scent of cut timber.

I stopped at an old log hotel to quench a desert 7 thirst. A sign on the door: NO LIVE ANIMALS ALLOWED. I guess you could bring in all the dead ones you wanted. A woman shouted, "Ain't servin' now." Her unmoving eyes, heavy as if cast from lead, watched suspiciously for a live badger under my jacket or a weasel up my pantleg.

"This is a fine old hotel," I said. She ignored me. 8 "Do you mind if I look at your big map?" She shrugged and moved away, safe from any live animal attack. I was hunting a place to go next. Someone had marked the Hopi Reservation to the north in red. Why not? As I left, I asked where I could water my lizard. She ignored that too.

Highway 260, winding through the pine forests of 9 central Arizona, let the mountains be boss as it followed whatever avenues they left open, crossing ridges only when necessary, slipping unobtrusively on narrow spans over streams of rounded boulders. But when 260 reached the massive escarpment called the Mogollon Rim, it had to challenge geography and climb the face.

I shifted to low, and Ghost Dancing pulled hard. A 10 man with a dusty, leathery face creased like an old boot strained on a bicycle—the old style with fat tires. I called a hello, he said nothing. At the summit, I waited to see whether he would make the ascent. Far below lay two cars, crumpled wads. Through the clear air I could count nine ranges of mountains, each successively grayer in a way reminiscent of old Chinese woodblock prints. The Mogollon was a spectacular place; the more so because I had not been anesthetized to it by endless Kodachromes. When the cyclist passed, I called out, "Bravo!" but he acknowledged nothing. I would have liked to talk to a man who, while his contemporaries were consolidating their little empires, rides up the Mogollon Rim on a child's toy. Surely he knew something about desperate men.

The top of the great scarp, elevation sixty-five hundred 11

feet, lay flat and covered with big ponderosas standing between dirty snowdrifts and black pools of snowmelt. I began anticipating Heber, the next town. One of the best moments of any day on the road was, toward sunset, looking forward to the last stop. At Heber I hoped for an old hotel with a little bar off to the side where they would serve A-1 on draft under a stuffed moosehead; or maybe I'd find a grill dishing up steak and eggs on blue-rimmed platters. I hoped for people who had good stories, people who sometimes took you home to see their collection of carved peach pits.

That was the hope. But Heber was box houses and 12 a dingy sawmill, a couple of motels and filling stations, a glass-and-Formica cafe. Heber had no center, no focus for the eye and soul: neither a courthouse, nor high church steeple, nor hotel. Nothing has done more to take a sense of civic identity, a feeling of community, from small-town America than the loss of old hotels to the motel business. The hotel was once where things coalesced, where you could meet both townspeople and travelers. Not so in a motel. No matter how you build it, the motel remains a haunt of the quick and dirty, where the only locals are Chamber of Commerce boys every fourth Thursday. Who ever heard the returning traveler exclaim over one of the great motels of the world he stayed in? Motels can be big, but never grand.

BUILDING VOCABULARY

1. *Compound words* are made up of two separate words joined together. They help intensify description by focusing on the connection between two words. Some compounds are formed by joining two nouns (*photograph, chairperson*); others combine nouns with nonnoun prefixes, suffixes, or combining forms (*childlike, self-pity*). Some compounds use hyphens between the two words, although the general current trend is to omit the hyphens. For example, such words as *today* or *tomorrow* were regularly hyphenated just 100 years ago. However, many compound words are still acceptable in all three steps of development: two separate words, a single hyphenated word, a single nonhyphenated word (*war monger, war-monger, warmonger*).

Locate at least ten compound words that in Least Heat Moon's essay are formed by joining two nouns. Use each in a sentence of your own.

2. *Denotation* refers to the dictionary definition of a word; *connotation* refers to the various shades of meaning and feeling readers bring to a word or phrase. Look up and write dictionary definitions for each of the words in italics. Then, explain in your own words the connotative meaning of each sentence or phrase.

    a. "the otherwise *solemn* face of the desert" (par. 1)
    b. "to *quench* a desert thirst" (par. 7)
    c. "it had to *challenge* geography (par. 9)
    d. "I had not been *anesthetized* by endless *Kodachromes*" (par. 10)
    e. "glass-and-*Formica* cafe" (par. 12)

3. Least Heat Moon is a careful observer of the plants, rocks, and wildlife of the Arizona landscape. List six of the words drawn from this landscape and write dictionary definitions of them.

UNDERSTANDING THE WRITER'S IDEAS

1. What are the saguaros? What are the odds of their reaching full growth? How old may saguaros become? At what age do they begin to sprout arms?

2. For what purpose do the cactus wrens use the saguaros? What is the major danger to these birds?

3. Explain the sentence: "The only shade along Arizona 87 lay under the bottom sides of rocks." (par. 4)

4. What is the American Indian legend about Superstition Mountains? Explain the "diabolic possession." What is supposedly hidden in these mountains and what is its importance? What is meant by "a white dream"?

5. How was the weather in Payson different from the weather when the writer started driving through the desert? What used to be the atmosphere in Payson? What is it like now?

6. Paragraph 9 describes the route of Highway 260.

In your own words, how does the highway relate to the environment that surrounds it?

7. What is Moon's attitude toward the man on the bicycle? What do we learn about the man's appearance? How does the man react to Moon? What does Moon describe as "a child's toy"? Why?

8. How do we know that some cars fell off the Mogollon Rim?

UNDERSTANDING THE WRITER'S TECHNIQUES

1. Writers often sharpen descriptions by making unusual comparisons. In this essay Least Heat Moon makes many such comparisons. Locate and explain the meaning of what each of the following things is compared to:

    a. The shape and look of the saguaros
    b. The saguaro blossoms
    c. The dives of the cactus wrens
    d. The appearance of the nine mountain ranges

Locate and explain other comparisons in the essay.

2. How does Moon use elements of space and time to order details in this description? Why is this method effective? Why does he introduce himself ("I drove") in paragraph 3? Why does he wait until then to introduce himself?

3. What is the effect of the short sentence "It was hot" (par. 4) coming as it does after a number of much longer sentences in preceding paragraphs?

4. *Imagery* refers to clear, vivid description rooted in sensory detail. List several images of vivid details that employ the senses: sight (color and action), sound, smell, touch, and taste.

5. In describing the old log hotel in paragraphs 7 and 8, Moon uses *dialogue,* or accurate recordings of actual conversations (see Glossary). What is the effect of dialogue on that descriptive scene?

6. Least Heat Moon makes use of humor to make

biting observations about the hotel in Payson. Explain what he means by "I guess you could bring in all the dead ones you wanted" (par. 7) and "As I left, I asked where I could water my lizard" (par. 8). Why does the woman ignore him? Why does he use biting humor in this way?

7. Least Heat Moon does not simply present factual details of the Arizona desert. Instead, his descriptions are highly subjective, colored with personal emotions. Locate five sentences of highly subjective description. Why is he so subjective? What impression does he give you of the scenes he describes? How does his subjectivity help create the *tone* of this essay? What is that tone?

8. Do you find the ending suitable? Is it too abrupt or is it consistent with the rest of the selection? Explain. Remember, this selection is a complete chapter of a book by the author.

EXPLORING THE WRITER'S IDEAS

1. In the final paragraph Least Heat Moon writes about the disappearance of "civic identity" or "a feeling of community" from small-town America. He blames this loss on the replacement of once-bustling hotels with impersonal motels. Do you think the writer believes this is the only reason for the change? In your experience, how else have American small towns lost their unique flavors or identities?

2. In paragraph 10, in discussing the bicyclist, the author writes, "Surely he knew something about desperate men." Why do you think he feels this way about the cyclist?

IDEAS FOR WRITING

Write a short essay describing a landscape you traveled through at one time. This can be a city, suburban, or countryside landscape.

1. Begin by concentrating on a particular or dominant element of the landscape.

2. Focus on the environmental conditions and the weather. Note any changes of the climate.

3. Arrange your description as you travel in time from place to place in the landscape.

4. Include at least one interaction with another person who helped you to formulate your feelings about the place.

5. Use concrete sensory detail as you write images of color, action, sound, smell, touch, and taste.

6. Use vivid and varied comparisons to describe what you saw.

7. Conclude your essay with a description and explanation of something that either greatly disappointed or excited you about your travels through this place.

MORE WRITING PROJECTS

1. Concentrating on both the setting and the person, write a short description of a chance encounter with someone, as Least Heat Moon does with the bicyclist on the Mongollon Rim. End by coming to a conclusion about this person's personality.

2. Describe a particular place that you feel has been changed very much by modernization. Include descriptions of both the old and the new ways the place looks and feels. Also include your reactions to both the old and the new.

Richard Selzer

THE DISCUS THROWER

Richard Selzer, a surgeon, gives his readers vivid insights into the excitement as well as the pathos of the world of medicine. His books include *Rituals of Surgery* (1974) and *Mortal Lesions* (1977). His essays are widely published in magazines, including *Esquire, Harper's,* and *Redbook.* In this essay, Selzer dramatically describes a patient's final day.

Words to Watch

furtive (par. 1): sly
pruned (par. 2): cut back; trimmed
facsimile (par. 2): an exact copy
shard (par. 20): a broken piece; fragment
forceps (par. 20): an instrument used in operations for holding or pulling
athwart (par. 21): leaning across
probes (par. 33): investigates thoroughly
hefts (par. 33): tosses; heaves

$\mathbf{I}$ spy on my patients. Ought not a doctor to observe 1
his patients by any means and from any stance, that he might the more fully assemble evidence? So I stand in the doorways of hospital rooms and gaze. Oh, it is not all that

furtive an act. Those in bed need only look up to discover me. But they never do.

From the doorway of Room 542 the man in the bed 2 seems deeply tanned. Blue eyes and close-cropped white hair give him the appearance of vigor and good health. But I know that his skin is not brown from the sun. It is rusted, rather, in the last stage of containing the vile repose within. And the blue eyes are frosted, looking inward like the windows of a snowbound cottage. This man is blind. This man is also legless—the right leg missing from midthigh down, the left from just below the knee. It gives him the look of a bonsai, roots and branches pruned into the dwarfed facsimile of a great tree.

Propped on pillows, he cups his right thigh in both 3 hands. Now and then he shakes his head as though acknowledging the intensity of his suffering. In all of this he makes no sound. Is he mute as well as blind?

The room in which he dwells is empty of all posses- 4 sions—no get-well cards, small, private caches of food, day-old flowers, slippers, all the usual kick-shaws of the sickroom. There is only the bed, a chair, a nightstand, and a tray on wheels that can be swung across his lap for meals.

"What time is it?" he asks. 5

"Three o'clock." 6

"Morning or afternoon?" 7

"Afternoon." 8

He is silent. There is nothing else he wants to know. 9

"How are you?" I say. 10

"Who is it?" he asks. 11

"It's the doctor. How do you feel?" 12

He does not answer right away. 13

"Feel?" he says. 14

"I hope you feel better," I say. 15

I press the button at the side of the bed. 16

"Down you go," I say. 17

"Yes, down, " he says. 18

He falls back upon the bed awkwardly. His stumps, 19 unweighted by legs and feet, rise in the air, presenting themselves. I unwrap the bandages from the stumps, and begin to cut away the black scabs and the dead, glazed fat with scissors and forceps. A shard of white bone comes loose. I pick it away. I wash the wounds with disinfectant and redress the stumps. All this while, he does not speak. What is he thinking behind those lids that do not blink? Is he remembering a time when he was whole? Does he dream of feet? Of when his body was not a rotting log?

He lies solid and inert. In spite of everything, he 20 remains impressive, as though he were a sailor standing athwart a slanting deck.

"Anything more I can do for you?" I ask.   21

For a long moment he is silent.   22

"Yes," he says at last and without the least irony.   23 "You can bring me a pair of shoes."

In the corridor, the head nurse is waiting for me.   24

"We have to do something about him," she says.   25 "Every morning he orders scrambled eggs for breakfast, and, instead of eating them, he picks up the plate and throws it against the wall."

"Throws his plate?"   26

"Nasty. That's what he is. No wonder his family   27 doesn't come to visit. They probably can't stand him any more than we can."

She is waiting for me to do something.   28

"Well?"   29

"We'll see," I say.   30

The next morning I am waiting in the corridor when   31 the kitchen delivers his breakfast. I watch the aide place the tray on the stand and swing it across his lap. She presses the button to raise the head of the bed. Then she leaves.

In time the man reaches to find the rim of the tray,   32 then on to find the dome of the covered dish. He lifts off the cover and places it on the stand. He fingers across the plate until he probes the eggs. He lifts the plate in both hands, sets it on the palm of his right hand, centers it, balances it. He hefts it up and down slightly, getting the feel of it. Abruptly, he draws back his right arm as far as he can.

There is the crack of the plate breaking against the   33 wall at the foot of his bed and the small wet sound of the scrambled eggs dropping to the floor.

And then he laughs. It is a sound you have never 34
heard. It is something new under the sun. It could cure
cancer.

Out in the corridor, the eyes of the head nurse 35
narrow.

"Laughed, did he?" 36

She writes something down on her clipboard. 37

A second aide arrives, brings a second breakfast 38
tray, puts it on the nightstand, out of his reach. She looks
over at me shaking her head and making her mouth go. I
see that we are to be accomplices.

"I've got to feed you," she says to the man. 39

"Oh, no you don't," the man says. 40

"Oh, yes I do," the aide says, "after the way you just 41
did. Nurse says so."

"Get me my shoes," the man says. 42

"Here's oatmeal," the aide says. "Open." And she 43
touches the spoon to his lower lip.

"I ordered scrambled eggs," says the man. 44

"That's right," the aide says. 45

I step forward. 46

"Is there anything I can do?" I say. 47

"Who are you?" the man asks. 48

In the evening I go once more to that ward to make 49
my rounds. The head nurse reports to me that Room 542 is
deceased. She has discovered this quite by accident, she says.
No, there had been no sound. Nothing. It's a blessing, she
says.

I go into his room, a spy looking for secrets. He is 50
still there in his bed. His face is relaxed, grave, dignified.
After a while, I turn to leave. My gaze sweeps the wall at
the foot of the bed, and I see the place where it has been
repeatedly washed, where the wall looks very clean and
very white.

BUILDING VOCABULARY

1. In this essay, Selzer uses a few words that derive
from languages other than English. Look up the following

words and tell what language they come from. Then, write a definition for each:

   a. *bonsai*
   b. *kick-shaws*
   c. *caches*

2. Use these words from the essay in complete sentences of your own: *vile, repose, dwarfed, glazed, inert, accomplices.*

UNDERSTANDING THE WRITER'S IDEAS

1. What reason does Selzer give for a doctor's spying on his patients?

2. What does the man in Room 542 look like? Why is his skin brown? How does Selzer know he is blind? Why does Selzer think the patient may be mute? When do we know that he is not mute?

3. What is the author's meaning of the phrase "vile repose"?

4. How do we know that this patient does not receive many visitors?

5. Aside from wanting to know the time of day, what is the patient's one request? Do you think he is serious about his request? Why?

6. Why does the patient hurl his food tray against the wall?

7. For what reason does the head nurse complain about the patient?

8. What does Selzer feel and think about the patient? How do you know?

UNDERSTANDING THE WRITER'S TECHNIQUES

1. Throughout the essay, Selzer asks a number of questions. Locate at least three of these questions that are not a part of the dialogue. To whom do you think they are addressed? What is their effect on the reader?

2. Like William Least Heat Moon, Selzer heightens

the description by making vivid and unusual comparisons. Locate and explain in your own words three comparisons that you feel are especially descriptive and intriguing.

3. Selzer uses some very short sentences interspersed among longer ones. Locate at least four very short sentences. How do they draw your attention to the description?

4. Locate in Selzer's essay at least five examples of vivid description (imagery) relating to illness. What is their emotional effect on the reader?

5. How does Selzer use *dialogue* to reveal the personality of the patient? of the doctor? of the head nurse?

6. In paragraph 24, Selzer states that the patient delivers his request "without the least irony." *Irony* (see Glossary) is saying what is opposite to what one means. Why might Selzer have expected irony from the patient? Why might someone in the sick man's condition use irony? What do you think the man means by his request "You can bring me a pair of shoes"—if, in fact, the remark is not an ironical one?

7. What does the title of the essay mean? What is a discus thrower? Why has Selzer chosen an ancient image of an athlete as the title of this essay? In what way is the title ironic?

8. Why does Selzer use such an unusual word as *kick-shaws* (par. 4)?

9. *Double entendre* (see Glossary) is a French expression that indicates that something has a double meaning, each equally valid. What might be the two meanings of the nurse's words "It's a blessing"?

10. In this essay, the author uses a *framing* device: that is, he opens and closes the essay with a similar image or idea. What is that idea? Why is it effective? What are the differences in the use of this idea in the opening and closing paragraphs?

11. The heart of this essay is the patient's insistence upon throwing his breakfast plate at the wall, and yet Selzer does not attempt to explain the man's reasons for such an act. Why do you think the man hurls his breakfast across

the room each morning—and why does he laugh? Why does Selzer not provide an analysis of the action? How does the title help us see Selzer's attitude toward the man's act?

EXPLORING THE WRITER'S IDEAS

1. In the beginning of the essay Selzer asks, "Ought not a doctor to observe his patients by any means from any stance, that he might more fully assemble evidence?" Do you feel that a doctor should have this right? Why? What rights do you believe patients should have in a hospital?

2. The head nurse in Selzer's description seems fed up with the patient in Room 542. Why do you think she feels this way? Do you think that a person in her position has the right to express this feeling on his or her job? Why or why not?

3. The patient's attitude is influenced by his physical state and his nearness to death. How have physical ailments or handicaps changed the attitudes of people you have known? How has an illness influenced your thoughts at any time?

IDEAS FOR WRITING

Guided Writing

Describe a person you have observed who was seriously ill, in danger, or under great stress.

1. Base your description upon close observation of the person during a short but concentrated span of time: a morning or afternoon, an hour or two, even a few minutes.

2. Begin with a short, direct paragraph in which you introduce the person and the critical situation he or she faces.

3. Include yourself ("I") in the description.

4. Describe the vantage point from which you are "spying" or observing, and focus on the particular subject of the scene.

5. Throughout your essay, ask key questions.

6. Use imagery and original comparisons to highlight the description of your subject.

7. Include some dialogue with either the subject or another person.

8. Describe at least one very intense action performed by your subject.

9. Tell how the subject and scene had changed when you next saw them.

MORE WRITING PROJECTS

1. Describe a hospital room in which you stayed or visited some other person. Focus on your sensory perceptions of the place.

2. Describe an interaction you had with a person who was blind or deaf or was disabled in some other way. In your description, focus closely on the person's features. Write about your reactions during and after the interaction.

2

Narration

Narration is the telling of a story. As a technique in essay writing, it normally involves a discussion of events that are "true" or real, events that take place over a period of time. Narration helps a writer explain things and, as such, it is an important skill for the kind of writing often required of you.

Writers who use narration usually rely on descriptive details to advance their stories. Moreover, in the narrative essay, there always must be some purpose in the telling, a purpose that goes beyond mere enjoyment of the story itself. Consequently, narration in an essay advances a thesis, or main idea. For example, if you had to write an essay on the happiest event in your life, you might choose to narrate the day your team won the state championship. You would establish your thesis—your main point—quickly, and then go on to tell about the event itself. In short, you would use narration as a means to an end—to make a significant statement about an important moment in your life.

The manner in which you relate this event depends on the simplicity or complexity of the story that you want to tell. If the season before the winning game was itself filled with excitement, you certainly would want to explain that and to trace the exciting events over a period of time. If the championship itself provided most of the thrills, you would want to concentrate on a much shorter period of time, breaking your narration down to days, hours, even minutes, instead of months. Learning to present time—whether in a single personal event, a series of related events, a historical occurrence, or an aging process—is one of the key elements in narrative prose.

Normally in a narrative essay you would start at the beginning and move to the end, or from past to present, or from old to new, but there are many other ways to relate events in the narrative essay. For instance, you could begin an essay on the death of someone important to you by detailing the day of the funeral, and then moving backward in time to flesh out the events leading up to the funeral. For beginners this "flashback" technique often causes very confused writing; but skilled writers know how to "jump around" in time without confusing the reader, blurring the thesis, or destroying the progression of the essay.

As with descriptive writing, the narrative essay requires a careful selection of details. Certain moments within any time order are more important than others, and these crucial moments will be emphasized and developed fully by a good writer. Other moments, significant but less important than the main moments, will take up less space, while unimportant items will be eliminated entirely. However, the writer must connect each event in the time span to other events that come before or after. Here, transitions of time—words like "afterwards," "soon," "a day later," "suddenly"—serve as bridges to connect the various moments in the narrative pattern.

There are other aspects of narration that appear in this chapter. For example, you must select a point of view for your story—whether presenting events through your own eyes or from a more objective or detached position. You must also decide on the value of dialogue (recording of conversations). Finally, you must be aware that other techniques of prose writing (like description) can reinforce your narrative pattern. Fortunately, most individuals have a basic storytelling ability and know how to develop stories that make a point. Once you master narration as a writing pattern, you will be able to use it in a variety of situations.

Elizabeth Wong

THE STRUGGLE TO BE AN ALL AMERICAN GIRL

In this poignant remembrance, Elizabeth Wong tells of the hurts and sorrows of her bicultural upbringing. Wong effectively blends concrete description and imaginative comparisons to give a vivid look into the life of a child who felt she had a Chinese exterior but an American interior.

Words to Watch

stoically (par. 1): without showing emotion
dissuade (par. 2): to talk out of doing something
ideographs (par. 7): Chinese picture symbols used to form words
disassociate (par. 8): to detach from association
vendors (par. 8): sellers of goods
gibberish (par. 9): confused, unintelligible speech or language
pidgin (par. 10): simplified speech that is usually a mixture of two
　　　or more languages

It's still there, the Chinese school on Yale Street 1
where my brother and I used to go. Despite the new coat of
paint and the high wire fence, the school I knew 10 years
ago remains remarkably, stoically the same.

Every day at 5 P.M., instead of playing with our 2
fourth- and fifth-grade friends or sneaking out to the empty
lot to hunt ghosts and animal bones, my brother and I had
to go to Chinese school. No amount of kicking, screaming,
or pleading could dissuade my mother, who was solidly
determined to have us learn the language of our heritage.

Forcibly, she walked us the seven long, hilly blocks 3
from our home to school, depositing our defiant tearful faces
before the stern principal. My only memory of him is that
he swayed on his heels like a palm tree, and he always
clasped his impatient twitching hands behind his back. I
recognized him as a repressed maniacal child killer, and
knew that if we ever saw his hands we'd be in big trouble.

We all sat in little chairs in an empty auditorium. 4
The room smelled like Chinese medicine, an imported
faraway mustiness. Like ancient mothballs or dirty closets.
I hated that smell. I favored crisp new scents. Like the soft
French perfume that my American teacher wore in public
school.

There was a stage far to the right, flanked by an 5
American flag and the flag of the Nationalist Republic of
China, which was also red, white and blue but not as pretty.

Although the emphasis at the school was mainly 6
language—speaking, reading, writing—the lessons always
began with an exercise in politeness. With the entrance of
the teacher, the best student would tap a bell and everyone
would get up, kowtow, and chant, "Sing san ho," the phonetic
for "How are you, teacher?"

Being ten years old, I had better things to learn 7
than ideographs copied painstakingly in lines that ran right
to left from the tip of a *moc but,* a real ink pen that had to
be held in an awkward way if blotches were to be avoided.
After all, I could do the multiplication tables, name the
satellites of Mars, and write reports on "Little Women" and
"Black Beauty." Nancy Drew, my favorite book heroine,
never spoke Chinese.

The language was a source of embarrassment. More 8
times than not, I had tried to disassociate myself from the
nagging loud voice that followed me wherever I wandered

in the nearby American supermarket outside Chinatown. The voice belonged to my grandmother, a fragile woman in her seventies who could outshout the best of the street vendors. Her humor was raunchy, her Chinese rhythmless, patternless. It was quick, it was loud, it was unbeautiful. It was not like the quiet, lilting romance of French or the gentle refinement of the American South. Chinese sounded pedestrian. Public.

In Chinatown, the comings and goings of hundreds 9 of Chinese on their daily tasks sounded chaotic and frenzied. I did not want to be thought of as mad, as talking gibberish. When I spoke English, people nodded at me, smiled sweetly, said encouraging words. Even the people in my culture would cluck and say that I'd do well in life. "My, doesn't she move her lips fast," they would say, meaning that I'd be able to keep up with the world outside Chinatown.

My brother was even more fanatical than I about 10 speaking English. He was especially hard on my mother, criticizing her, often cruelly, for her pidgin speech—smatterings of Chinese scattered like chop suey in her conversation. "It's not 'What it is,' Mom," he'd say in exasperation. "It's 'What *is* it, what *is* it, what *is* it!'" Sometimes Mom might leave out an occasional "the" or "a," or perhaps a verb of being. He would stop her in mid-sentence: "Say it again, Mom. Say it right." When he tripped over his own tongue, he'd blame it on her: "See, Mom, it's all your fault. You set a bad example."

What infuriated my mother most was when my 11 brother cornered her on her consonants, especially "r." My father had played a cruel joke on Mom by assigning her an American name that her tongue wouldn't allow her to say. No matter how hard she tried, "Ruth" always ended up "Luth" or "Roof."

After two years of writing with a *moc but* and 12 reciting words with multiples of meanings, I finally was granted a cultural divorce. I was permitted to stop Chinese school.

I thought of myself as multicultural. I preferred 13 tacos to egg rolls; I enjoyed Cinco de Mayo more than Chinese New Year.

At last, I was one of you; I wasn't one of them.   14
Sadly, I still am.   15

BUILDING VOCABULARY

For each of the words in italics, choose the letter of the word or expression that most closely matches its meaning.

1. the *stern* principal (par. 3)
a. military
b. very old
c. immoral
d. strict

2. *repressed* maniacal child killer (par. 3)
a. quiet
b. ugly
c. held back
d. retired

3. an imported faraway *mustiness* (par. 4)
a. country
b. moth balls
c. chair
d. staleness

4. a *fragile* woman (par. 8)
a. elderly
b. frail
c. tall
d. inconsistent

5. her humor was *raunchy* (par. 8)
a. obscene
b. unclear
c. childish
d. very funny

6. thought of as *mad* (par. 9)
a. foreign
b. angry
c. stupid
d. crazy

7. quiet *lilting* romance of French (par. 8)
a. musical
b. tilting
c. loving
d. complicated

8. what *infuriated* my mother most (par. 11)
a. angered
b. humiliated
c. made laugh
d. typified

UNDERSTANDING THE WRITER'S IDEAS

1. What did Elizabeth Wong and her brother do every day after school? How did that make them different from their friends? What was their attitude toward what they did? How do you know?

2. What does Wong mean when she says of the

principal "I recognized him as a repressed child killer"? Why were she and her brother afraid to see his hands?

3. What was the main purpose of going to Chinese school? What did Wong feel she had learned at "regular" American school? Which did she feel was more important? What are *Little Women, Black Beauty,* and *Nancy Drew*?

4. In the first sentence of paragraph 8, what language is "the language"?

5. What was Wong's grandmother like? What was Wong's attitude toward her? Why?

6. When Wong spoke English in Chinatown, why did the others think it was good that she moved her lips quickly?

7. What was her brother's attitude toward speaking English? How did he treat their mother when she tried to speak English? Why was it unfortunate that the mother had the American name *Ruth*? Who gave her that name? Why?

8. Explain the expression "he tripped over his own tongue" (par. 10).

9. In paragraph 13, Wong states, "I thought of myself as multicultural." What does that mean? What are tacos, egg rolls, and Cinco de Mayo? Why is it surprising that Wong includes those items as examples of her multiculturalism?

10. Who are the "you" and "them" of paragraph 14? Explain the significance of the last sentence. What does it indicate about Wong's attitude toward Chinese school from the vantage point of being an adult?

UNDERSTANDING THE WRITER'S TECHNIQUES

1. What is the author's purpose in writing this narrative? Is the technique of narration an appropriate one to her purpose? Why or why not?

2. Wong does not state a thesis directly in a thesis sentence. How does her title imply a thesis? If you were writing a thesis sentence of your own for this essay, what would it be?

3. This narrative contains several stories really. The first one ends after paragraph 7 and tells about Wong's routine after 5:00 P.M. on school days. Paragraphs 8 and 9, 10 and 11, and 12 and 13 offer other related narratives. Summarize each of these briefly. How does Wong help the reader shift from story to story?

4. The writer of narration will present *time* in a way that best fulfills the purpose of the narration. This presentation may take many forms: a single, personal event; a series of related events; a historical occurrence; an aging process. Obviously Wong chose a series of related events. Why does she use such a narrative structure to make her point? Could she have chosen an alternative plan, do you think? Why or why not?

5. Writers of narration often rely upon descriptive details to flesh out their stories. Find examples of sensory language here that makes the scene come alive for the reader.

6. Writers often use figurative comparisons to enliven their writing and to make it more distinctive. A *simile* is an imaginative form of figurative comparison using "like" or "as" to connect two items. One thing is similar to another in this figure. A *metaphor* is a figure of speech in which the writer compares two items not normally thought of as similar, but unlike in a simile, the comparison is direct— that is, it does not use "like" or "as." In other words, one thing is said to be the other thing, not merely to be like it. For example, if you wanted to compare love to a rose, you might use these two comparisons:

(simile)   My love is *like* a red, red rose.
(metaphor)   My love *is* a red, red rose.

In Wong's essay, find the similes and metaphors in paragraphs 2, 3, 4, 10, and 12. For each, name the two items compared and explain the comparison in your own words.

7. Narratives often include lines of spoken language, that is, one person in the narrative talking alone or to another. Wong uses quoted detail sparsely here. Why did she choose to limit the dialogue? How effective is the dialogue

that appears here? Where do you think she might have used more dialogue to advance the narrative?

8. The last two paragraphs are only one sentence each. Why do you think the author chose this technique?

9. What is the irony in the last sentence of the essay? (See Glossary). How would the meaning of the last sentence change if you eliminated the word *sadly*? What is the irony in the title of the essay?

10. What is the tone (see Glossary) of this essay? How does the tone here compare with the tone in Jade Snow Wong's description of Uncle Kwok?

EXPLORING THE WRITER'S IDEAS

1. Wong and her brother deeply resented being forced to attend Chinese school. When children very clearly express displeasure or unhappiness, should parents force them to do things anyway? Why or why not?

2. On one level this essay is about a clash of cultures, here the ancient Chinese culture of Wong's ancestry and the culture of the twentieth-century United States. Is it possible for someone to maintain connections to his or her ethnic or cultural backgrounds and at the same time to become an "all American" girl or boy? What do people of foreign backgrounds gain when they become completely Americanized? What do they lose?

3. Because of their foreign ways, the mother and grandmother clearly embarrassed the Wong children. Under what other conditions that you can think of do parents embarrass children? Children, parents?

IDEAS FOR WRITING

Write a narration in which you tell about some difficult moment that took place in grade school or high school, a moment that taught you something about yourself, your needs, or your cultural background.

1. Provide a concrete description of the school.
2. Tell in correct sequence about the event.

3. Identify people who play a part in this moment.

4. Use concrete, sensory description throughout your essay.

5. Use original similes and metaphors to make your narrative clearer and more dramatic.

6. Use dialogue (or spoken conversation) appropriately in order to advance the narrative.

7. In your conclusion, indicate what your attitude toward this moment is now that you are an adult.

8. Write a title that implies your thesis.

MORE WRITING PROJECTS

1. In an essay, tell about your happiest childhood memory and explain why it made you so happy.

2. Write a short narration about an experience you had with a person of another culture.

Langston Hughes

SALVATION

For more than forty years, Langston Hughes (1902–1967) was a major figure in American literature. In poetry, essays, drama, and fiction he attempted, as he said himself, "to explain and illuminate the Negro condition in America." This selection from his autobiography, *The Big Sea* (1940), tells the story of his "conversion" to Christ. Salvation was a key event in the life of his community, but Hughes tells comically how he bowed to pressure by permitting himself to be "saved from sin."

Words to Watch

dire (par. 3): terrible; disastrous
gnarled (par. 4): knotty; twisted
rounder (par. 6): watchman; policeman
deacons (par. 6): clergymen or laymen appointed to help the minister
serenely (par. 7): calmly; tranquilly
knickerbockered (par. 11): dressed in short, loose trousers that are gathered below the knees

I was saved from sin when I was going on thirteen. 1
But not really saved. It happened like this. There was a big revival at my Auntie Reed's church. Every night for weeks

there had been much preaching, singing, praying, and shouting, and some very hardened sinners had been brought to Christ, and the membership of the church had grown by leaps and bounds. Then just before the revival ended, they held a special meeting for children, "to bring the young lambs to the fold." My aunt spoke of it for days ahead. That night I was escorted to the front row and placed on the mourners' bench with all the other young sinners, who had not yet been brought to Jesus.

2　My aunt told me that when you were saved you saw a light, and something happened to you inside! And Jesus came into your life! And God was with you from then on! She said you could see and hear and feel Jesus in your soul. I believed her. I had heard a great many old people say the same thing and it seemed to me they ought to know. So I sat there calmly in the hot, crowded church, waiting for Jesus to come to me.

3　The preacher preached a wonderful rhythmical sermon, all moans and shouts and lonely cries and dire pictures of hell, and then he sang a song about the ninety and nine safe in the fold, but one little lamb was left out in the cold. Then he said: "Won't you come? Won't you come to Jesus? Young lambs, won't you come?" And he held out his arms to all us young sinners there on the mourners' bench. And the little girls cried. And some of them jumped up and went to Jesus right away. But most of us just sat there.

4　A great many old people came and knelt around us and prayed, old women with jet-black faces and braided hair, old men with work-gnarled hands. And the church sang a song about the lower lights are burning, some poor sinners to be saved. And the whole building rocked with prayer and song.

5　Still I kept waiting to *see* Jesus.

6　Finally all the young people had gone to the altar and were saved, but one boy and me. He was a rounder's son named Westley. Westley and I were surrounded by sisters and deacons praying. It was very hot in the church, and getting late now. Finally Westley said to me in a whisper: "God damn! I'm tired o' sitting here. Let's get up and be saved." So he got up and was saved.

Then I was left all alone on the mourners' bench. 7
My aunt came and knelt at my knees and cried, while
prayers and songs swirled all around me in the little church.
The whole congregation prayed for me alone, in a mighty
wail of moans and voices. And I kept waiting serenely for
Jesus, waiting, waiting—but he didn't come. I wanted to see
him, but nothing happened to me. Nothing! I wanted something to happen to me, but nothing happened.

I heard the songs and the minister saying: "Why 8
don't you come? My dear child, why don't you come to Jesus?
Jesus is waiting for you. He wants you. Why don't you come?
Sister Reed, what is this child's name?"

"Langston," my aunt sobbed. 9

"Langston, why don't you come? Why don't you come 10
and be saved? Oh, Lamb of God! Why don't you come?"

Now it was really getting late. I began to be ashamed 11
of myself, holding everything up so long. I began to wonder
what God thought about Westley, who certainly hadn't seen
Jesus either, but who was now sitting proudly on the
platform, swinging his knickerbockered legs and grinning
down at me, surrounded by deacons and old women on their
knees praying. God had not struck Westley dead for taking
his name in vain or for lying in the temple. So I decided that
maybe to save further trouble, I'd better lie, too, and say
that Jesus had come, and get up and be saved.

So I got up. 12

Suddenly the whole room broke into a sea of shouting, 13
as they saw me rise. Waves of rejoicing swept the place.
Women leaped in the air. My aunt threw her arms around
me. The minister took me by the hand and led me to the
platform.

When things quieted down, in a hushed silence, 14
punctuated by a few ecstatic "Amens," all the new young
lambs were blessed in the name of God. Then joyous singing
filled the room.

That night, for the last time in my life but one—for 15
I was a big boy twelve years old—I cried. I cried, in bed
alone, and couldn't stop. I buried my head under the quilts,
but my aunt heard me. She woke up and told my uncle I was
crying because the Holy Ghost had come into my life, and

because I had seen Jesus. But I was really crying because I couldn't bear to tell her that I had lied, that I had deceived everybody in the church, that I hadn't seen Jesus, and that now I didn't believe there was a Jesus any more, since he didn't come to help me.

BUILDING VOCABULARY

1. Throughout this essay, Hughes selects words dealing with religion to emphasize his ideas. Look these words up in a dictionary. Then tell what *connotations* the following words have for you. (See Glossary).

    a. sin (par. 1)
    b. mourner (par. 1)
    c. lamb (par. 3)
    d. salvation (title)

2. Locate additional words that deal with religion.
3. When Hughes talks about lambs in the fold—and lambs in general—he is using a figure of speech, a comparison. What is being compared? How does religion enter into the comparison? Why is it useful as a figure of speech?

UNDERSTANDING THE WRITER'S IDEAS

1. According to Hughes' description, what is a revival meeting like? What is the effect of the "preaching, singing, praying, and shouting" on the "sinners" and the "young lambs"?
2. Why does Westley "see" Jesus? Why does Langston Hughes come to Jesus?
3. How does the author feel after his salvation? Does Hughes finally believe in Christ after his experience? How do you know?

UNDERSTANDING THE WRITER'S TECHNIQUES

1. Is there a thesis statement in the essay? Where is it located?

2. How does the first paragraph serve as an introduction to the narrative?

3. What is the value of description in this essay? List several instances of vivid description that contribute to the narrative.

4. Where does the main narration begin? How much time passes in the course of the action?

5. In narration, it is especially important to have effective *transitions*—or word bridges—from stage to stage in the action. Transitions help the reader shift easily from idea to idea, event to event. List several transition words that Hughes uses.

6. A piece of writing has *coherence* if all its parts relate clearly and logically to each other. Each sentence grows naturally from the sentence before it; each paragraph grows naturally from the paragraph before it. Is Hughes' essay coherent? Which transitions help advance the action and relate the parts of a single paragraph to each other? Which transitions help connect paragraphs together? How does the way Hughes organized this essay help establish coherence?

7. A story (whether it is true or fiction) has to be told from the first-person ("I, we"), second-person ("you"), or third-person ("he, she, it, they") *point of view*. Point of view in narration sets up the author's position in regard to the action, making him either a part of the action or an observer of it.

a. What is the point of view in "Salvation"—is it first, second, or third person?

b. Why has Hughes chosen this point of view instead of any other? Can you think of any advantages to this point of view?

8. What is your opinion about the last paragraph, the conclusion of this selection? What does it suggest about the mind of a twelve-year-old boy? What does it say about adults' misunderstanding of the activities of children?

9. What does the word "conversion" mean? What conversion really takes place in this piece? How does that

compare to what people usually mean when they use "conversion" in a religious sense?

EXPLORING THE WRITER'S IDEAS

1.   Hughes seems to suggest that we are forced to do things because of social pressures. Do you agree with his suggestion? Do people do things because their friends or families expect them to? To what extent are we part of the "herd"? Is it possible for a person to retain individuality under pressure from a group? When did you bow to group pressures? When did you resist?

2.   Do you find the religious experience in Hughes' essay unusual or extreme? Why or why not? How do *you* define religion?

3.   Under what circumstances might a person lie in order to satisfy others? Try to recall a specific episode in which you or someone you know was forced to lie in order to please others.

IDEAS FOR WRITING

Guided Writing

Narrate an event in your life where you (or someone you know) gave in to group pressure or were forced to lie in order to please those around you.

1.   Start with a thesis statement.

2.   Set the stage for your narrative in the opening paragraph by telling where and when the incident took place. Use specific names for places.

3.   Try to keep the action within as brief a time period as possible. If you can write about an event that took no more than a few minutes, so much the better.

4.   Use description to sketch in the characters around you. Use colors, actions, sounds, smells, sensations of touch to fill in details of the scene.

5.   Use effective transitions of time to link sentences and paragraphs.

6.   Use the last paragraph to explain how you felt immediately after the incident.

More Writing Projects

1.   Explain an abstract word like "salvation," "sin," "love," or "hatred" by narrating an event that reveals the meaning of the word to you.

2.   Narrate an important event that affected your relationship to family, friends, or your community during your childhood.

3.   Tell about an important religious experience you remember. You might want to narrate an event about your own "conversion."

Andrea Lee

BLACK AND WELL-TO-DO

In this essay, Andrea Lee, a staff writer for the *New
Yorker* magazine and the author of *Russian Journal,* tells
fondly of her experiences from childhood to adulthood in
a black, middle-class Philadelphia suburb. As you read
this essay, consider the nature of the historical and
sociological evidence that she uses to support her idea of
a "black upper-middle class."

Words to Watch

bourgeoisie (par. 1): the middle class
enclaves (par. 2): distinctly enclosed area
pastoral (par. 4): very calm and uncomplicated
idyll (par 5): a romantic interlude
vague (par. 6): not clear
radicalized (par. 6): made radical in politics
vied (par. 8): competed for
complacency (par. 8): a feeling of self-satisfaction
repository (par. 9): a place where something is stored

I grew up in the kind of town few people believe 1
exists: a black upper-middle-class suburb full of colonial-
style houses and Volkswagen Rabbits. Yes, Virginia, there
is a black bourgeoisie, it has existed for years, and it summers
on Martha's Vineyard.

The Philadelphia suburb of Yeadon, my home 2
through childhood and adolescence, is one of many black
enclaves that someday will make a very interesting study
for a sociologist.

After World War II, housing speculators found it 3
profitable to scare off white residents and sell whole streets
of Yeadon to black professionals who were as eager as
anyone else at that time to pursue the romantic suburban
dream of fieldstone patios and eye-level ovens. In the 1950's,
half the black doctors and lawyers in Philadelphia crowded
into this rather small town, which was one of the few
integrated suburbs, and we Yeadon kids grew up with tree
houses and two-car garages and fathers who commuted into
the city.

Our parents had a vision of pastoral normalcy for 4
their children that was little different from the white ideal
laid out in the Dick and Jane readers. Their attempts to
provide this and to protect us from the slightest contact
with race prejudice left us extraordinarily, perhaps un-
healthily, sheltered: We were sent to Quaker schools and
camps where race and class were discounted with eager
innocence. When the Yeadon Civic Association (my father
was president) discovered that a local swimming club was
discriminating against blacks, the parents in my neighborhood simply built another club, which they christened "The
Nile Swim Club." When we asked about the name, my
father explained gravely: "This is a club only for Egyptians."

Childhood in Yeadon was a suburban idyll of shady 5
streets and bicycles and ice cream from a drugstore called
Doc's. This was the early 1960's, and as my friends and I
grew older, we became dimly aware that the rest of the
world was not necessarily Yeadon. Most of our parents were
active in the civil rights movement, and at gatherings we
listened avidly to their campaign references: Birmingham,
Selma, Greensboro.

Occasionally, we kids would travel into the city and 6
stare in horrified fascination at slums. When my generation
of Yeadon preppies was graduated from high school in the
late 1960's and early 1970's, however, we quickly realized

that our vague concern was not enough, and many of us became radicalized. (Most of us were attending Ivy League colleges, and this increased our sense of guilt.)

During college holidays, Yeadon's driveways were 7 colorful with dashikis and other, more complicated African garments, and a great deal of talk went on about the brothers and sisters of the urban community. Yeadon parents were edgy and alienated from their children at this time, and a common conversation between mothers began: "Yes, she used to look so *sweet,* and now she's gone and gotten one of those . . . Afros."

In the 1970's, our guilt evaporated, and Yeadon 8 became a place where parents vied with one another to produce tidbits about surgeon daughters and M.B.A. sons. Now, early in the 1980's, I find that in some circles, Yeadon is a synonym for conservatism and complacency, a place famed as being the hunting-ground of the AAP (Afro-American Prince or Princess), but I don't care.

Yeadon was a great town to grow up in, was as solid 9 a repository of American virtues and American flaws as any other close-knit suburban community; moreover, it had, and still has, its own peculiar flavor—a lively mixture of materialism, idealism, and ironic humor that prevents the minds of its children from stagnating. I feel a surge of well-being when I return there in the summer to hear the symphony of lawn mowers and to find that the Nile Swim Club remains "for Egyptians only."

BUILDING VOCABULARY

1. Lee makes use of a number of *allusions* (references to literary, biographical, historical, or sociological places, events, or items—see Glossary). Write explanations of the following allusions:

    a. Volkswagen Rabbits (par. 1)
    b. "Yes, Virginia . . ." (par. 1)
    c. Martha's Vineyard (par. 1)
    d. Dick and Jane readers (par. 4)

        e. the civil rights movement (par. 5)
        f. Ivy League colleges (par. 6)
        g. M.B.A. (par. 8)

    2. The writer uses some *hyphenated* words (a type of *compound* word—see Glossary) in this selection. Explain the meaning of each of the following phrases; then use each hyphenated word in a sentence of your own:

        a. *upper-middle-class* suburb (par. 1)
        b. *colonial-style* houses (par. 1)
        c. *two-car* garage (par. 3)
        d. *Afro-American* Prince or Princess (par. 8)
        e. *close-knit* suburban community (par. 9)
        f. a surge of *well-being* (par. 9)

    3. Write definitions for the three *-isms* that Lee refers to: *conservatism* (par. 8); *materialism* (par. 9); *idealism* (par. 9).

UNDERSTANDING THE WRITER'S IDEAS

    1. What does Lee say exists in spite of what most people believe?

    2. Why does the author say that her neighborhood "someday will make a very interesting study for a sociologist"?

    3. What are "housing speculators"? Why does Lee think that they "found it profitable to scare off white residents" of Yeadon after World War II?

    4. In this essay Lee states that she is describing an "upper-middle-class suburb." Find at least five details that show that Yeadon is such a place. Why does she say that it is "the kind of town few people believe exists"?

    5. Explain the sentence "We were sent to Quaker schools and camps where race and class were discounted with eager innocence." (par. 4)

    6. For what reason do the black parents of Yeadon build "the Nile Swim Club"? For whom is the swim club intended?

7. Explain what Lee means when she writes, "Occasionally, we kids would travel into the city and stare in horrified fascination at slums." (par. 6)

8. Why did Lee and her friends feel guilty?

9. How did the attitudes of Lee and her friends change in the late 1960s and early 1970s? Why did they change?

UNDERSTANDING THE WRITER'S TECHNIQUES

1. What *thesis* does Lee want to illustrate with her narrative? Where is the thesis statement placed? Why is this an effective placement?

2. In her opening paragraphs, Lee asserts that something people do not believe true in fact really is true. Why does she begin this way? How does this introduction hold the reader's attention?

3. How does Lee use *chronological order* (the arrangement of events in the order that they happened) in the essay? What periods are covered in each of paragraphs 3 through 8? How are the main events in this narrative related?

4. Does the writer *subjectively* or *objectively* narrate the series of events in this essay? Why, do you think, has she chosen that particular strategy? Is it the appropriate one for this kind of narrative?

5. What evidence does Lee build into her narrative to support her concept of the black upper-middle class?

6. In the last paragraph, Lee speaks of the "ironic humor" that permitted children in Yeadon to develop successfully. What is ironic humor (see Glossary under *Irony*)? Locate and explain examples of Lee's own ironic humor in this essay.

7. To what extent does the last paragraph confirm Lee's thesis? Explain.

8. What is Lee's *purpose* in narrating the history of Yeadon? Does she want to inform, argue, persuade, amuse, entertain? Explain your response.

9. What is Lee's attitude toward Yeadon? How do

words like "flavor" and "symphony" project that attitude? Compare the *tone* (see Glossary) of Lee's essay about a neighborhood with the tone of Patricia Cayo Sexton's essay "Backdrop of Poverty" (see pages 9–11). How are they different? What are the similarities?

10. What is Lee's intended audience for this essay? How do you know?

EXPLORING THE WRITER'S IDEAS

1. In this essay about growing up in Yeadon, Andrea Lee includes herself and her family as members of "a black upper-middle class." Why does she say that few people believe that a place like Yeadon exists? Why does the author suggest that the idea of a black bourgeoisie is improbable?

2. In paragraph 6, Lee speaks of the civil rights movement and mentions such places as Birmingham (Alabama), Selma (Alabama), and Greensboro (North Carolina). Try to find information about the civil rights movement of the 1960s. Then, find out why these three cities were important at that time.

3. Lee uses a number of specialized cultural terms in her essay, particularly terms that relate to the black cultural identity movements of the 1960s and 1970s. Find out the meanings of the expressions "dashikis," "brothers and sisters," and "Afros." (par. 7)

4. Lee implies the importance of a neighborhood or a town in a person's growth to maturity. What role did your neighborhood, town, or city play in your growing up? What values did it help develop?

5. The essay makes clear that blacks and whites of similar economic status are not much different in their goals and aspirations. Given the stress on ethnic identity in our culture, this point is an unusual one. Do you agree that social class differences are not that strong among different ethnic groups? What is gained when neighborhoods with different ethnic makeups grow more and more alike? What is lost?

IDEAS FOR WRITING

Guided Writing

Write a narrative essay about the neighborhood or area in which you grew up.

1. Begin with a catchy opening to attract the reader's attention. Try to tell readers that something exists about your neighborhood that few people would believe is true.

2. Use a clear thesis statement to indicate why your neighborhood was, is, or will be especially interesting to others who did not live there.

3. Use the first person ("I") point of view.

4. Divide your narration chronologically into important time periods and explain your attitudes toward the area in each time.

5. Throughout your essay, make use of a number of allusions to make the narrative more vivid.

6. Use some expressions that were special to your neighborhood.

7. Conclude by explaining what your present attitude is toward the place. If you have recently visited the area, tell how it has or has not changed.

More Writing Projects

1. Bring to class two other writers' narrative pieces about places where they grew up. Be prepared to discuss what each has in common and how each is different.

2. Narrate an experience of prejudice—either against you or against someone else—that you witnessed.

3. In a brief essay narrate a moment about an urban or suburban neighborhood that you do not live in but that you visited.

4. Select some community that interests you and with narrative techniques like Lee's trace the evolution of that neighborhood over a span of time. Focus your narrative on the people, the scenery, the physical appearance, or a combination of these.

George Orwell

A HANGING

One of the masters of English prose, George Orwell (1903–1950) often used narration of personal events to explore important social issues. Notice here how he involves the reader in a simple yet fascinating and tragic story, almost as if he were writing fiction. Orwell takes a brief time span and expands that moment with specific language. At one point, as you will see, the purpose of the narrative comes into sharp focus.

Words to Watch

sodden (par. 1): heavy with water
absurdly (par. 2): ridiculously
desolately (par. 3): gloomily; lifelessly; cheerlessly
prodding (par. 3): poking or thrusting at something
Dravidian (par. 4): any member of a group of intermixed races of southern India and Burma
pariah (par. 6): outcast; a member of a low caste of southern India and Burma
servile (par. 11): slave-like; lacking spirit or independence
reiterated (par. 12): repeated
abominable (par. 13): hateful; disagreeable; unpleasant
timorously (par. 15): fearfully
oscillated (par. 16): moved back and forth between two points
garrulously (par. 20): in a talkative manner
refractory (par. 22): stubborn
amicably (par. 24): friendly; peaceably

It was in Burma, a sodden morning of the rains. A 1
sickly light, like yellow tinfoil, was slanting over the high
walls into the jail yard. We were waiting outside the
condemned cells, a row of sheds fronted with double bars,
like small animal cages. Each cell measured about ten feet
by ten and was quite bare within except for a plank bed and
a pot of drinking water. In some of them brown silent men
were squatting at the inner bars, with their blankets draped
round them. These were the condemned men, due to be
hanged within the next week or two.

One prisoner had been brought out of his cell. He 2
was a Hindu, a puny wisp of a man, with a shaven head and
vague liquid eyes. He had a thick, sprouting moustache,
absurdly too big for his body, rather like the moustache of
a comic man on the films. Six tall Indian warders were
guarding him and getting him ready for the gallows. Two
of them stood by with rifles with fixed bayonets, while the
others handcuffed him, passed a chain through his handcuffs
and fixed it to their belts, and lashed his arms tight to his
sides. They crowded very close about him, with their hands
always on him in a careful, caressing grip, as though all the
while feeling him to make sure he was there. It was like
men handling a fish which is still alive and may jump back
into the water. But he stood quite unresisting, yielding his
arms limply to the ropes, as though he hardly noticed what
was happening.

Eight o'clock struck and a bugle call, desolately thin 3
in the wet air, floated from the distant barracks. The
superintendent of the jail, who was standing apart from the
rest of us, moodily prodding the gravel with his stick, raised
his head at the sound. He was an army doctor, with a grey
toothbrush moustache and a gruff voice. "For God's sake
hurry up, Francis," he said irritably. "The man ought to
have been dead by this time. Aren't you ready yet?"

Francis, the head jailer, a fat Dravidian in a white 4
drill suit and gold spectacles, waved his black hand. "Yes
sir, yes sir," he bubbled. "All iss satisfactorily prepared. The
hangman iss waiting. We shall proceed."

"Well, quick march, then. The prisoners can't get 5 their breakfast till this job's over."

We set out for the gallows. Two warders marched on 6 either side of the prisoner, with their files at the slope; two others marched close against him, gripping him by arm and shoulder, as though at once pushing and supporting him. The rest of us, magistrates and the like, followed behind. Suddenly, when we had gone ten yards, the procession stopped short without any order or warning. A dreadful thing had happened—a dog, come goodness knows whence, had appeared in the yard. It came bounding among us with a loud volley of barks, and leapt round us wagging its whole body, wild with glee at finding so many human beings together. It was a large woolly dog, half Airedale, half pariah. For a moment it pranced round us, and then, before anyone could stop it, it had made a dash for the prisoner, and jumping up tried to lick his face. Everyone stood aghast, too taken aback even to grab at the dog.

"Who let that bloody brute in here?" said the super- 7 intendent angrily. "Catch it, someone!"

A warder, detached from the escort, charged clumsily 8 after the dog, but it danced and gambolled just out of his reach, taking everything as part of the game. A young Eurasian jailer picked up a handful of gravel and tried to stone the dog away, but it dodged the stones and came after us again. Its yaps echoed from the jail walls. The prisoner, in the grasp of the two warders, looked on incuriously, as though this was another formality of the hanging. It was several minutes before someone managed to catch the dog. Then we put my handkerchief through its collar and moved off once more, with the dog still straining and whimpering.

It was about forty yards to the gallows. I watched 9 the bare brown back of the prisoner marching in front of me. He walked clumsily with his bound arms, but quite steadily, with that bobbing gait of the Indian who never straightens his knees. At each step his muscles slid neatly into place, the lock of hair on his scalp danced up and down, his feet printed themselves on the wet gravel. And once, in spite of the men who gripped him by each shoulder, he stepped slightly aside to avoid a puddle on the path.

It is curious, but till that moment I had never 10 realised what it means to destroy a healthy, conscious man. When I saw the prisoner step aside to avoid the puddle, I saw the mystery, the unspeakable wrongness, of cutting a life short when it is in full tide. This man was not dying, he was alive just as we were alive. All the organs of his body were working—bowels digesting food, skin renewing itself, nails growing, tissues forming—all toiling away in solemn foolery. His nails would still be growing when he stood on the drop, when he was falling through the air with a tenth of a second to live. His eyes saw the yellow gravel and the grey walls, and his brain still remembered, foresaw, reasoned—reasoned even about puddles. He and we were a party of men walking together, seeing, hearing, feeling, understanding the same world; and in two minutes, with a sudden snap, one of us would be gone—one mind less, one world less.

The gallows stood in a small yard, separate from the 11 main grounds of the prison, and overgrown with tall prickly weeds. It was a brick erection like three sides of a shed, with planking on top, and above that two beams and a crossbar with the rope dangling. The hangman, a grey-haired convict in the white uniform of the prison, was waiting beside his machine. He greeted us with a servile crouch as we entered. At a word from Francis the two warders, gripping the prisoner more closly than ever, half led, half pushed him to the gallows and helped him clumsily up the ladder. Then the hangman climbed up and fixed the rope round the prisoner's neck.

We stood waiting, five yards away. The warders had 12 formed in a rough circle round the gallows. And then, when the noose was fixed, the prisoner began crying out on his god. It was a high, reiterated cry of "Ram! Ram! Ram! Ram!", not urgent and fearful like a prayer or a cry for help, but steady, rhythmical, almost like the tolling of a bell. The dog answered the sound with a whine. The hangman, still standing on the gallows, produced a small cotton bag like a flour bag and drew it down over the prisoner's face. But the sound, muffled by the cloth, still persisted, over and over again: "Ram! Ram! Ram! Ram! Ram!"

The hangman climbed down and stood ready, holding 13 the lever. Minutes seemed to pass. The steady, muffled crying from the prisoner went on and on, "Ram! Ram! Ram!" never faltering for an instant. The superintendent, his head on his chest, was slowly poking the ground with his stick; perhaps he was counting the cries, allowing the prisoner a fixed number—fifty, perhaps, or a hundred. Everyone had changed colour. The Indians had gone grey like bad coffee, and one or two of the bayonets were wavering. We looked at the lashed, hooded man on the drop, and listened to his cries—each cry another second of life; the same thought was in all our minds: oh, kill him quickly, get it over, stop that abominable noise!

Suddenly the superintendent made up his mind. 14 Throwing up his head he made a swift motion with his stick. "Chalo!" he shouted almost fiercely.

There was a clanking noise, and then dead silence. 15 The prisoner had vanished, and the rope was twisting on itself. I let go of the dog, and it galloped immediately to the back of the gallows; but when it got there it stopped short, barked, and then retreated into a corner of the yard, where it stood among the weeds, looking timorously out at us. We went round the gallows to inspect the prisoner's body. He was dangling with his toes pointed straight downwards, very slowly revolving, as dead as a stone.

The superintendent reached out with his stick and 16 poked the bare body; it oscillated, slightly. "*He's* all right," said the superintendent. He backed out from under the gallows, and blew out a deep breath. The moody look had gone out of his face quite suddenly. He glanced at his wristwatch. "Eight minutes past eight. Well, that's all for this morning, thank God."

The warders unfixed bayonets and marched away. 17 The dog, sobered and conscious of having misbehaved itself, slipped after them. We walked out of the gallows yard, past the condemned cells with their waiting prisoners, into the big central yard of the prison. The convicts, under the command of warders armed with lathis, were already receiving their breakfast. They squatted in long rows, each man holding a tin pannikin, while two warders with buckets marched round ladling out rice; it seemed quite a homely, jolly scene, after the hanging. An enormous relief had come upon us now that the job was done. One felt an impulse to sing, to break into a run, to snigger. All at once everyone began chattering gaily.

The Eurasian boy walking beside me nodded towards 18 the way we had come, with a knowing smile: "Do you know, sir, our friend (he meant the dead man), when he heard his appeal had been dismissed, he pissed on the floor of his cell. From fright.—Kindly take one of my cigarettes, sir. Do you not admire my new silver case, sir? From the boxwallah, two rupees eight annas. Classy European style."

Several people laughed—at what, nobody seemed 19 certain.

Francis was walking by the superintendent, talking 20 garrulously: "Well, sir, all hass passed off with the utmost satisfactoriness. It wass all finished—flick! like that. It iss not always so—oah, no! I have known cases where the doctor wass obliged to go beneath the gallows and pull the prisoner's legs to ensure decease. Most disagreeable!"

"Wriggling about, eh? That's bad," said the super- 21 intendent.

"Ach, sir, it iss worse when they become refractory! 22 One man, I recall, clung to the bars of hiss cage when we went to take him out. You will scarcely credit, sir, that it took six warders to dislodge him, three pulling at each leg. We reasoned with him. 'My dear fellow,' we said, 'think of all the pain and trouble you are causing to us!' But no, he would not listen! Ach, he wass very troublesome!"

I found that I was laughing quite loudly. Everyone 23 was laughing. Even the superintendent grinned in a tolerant way. "You'd better all come out and have a drink," he said quite genially. "I've got a bottle of whisky in the car. We could do with it."

We went through the big double gates of the prison, 24

into the road. "Pulling at his legs!" exclaimed a Burmese magistrate suddenly, and burst into a loud chuckling. We all began laughing again. At that moment Francis's anecdote seemed extraordinarily funny. We all had a drink together, native and European alike, quite amicably. The dead man was a hundred yards away.

BUILDING VOCABULARY

1. It is often possible to figure out the meaning of a difficult word by using context clues—clues in surrounding words and sentences. Without a dictionary, make an "educated guess" on the definitions of the words in italics below. Before you guess, look back to the paragraph for clues. Afterward, check your guess in a dictionary.

    a. *condemned* men (par. 1)
    b. puny *wisp* of a man (par. 2)
    c. Indian *warders* (par. 2)
    d. careful *caressing* grip (par. 2)
    e. stood *aghast* (par. 6)
    f. it danced and *gambolled* (par. 7)
    g. *solemn* foolery (par. 10)
    h. armed with *lathis* (par. 17)
    i. a tin *pannikin* (par. 17)
    j. quite *genially* (par. 23)

2. What are definitions for the words below? Look at words within them, which you may be able to recognize.

    a. moodily
    b. dreadful
    c. Eurasian
    d. incuriously
    e. formality

3. a. Select any five words from the Words to Watch section on page 54 and write a sentence of your own for each.

    b. Select any five words from Exercises 1 and 2 above and write a sentence of your own for each.

UNDERSTANDING THE WRITER'S IDEAS

1. What is the main point that the writer wishes to make in this essay? Which paragraph tells the author's purpose most clearly? Which sentence in that paragraph best states the main idea of the essay?

2. The events in the essay occur in Burma, a country in Asia. Describe in your own words the specific details of the action.

3. Who are the major characters in this essay? Why might you include the dog as a major character?

4. In a narrative essay the writer often tells the events in chronological order. Examine the following events from "A Hanging." Arrange them in the order in which they occurred.

a. A large wooly dog tries to lick the prisoner's face.

b. A Eurasian boy talks about his silver case.

c. The superintendent signals "Chalo!" to the hangman.

d. One prisoner, a Hindu, is brought from his cell.

e. Francis discusses with the superintendent a prisoner who had to be pulled off the bars of his cage.

f. The prisoner steps aside to avoid a puddle as he marches to the gallows.

5. What is the author's opinion of *capital punishment* (legally killing someone who has disobeyed the laws of society)? How does the incident with the puddle suggest that opinion, even indirectly?

UNDERSTANDING THE WRITER'S TECHNIQUES

1. In the first paragraph of the essay, we see clear images such as "brown silent men were squatting at the inner bars, with their blankets draped around them." The use of color and action make an instant appeal to our sense of sight.

a. What images in the rest of the essay do you find most vivid?

b. Which sentence gives the best details of sound?

c. What word pictures suggest action and color?

d. Where do you find words that describe a sensation of touch?

2. In order to make their images clearer, writers use *figurative language* (see Glossary). "A Hanging" is especially rich in *similes,* which are comparisons using the word *like* or *as.*

a. What simile does Orwell use in the first paragraph in order to let us see how the light slants over the jail yard walls? How does the simile make the scene clearer?

b. What other simile does Orwell use in the first paragraph?

c. Discuss the similes in the paragraphs listed below. What are the things being compared? Are the similes, in your opinion, original? How do they contribute to the image the author intends to create?

(1) "It was like man handling a fish. . . ." (par. 2)

(2) "A thick sprouting moustache . . . rather like the moustache of a comic man in the films." (par. 2)

(3) "It was a high, reiterated cry . . . like the tolling of a bell." (par. 12)

(4) "The Indians had gone grey like bad coffee. . . ." (par. 13)

(5) "He was dangling with his toes pointed straight downwards, slowly revolving, as dead as a stone." (par. 15)

3. You know that an important feature of narration is the writer's ability to look at a brief span of time and to expand that moment with specific language.

a. How has Orwell limited the events in "A Hanging" to a specific moment in time and place?

b. How does the image "a sodden morning of the rains" in paragraph 1 set the mood for the main event portrayed in the essay? What is the effect of the image "brown silent men"? Why does Orwell describe the prisoner as "a puny wisp of a man, with a shaven head and vague liquid eyes"? (par. 2) Why does the author present him in almost a comic way?

c. What is the effect of the image about the bugle call in paragraph 3? Why does Orwell create the image of the dog trying to lick the prisoner's face (par. 6)? How does it contribute to his main point? In paragraph 12, Orwell tells us that the dog whines. Why does he give that detail? Discuss the value of the images about the dog in paragraphs 15 and 17.

d. Why does Orwell offer the image of the prisoner stepping aside "to avoid a puddle on the path"? How does it advance the point of the essay? What is the effect of the image of the superintendent poking the ground with his stick (par. 13)?

e. What is the importance of the superintendent's words in paragraph 3? What is the value of the Eurasian boy's conversation in paragraph 18? How does the dialogue in paragraphs 20 to 24 contribute to Orwell's main point?

f. Why has Orwell left out information about the crime the prisoner committed? How would you feel about the prisoner if you knew he were, say, a rapist, a murderer, a molester of children, or a heroin supplier?

4. Analyze the point of view in the essay. Is the "I" narrator an observer, a participant, or both? Is he neutral or involved? Support your opinion.

5. In "A Hanging," Orwell skillfully uses several forms of *irony* to support his main ideas. Irony, in general, is the use of language to suggest the opposite of what is said. First, there is *verbal irony,* which involves a contrast between what is said and what is actually meant. Second, there is *irony of situation,* where there is a contrast between what is expected or thought appropriate and what actually happens. Then, there is *dramatic irony,* in which there is a contrast between what a character says and what the reader (or the audience) actually knows or understands.

a. Look at paragraph 2. Why does Orwell describe the prisoner as a *comic* type? Why does he emphasize the prisoner's *smallness?* Why does Orwell write that the prisoner "hardly noticed what was happening"? Why might this be called ironic?

b. When the dog appears in paragraph 6, how is its behavior described? How do the dog's actions contrast with the situation?

c. What is the major irony that Orwell analyzes in paragraph 10?

d. In paragraph 11, how does the fact that one prisoner is being used to execute another prisoner strike you?

e. Why is the Superintendent's remark in paragraph 11—"*He's* all right"—a good example of verbal irony?

f. After the hanging, the men engage in seemingly normal actions. However, Orwell undercuts these actions through the use of irony. Find at least three examples of irony in paragraphs 17 to 24.

EXPLORING THE WRITER'S IDEAS

1. Orwell is clearly against capital punishment. Why might you agree or disagree with him? Are there any crimes for which capital punishment is acceptable to you? If not, what should society do with those convicted of serious crimes?

2. Do you think the method used to perform capital punishment has anything to do with the way we view it? Is death by hanging or firing squad worse than death by gas or by the electric chair? Or are they all the same? Socrates— a Greek philosopher convicted of conspiracy—was forced to drink *hemlock,* a fast acting poison. Can you accept that?

3. Orwell shows a variety of reactions people have to an act of execution. Can you believe the way the people behave here? Why? How do you explain the large crowds that gathered to watch public executions in Europe in the sixteenth and seventeenth centuries?

IDEAS FOR WRITING

Guided Writing

Write a narrative theme of four or five paragraphs in which you tell about a punishment you either saw or received. Use sensory language, selecting your details carefully. At one point in your paper—as Orwell does in paragraph 10—state your opinion or interpretation of the punishment clearly.

1. Use a number of images that name colors, sounds, smells, and actions.

2. Try to write at least three original similes. Think through your comparisons carefully. Make sure they are logical. Avoid overused comparisons like "He was white as a ghost."

3. Set your narrative in time and place. Tell the season of the year and the place in which the event occurred.

4. Fill in details of the setting. Show what the surroundings look like.

5. Name people by name. Show details of their actions. Quote some of their spoken dialogue.

6. Use the first-person point of view.

More Writing Projects

1. Write a narrative essay in which you tell the story of an execution from the point of view of either the executioner or the person condemned to die. Focus on the last moments before the execution.

2. Write an essay in which you narrate an event that turned out differently from what you expected—a blind date, a picnic, a holiday. Try to stress the irony of the situation.

3. Write a narrative that describes a vivid event in which you hid your true feelings about the event, such as a postelection party, the wedding of someone you disliked, a job interview, a visit to the doctor.

3

Illustration

One convenient way for writers to present and to support a point is through *illustration*—that is, by means of several examples to back up an idea. Illustration helps a writer put general or abstract thoughts into specific examples. It also holds a reader's interest: We all respond to concrete instances when we are trying to understand a point. Certainly, you are no stranger to illustration as a way to present information. Every time you try to explain why you believe or feel something to be true, and you give more than one case to back it up, you are using this technique.

Suppose you want to share with a friend your belief that the Los Angeles Dodgers are a great baseball team. First you might point out the pitching staff; then you might bring up the quality hitters; then the fielders; then the management. Your friend would, no doubt, expect you to explain each of those illustrations by giving some details. And so you would name a couple of first-rate pitchers, perhaps describe them and state their won-lost record; you would tell which of the hitters you thought outstanding and point out their runs-batted-in and their hitting averages; you would describe a good fielder or two in action, even telling a story, perhaps, of one really first-rate play you saw when the Dodgers pounded the Reds.

When you present illustrations, it is best to have *several* reasons that lead you to a certain conclusion. A single, isolated example might not convince anyone easily, unless it is a strong, extended example. You have to make decisions, of course, about the number and kinds of details to offer for each example. Sometimes each illustration will itself require a few different examples to make the point. And you have to decide which illustration to give first: No doubt you would save the most important for last.

As you have probably guessed, when you write an essay of illustration you will be using much of what you have already learned so far. Techniques of description and narration will help you support and organize your examples clearly and strongly. In fact, a number of ways to develop essays discussed later on—comparison, cause and effect, process analysis, definition, and classification—lend themselves to development by illustration. The selections you will read in this section show how four writers use illustration to advance their ideas.

ILLUSTRATION 67

Randall Williams

DADDY TUCKED THE BLANKET

Randall Williams was a reporter for *The Alabama Journal* when he wrote this autobiographical essay. He is trying here to show how the social conditions of the poor have an ugly effect upon personal relationships. A number of examples point out how his family reacted to each other and to the environment created by poverty.

Words to Watch

humiliating (par. 5): lowering the pride or dignity of someone
shiftless (par. 7): incapable; inefficient; lazy
articulate (par. 7): able to speak clearly
teetering (par. 8): wavering; moving unsteadily
deteriorating (par. 12): becoming worse
futility (par. 13): the quality of being useless
abuse (par. 16): mistreatment
psyche (par. 20): the mind
affluent (par. 21): wealthy
grandeur (par. 23): magnificence

About the time I turned 16, my folks began to 1 wonder why I didn't stay home any more. I always had an excuse for them, but what I didn't say was that I had found my freedom and I was getting out.

I went through four years of high school in semirural 2
Alabama and became active in clubs and sports; I made a
lot of friends and became a regular guy, if you know what
I mean. But one thing was irregular about me: I managed
those four years without ever having a friend visit at my
house.

I was ashamed of where I lived. I had been ashamed 3
for as long as I had been conscious of class.

We had a big family. There were several of us 4
sleeping in one room, but that's not so bad if you get along,
and we always did. As you get older, though, it gets worse.

Being poor is a humiliating experience for a young 5
person trying hard to be accepted. Even now—several years
removed—it is hard to talk about. And I resent the weakness
of these words to make you feel what it was really like.

We lived in a lot of old houses. We moved a lot 6
because we were always looking for something just a little
better than what we had. You have to understand that my
folks worked harder than most people. My mother was
always at home, but for her that was a full-time job—and
no fun, either. But my father worked his head off from the
time I can remember in construction and shops. It was hard,
physical work.

I tell you this to show that we weren't shiftless. No 7
matter how much money Daddy made, we never made much
progress up the social ladder. I got out thanks to a college
scholarship and because I was a little more articulate than
the average.

I have seen my Daddy wrap copper wire through the 8
soles of his boots to keep them together in the wintertime.
He couldn't buy new boots because he had used the money
for food and shoes for us. We lived like hell, but we went to
school well-clothed and with a full stomach.

It really is hell to live in a house that was in bad 9
shape 10 years before you moved in. And a big family puts
a lot of wear and tear on a new house, too, so you can
imagine how one goes downhill if it is teetering when you
move in. But we lived in houses that were sweltering in
summer and freezing in winter. I woke up every morning

for a year and a half with plaster on my face where it had fallen out of the ceiling during the night.

This wasn't during the Depression; this was in the late 60's and early 70's. 10

When we boys got old enough to learn trades in 11 school, we would try to fix up the old houses we lived in. But have you ever tried to paint a wall that crumbled when the roller went across it? And bright paint emphasized the holes in the wall. You end up more frustrated than when you began, especially when you know that at best you might come up with only enough money to improve one of the six rooms in the house. And we might move out soon after, anyway.

The same goes for keeping a house like that clean. 12 If you have a house full of kids and the house is deteriorating, you'll never keep it clean. Daddy used to yell at Mama about that, but she couldn't do anything. I think Daddy knew it inside, but he had to have an outlet for his rage somewhere, and at least yelling isn't as bad as hitting, which they never did to each other.

But you have a kitchen which has no counter space 13 and no hot water, and you will have dirty dishes stacked up. That sounds like an excuse, but try it. You'll go mad from the sheer sense of futility. It's the same thing in a house with no closets. You can't keep clothes clean and rooms in order if they have to be stacked up with things.

Living in a bad house is generally worse on girls. 14 For one thing, they traditionally help their mother with the housework. We boys could get outside and work in the field or cut wood or even play ball and forget about living conditions. The sky was still pretty.

But the girls got the pressure, and as they got older 15 it became worse. Would they accept dates knowing they had to "receive" the young man in a dirty hallway with broken windows, peeling wallpaper and a cracked ceiling? You have to live it to understand it, but it creates a shame which drives the soul of a young person inward.

I'm thankful none of us ever blamed our parents for 16 this, because it would have crippled our relationships. As it worked out, only the relationship between our parents was damaged. And I think the harshness which they expressed to each other was just an outlet to get rid of their anger at the trap their lives were in. It ruined their marriage because they had no one to yell at but each other. I knew other families where the kids got the abuse, but we were too much loved for that.

Once I was about 16 and Mama and Daddy had had 17 a particularly violent argument about the washing machine, which had broken down. Daddy was on the back porch— that's where the only water faucet was—trying to fix it and Mamma had a washtub out there washing school clothes for the next day and they were screaming at each other.

Later that night everyone was in bed and I heard 18 Daddy get up from the couch where he was reading. I looked out from my bed across the hall into their room. He was standing right over Mama and she was already asleep. He pulled the blanket up and tucked it around her shoulders and just stood there and tears were dropping off his cheeks and I thought I could faintly hear them splashing against the linoleum rug.

Now they're divorced. 19

I had courses in college where housing was discussed, 20 but the sociologists never put enough emphasis on the impact living in substandard housing has on a person's psyche. Especially children's.

Small children have a hard time understanding 21 poverty. They want the same things children from more affluent families have. They want the same things they see advertised on television, and they don't understand why they can't have them.

Other children can be incredibly cruel. I was in 22 elementary school in Georgia—and this is interesting because it is the only thing I remember about that particular school—when I was about eight or nine.

After Christmas vacation had ended, my teacher 23 made each student describe all his or her Christmas presents. I became more and more uncomfortable as the privilege passed around the room toward me. Other children were reciting the names of the dolls they had been given, the kinds of bicycles and the grandeur of their games and toys. Some had lists which seemed to go on and on for hours.

It took me only a few seconds to tell the class that 24 I had gotten for Christmas a belt and a pair of gloves. And then I was laughed at—because I cried—by a roomful of children and a teacher. I never forgave them, and that night I made my mother cry when I told her about it.

In retrospect, I am grateful for that moment, but I 25 remember wanting to die at the time.

BUILDING VOCABULARY

1. For each expression in italics in Column A select from Column B the best definition. On a separate sheet of paper, write the correct letter after each number.

Column A	Column B
a. one thing was *irregular* about me	1. absolute
b. *conscious* of class	2. object to
c. I *resent* the weakness	3. way to express anger
d. houses that were *sweltering*	4. are expected to
e. an *outlet for his rage*	5. force
f. the *sheer* sense of futility	6. not correct
g. they *traditionally* help mother	7. very hot
h. the *impact* living in substandard housing has	8. unbelievably
i. *incredibly* cruel	9. aware
j. in *retrospect*	10. looking back

UNDERSTANDING THE WRITER'S IDEAS

1. Why did the author never have a friend visit his house? How did he explain to his parents the fact that, at sixteen, he did not stay home any more?

2. Describe some of the situations Williams remembers about the houses in which he lived as a child. Why

was it hard to keep the houses clean? Why was living in such a house so bad for the author's sisters? Why did the family keep moving around?

3. Why did the Williams family never "progress up the social ladder"? Why does he stress the idea that the family was not shiftless?

4. Why, according to the author, was his parent's relationship damaged? Why were they frequently having violent arguments? How does Williams show the love his father had for his mother?

5. Why does the author believe that children can be incredibly cruel?

6. What is the meaning of the last paragraph? For which moment do you think the author is grateful, the moment in school or the moment in which his mother cried? Why would he be grateful for either of those moments?

UNDERSTANDING THE WRITER'S TECHNIQUES

1. What is Williams's main point in this essay? Which sentence expresses the writer's *thesis?*

2. What details does Williams offer to illustrate the fact that he lived in bad houses? Which details are clearest to you?

3. How does Williams illustrate how little money his father had for himself?

4. How does Williams illustrate the way his parents argued? What elements of narration do you find in that example? Where else does the author use narrative as part of an illustration?

5. In which illustrations does the author use description? Where do you find good descriptive details in this essay? On the whole, though, the author has not used descriptive language very much. Why? Where would you have liked to see more concrete detail?

6. One way that the author has for tying together his ideas is by frequently reminding the reader of his thesis. Review your response to question 1 above; then, find words or word groups later on in the essay that repeat the main

point, either through the same words or through words that mean the same or similar things.

7. This essay is written in a very simple style. How does the author achieve this simplicity? Is it the vocabulary? How would you describe it? Is it the sentence structure? What kinds of sentences does Williams write most of the time? What is the effect of the numerous short paragraphs? What is your reaction to the two paragraphs that have only one sentence in each of them?

8. Do the author's illustrations support his main point successfully? Why do you think he chose illustration as a way to develop his idea? Which illustration do you find most effective? Why does he tell the story about his experience in school after Christmas one year at the *end* of the essay?

9. When a writer exaggerates emotions, he is often accused of *sentimentality*. In sentimental writing the author plays with the reader's emotions simply for their own sake. Would you call Williams sentimental? Why? Which images deliberately convey an emotional stance? Do you feel as if he is exaggerating emotions here? Where has he *avoided* sentimentality when he might have played up the scene for its emotional content?

EXPLORING THE WRITER'S IDEAS

1. Williams says that it is hard to talk about his humiliating past experiences, and then he says, "I resent the weakness of these words to make you feel what it was really like." Do you agree that words are weak in conveying feeling to someone who might not have experienced that feeling? Williams is talking about *humiliation* and how words are not strong enough to make people feel it. What other feeling have you had that might be hard to convey in words? Despite the fact that the author complains about words, he writes, nonetheless, about his experiences. How do you explain that?

2. Has Williams fairly presented the condition of poverty in America? How does his own situation show some

ways that a family or an individual may overcome certain features of poverty? Would you say that poverty in a rural area is the same as poverty in a large city like Atlanta, or Chicago, or New York?

3. Do you agree with Williams' analysis that his father and mother yelled at each other because they needed an outlet for their anger? Do you think the need for such an outlet can force apart two people who love each other? Is it possible for people to fight constantly and still to love each other? What instances from your own experience can you quote to demonstrate these points? How do you account for the fact that despite poverty and frequent fights, some parents stay together without divorcing?

4. The author suggests that housing plays an important part in the development of a person's psyche. Do you agree? Why? What ingredients would you list for perfect home conditions? Would you include anything other than simple physical conditions like walls that do not crumble or washing machines that work?

5. Williams' father and mother obviously sacrificed many of their own needs and comforts for their children. Do you believe that parents should make such sacrifices? Why or why not?

6. Do you agree that living in a bad house is more difficult for girls than boys? Why?

IDEAS FOR WRITING

Guided Writing

On a separate sheet of paper, fill in the blanks in this sentence and then write an essay of 350 to 500 words in which you use illustration to present your ideas:

Being _____ is a _____
experience for a young person.

1. For the blank spaces select words which reflect important aspects of your own experiences. You do not have to pick negative qualities: You might say, "Being *free* is an *important* experience for a young person." Or, you might

follow one of these other suggestions if you cannot think of one of your own. But be sure to avoid overused words like *good, bad, nice, fantastic,* or *interesting.*

      a. Being *lonely* is a *terrible* experience for a young person.

      b. Being *frightened* is an *unforgetable* experience for a young person.

      c. Being *loved* is a *vital* experience for a young person.

      d. Being *"different"* is a *sad* experience for a young person.

    2.   Use the sentence you have written as the thesis sentence of your paragraph. Build an introduction around it.

    3.   Illustrate your thesis with examples drawn from your own experience. Provide at least three illustrations.

    4.   If your illustrations require narrative, follow the techniques you learned in Chapter 2 about good narration.

    5.   If you have to use description, make sure you follow the suggestions in Chapter 1 about good description. Use concrete, sensory language to help your reader see your points clearly.

    6.   Connect the different illustrations in your essay by referring to the main point in your thesis sentence.

More Writing Projects

    1.   Write an essay of illustration in which you show how certain conditions affected your parents' relationship. You might show the effect of *poverty* on their lives; or you might show the effect of a *city, love, religion, education, superstition, fear, children* on their lives. Feel free to name any condition you choose.

    2.   Write an essay in which you provide illustrations to show the nature of poverty in your neighborhood, city, or state. You may want to select illustrations from your own experience or observation. Or, you might want to use other sources, like newspaper articles, books, magazines, presentations on radio or television.

Annette Dula

NO HOME IN AFRICA

On a visit to Africa, Annette Dula, a teacher, discovered some surprising things about her cultural roots as a black American. Presenting a wide range of personal experiences, she develops her essay by means of illustration. Notice how each illustration reinforces Dula's thesis in this essay.

Words to Watch

anonymity (par. 2): not being known by others
servile (par. 4): like or characteristic of a slave
Mensaab (par. 4): a word of Hindu origin meaning "lady" or "mistress"
mercenary (par. 5): working for money only; greedy
rejoiced (par. 11): made glad or happy; delighted
unescorted (par. 13): not accompanied
resented (par. 14): felt displeasure
galled (par. 14): irritated; annoyed
docile (par. 17): easy to teach or discipline
typify (par. 20): to be typical of
reciprocal (par. 20): on both sides; done, felt, or given in return

I have no cultural roots in Africa nor do I want any. 1
I have discovered that Egypt is not black Africa. The skin

isn't black enough and the hair isn't kinky enough. An Egyptian merchant put his light brown arm next to my black arm and said, "My skin isn't black but I'm African, too." Sincerity was not in his voice.

In Khartoum, the Sudan, a near-riot developed 2 when I appeared to be an African woman walking down the street in a leather miniskirt. I liked melting into the anonymity of hundreds of black faces, but I also wanted the freedom that tourists enjoy.

I went to Ethiopia with Kay, who is white. The 3 people were hostile. They pelted me with rotten tomatoes. They did not bother Kay. Didn't they realize that I was black like them?

In East Africa, the Africans were too servile toward 4 whites. I got extremely angry when a gnarled little old man would bow down and call my friend "Mensaab." An African woman would not become angry.

I hated the mercenary Indians of East Africa more 5 than the Africans hated them. Two years after the incident, I can still taste the bitterness. I wanted to buy material for a blouse. At the time, most shopkeepers in East Africa were Indians. I had walked in ahead of Kay. The shopkeeper continued talking to another Indian. Kay walked in. The shopkeeper rushed up to her.

"Can I help you, madam?" he asked, with the proper 6 servility.

"My friend wants to buy material," she said. 7

"How much does she want to pay for it?" he asked. 8

"Perhaps you'd better talk to her, sir." 9

Completely ignoring her suggestion, he continued 10 explaining to Kay the virtues of expensive imported materials over cheaper native ones. "You know, these Africans are lazy. They just aren't capable of the superior quality you get in Western work!"

I walked out. I knew what prejudice was—but not 11 this kind. This was the type my parents had known in North Carolina 25 years ago. I rejoiced when the Indians were kicked out of Uganda.

I do have the appearance of a black African. I have 12

even been asked by Africans. "To what tribe do you belong?" And, "From what part of Africa do you come?" When it was to my advantage to be considered African, it pleased me. At other times, embarrassing situations could develop.

Once when I was walking from a restaurant at 13 around 9:30 P.M., four or five policemen jumped out of a squad car, surrounded me, and pointed their loaded guns at me. Though they were speaking in Swahili, I soon gathered that I was being arrested on prostitution charges. The more I protested in English, the more incensed they became. I reacted as any American woman would. "Who do you think you are? Get those guns out of my face. I am an American. I want to call the Ambassador." (Later, I learned that Kenya had a new law making it illegal for unescorted African women to be on the street after 9:30 P.M.)

More often than not, I resented being treated as an 14 African by Africans. I was truly galled at the customs station between Zaire and the Central African Republic. Tourists usually pass customs by merely showing their passports. Africans are subjected to a thorough search. As I was about to move along with other tourists, I was roughly grabbed from behind and thrust back into the crowd. I had to be freed by other tourists. The mob attitude was: "Who do you think you are? You're not a tourist! You're one of us." Why didn't I protest the preferential treatment that tourists receive? Because I felt as the American tourists do: "We are entitled to these considerations."

When I understood that the average African male 15 has little respect for the female intellect, I was surprised. Ngimbus, a close friend of mine, decided that I was a militant feminist when I lectured him on male-female equality!

"She looks like an African, but she talks nonsense," 16 he said later.

Often, I found myself defending black Americans to 17 nationalist West-Africans. A favorite question was "Why do you call yourselves *Afro*-American?" I usually answered in terms of cultural heritage, identity oppression, and other nebulous words that explain nothing. The conversation would continue: "You have forfeited the right to call yourselves *Afro*-Americans. If you were worthy of the name *Afro-,* your people would never have taken all those years of such treatment. We sympathize with you, but you're too docile for us."

"What about South Africa and Mozambique?" I would always ask. 18

The question was usually ignored or if answered, the time factor was brought in: "We have accomplished more in eighty years than you have accomplished in 400 years." The conversation always left me with a need to explain our differences. But there never were acceptable explanations. 19

My experiences in Africa typify the reciprocal misunderstandings between black Americans and Africans. Our common color is not enough. Too much time has passed. 20

I am not patriotic, but I am a product of America. I believe in freedom of speech, even if it is only token. I take education for granted though we may not receive it equally. I believe in the working of democracy even though it never seems to work. I am forced to accept that I am an American and that here in America lie my cultural roots—whether I like it or not. 21

BUILDING VOCABULARY

1. For each word in italics below, select the correct meaning.

a. an Egyptian *merchant*
1. marcher   2. lover   3. businessperson   4. lawyer
5. police officer

b. *sincerity* was not in his voice
1. honesty   2. sweetness   3. love   4. lust
5. hoarseness

c. the people were *hostile*
1. farmers   2. horrible   3. unconcerned
4. unfriendly   5. peculiar

d. a *gnarled* little man
1. affectionate   2. twisted   3. graceful   4. weak
5. devoted

e. the more *incensed* they became

1. insensible   2. inspired   3. silent   4. angry
5. indirect

f. *preferential* treatment

1. special   2. predictable   3. poor   4. prejudiced
5. anonymous

g. a *militant* feminist

1. armed   2. aggressive   3. masculine   4. ridiculous
5. attractive

h. cultural *heritage*

1. finance   2. value   3. religion   4. fear
5. tradition

i. other *nebulous* words

1. vague   2. strong   3. clear   4. unimportant
5. undefinable

j. you have *forfeited*

1. fulfilled   2. forgiven   3. established   4. questioned
5. given up

UNDERSTANDING THE WRITER'S IDEAS

1.   Why, according to the author, is Egypt not part of black Africa?

2.   What happened in Khartoum? in Ethiopia?

3.   Why would an African woman not get angry if someone called a white person "Mensaab"?

4.   Why was the author bitter about the incident with East African Indians? Why did the shopkeeper ignore her? Why does Dula say that this incident reminded her of the prejudice her parents experienced in North Carolina?

5.   Why was the author treated differently from other tourists at the customs station between Zaire and the Central African Republic?

6.   What did Ngimbas mean when he said, "She looks like an African, but she talks nonsense"? (par. 16)

7.   How did Dula defend black Americans to West Africans? Why do you think she felt it necessary to do so?

8.   Why does the author say she is a product of America and that in America lie her cultural roots?

9. What is the main point of the essay? Which sentence states it most clearly?

UNDERSTANDING THE WRITER'S TECHNIQUES

1. In your own words explain the illustrations Dula offers to show that

a. it was hard to be a "free" tourist as a black in Africa

b. African men have little respect for the female intellect

c. there was hostility directed towards her

d. unescorted black women were not allowed on the streets after 9:30 p.m. in Kenya

e. she did not like being treated like an African by Africans

2. Dula developed her illustrations in different ways and with different degrees of detail. Where does she use narration? Where does she use description?

3. Which illustration does she develop with the most details? Why do you think she chose to emphasize that one? To develop the incidents in Khartoum and in Ethiopia, the author presents very few details. Why? How do they help build up to the incident with the Indians?

4. Where does Dula attempt to compare and/or contrast? How does her purpose in writing this essay almost *demand* certain comparisons and contrasts? (See pp. 105–106.)

5. Dula arranges her illustrations by *place* order; that is, she offers an example first about one geographical area and then about another. When she names a new place, it serves as a *transition* to a new example. However, she uses other techniques—words or phrases—to join her examples together smoothly. What transitions has she used in this way? Make a list of several. Where does Dula *repeat* or *refer back to* her main point in order to provide clear transitions?

6. From the kind of language and sentence struc-

ture she uses, to what kind of audience is Dula speaking? Why has she not used more informal language? How do her purpose and the quality of her style match?

EXPLORING THE WRITER'S IDEAS

1. Part of Dula's disappointment comes, it would seem, from what she expected her treatment to be like as a black in Africa. How do you think she expected to be treated?

2. Dula suggests enormous differences in the way black and white tourists are treated in Africa. Do these differences exist for black and white tourists in America? in Europe? Draw from your own experience, if you can, or check with friends or relatives who have traveled.

3. In several places (paragraphs 1, 12, 19), Dula questions the ability of skin color to join people together. Why might you agree (or disagree) with her comment, "Our common color is not enough"? Would you say that *religion* is not enough? *nationality?* What would you say *is* enough to join people together?

4. The author says, "When it was to my advantage to be considered African it pleased me." At other times she was not pleased to be considered African. How is Dula's position typical of the way most people would feel under similar circumstances? Do you think it all right to "straddle the fence," so to speak, to be one thing at a time when it serves you well and to be something else when it does not serve you well? (A black man or woman in white America is often denied that privilege. Why?)

5. Why do Africans question the phrase *Afro*-American for American blacks? Are their questions reasonable? Dula suggests that conditions in South Africa and Mozambique should be weighed against criticism that Afro-Americans are too docile. What happened in those countries? How did Africans respond to the author's point? Are their answers convincing to you? Why?

6. Do you agree with the points Dula makes in the last paragraph? How do you explain the last sentence?

IDEAS FOR WRITING

Guided Writing

Using illustration as your means of development, write an essay (500 to 750 words) in which you show how your race, religion, nationality, or sex makes people behave toward you in a special way.

1. Determine the way people react to you because of your race, religion, nationality or sex; try to state that reaction in a word or two. If you are black, for example, do people *fear* you or *talk down* to you? If you are a woman, do people think you are *unintelligent* or *passive*?

2. Make sure that the illustrations you present support your point. Draw examples from your own experience. Develop some examples more completely than others.

3. Use concrete, sensory detail to make your examples real for your reader.

4. Decide on your audience for this essay. Select your language and sentence structure to reach that audience most effectively.

5. Determine an effective order for the illustrations you present. You might want to discuss things according to time order, taking the incident or situation that occurred first. Or, you might want to arrange the examples, saving the most important for last. If you are drawing incidents from different geographical areas, you may want to use place order.

More Writing Projects

1. Write an illustrative essay in which you discuss disappointments you experienced as a traveler.

2. Write an essay in which you illustrate how your view of certain things is different from the view of most people of your age, sex, religion, race, or nationality.

Ray Bradbury

TRICKS! TREATS! GANGWAY!

Ray Bradbury (1920–   ) is noted for his science fiction writing—you may have read *Farenheit 451* or have seen the movie—but in this piece he is recalling a special time of year for a boy who grew up in the midwest in the 1920s and 1930s. Illustrations drawn from his childhood show what a grand time Halloween really was in Illinois.

Words to Watch

corrupted (par. 2): spoiled; ruined
induce (par. 2): cause; bring about
climax (par. 6): the highest point of interest or excitement
corn shocks (par. 7): a bunch of corn sheaves drawn together to dry
grisly renderings (par. 8): terrifying examples
crump-backed (par. 8): creased; humpbacked
caldron (par. 10): a large kettle
banshee (par. 10): a female spirit that warns of death
bereavements (par. 10): losses of people through death
serpentines (par. 10): coils
papier-mâché (par. 10): a material made of paper pulp that can be molded into objects when moist
vulnerable (par. 15): open to attack
disemboweled (par. 17): with the bowels or entrails removed

Halloweens I have always considered wilder and   1
richer and more important than even Christmas morn. The
dark and lovely memories leap back at me as I see once
again my ghostly relatives, and the lurks and things that
creaked stairs or sang softly in the hinges when you opened
a door.

For, you see, I have been most fortunate in the   2
selection of my aunts and uncles and midnight-minded
cousins. My grandma gave me her old black-velvet opera
cape to cut into batwings and fold about myself when I was
eight. My aunt gave me some white candy fangs to stick in
my mouth and make delicious and most terrible smiles. A
great-aunt encouraged me in my witchcrafts by painting my
face into a skull and stashing me in closets to induce cardiac
arrest in passing cousins or upstairs boarders. My mother
corrupted me completely by introducing me to Lon Chaney
in *The Hunchback of Notre Dame* when I was three.

In sum, Halloween has always been *the* celebration   3
for me and mine. And those Halloweens in the late 1920s
and early '30s come back to me now at the least scent of
candlewax or aroma of pumpkin pies.

Autumns were a combination of that dread moment   4
when you see whole windows of dime stores full of nickel
pads and yellow pencils meaning School is Here—and also
the bright promise of October, that stirring stuff which lurks
in the blood and makes boys break out in joyful sweats,
planning ahead.

For we *did* plan ahead in the Bradbury houses. We   5
were three families on one single block in Waukegan, Ill.
My grandma and, until he died in 1926, grandpa, lived in
the corner house; my mom and dad, and my brother Skip
and I, in the house next south of that; and around the block
my Uncle Bion, whose library was wise with Edgar Rice
Burroughs and ancient with H. Rider Haggard.

1928 was one of the prime Halloween years. Every-   6
thing that was grandest came to a special climax that
autumn.

My Aunt Neva was 17 and just out of high school,   7
and she had a Model-A Ford. "Okay, kiddo," she said around

about October 20. "It's coming fast. Let's make plans. How do we use the attics? Where do we put the witches? How many corn shocks do we bring in from the farms? Who gets bricked up in the cellar with the Amontillado?"

"Wait, wait, wait!" I yelled—and we made a list. 8 Neva drew pictures and made paintings of the costumes we would all wear to make the holiday truly fascinating and horrible. That was Costume Painting Night. When Neva finished, there were sketches of Grandma as the nice mother in "The Monkey's Paw," paintings of my dad as Edgar Allan Poe, some fine grisly renderings of my brother as crump-backed Quasimodo, and myself playing my own xylophone skeleton as Dr. Death.

After that came, in one flying downpour, Costume 9 Cutting Night, Mask Painting Night, Cider Making Night, Candle Dippling and Taffy Pulling Night, and Phonograph Playing Night, when we picked the spookiest music. Halloween, you see, didn't just stroll into our yards. It had to be seized and shaped and *made* to happen!

My grandparents' home, then, was a caldron to 10 which we might bring hickory sticks that looked like witches' broken arms and leaves from the family graveyard out where the banshee trains ran by at night souling the air with bereavements. To their house, upstairs and down, must be fetched corn shocks from fields just beyond the burying tombs, and pumpkins. And from Woolworth's, orange-black crepe serpentines, and bags of black confetti which you tossed on the wind, yelling, "A witch just sneezed!" and papier-mâché masks that smelled like a sour dog's fur after you had snuffed in and out while running. All of it had to be fetched, carried, touched, held, sniffed, crunched along the way.

October 29 and 30 were almost as great as October 11 31, for those were the late afternoons, the cool, spicy dusks when Neva and Skip and I went out for the Slaughter and final Gathering.

"Watch out, pumpkins!" 12

I stood by the Model A as the sun furnaced the 13 western sky and vanished, leaving spilled-blood and burnt-pumpkin colors behind. "Pumpkins, if they had any brains, would hide tonight!" said I.

"Yeah," said Skip. "Here comes the Smiler with the 14 Knife!" I beamed, feeling my Boy Scout knife in my pocket.

We reached our uncles' farms and went out to dance 15 around the corn shocks and grab great armfuls and wrestle them like dry Indian ghosts back to the rumble seat. Then we went back to get the harvest-moon pumpkins. They burrowed in the cereal grass, but they could not escape the Smiler and his friends. Then home, with the cornstalks waving their arms wildly in the wind behind us, and the pumpkins thudding and running around the floorboards trying to escape. Home toward a town that looked vulnerable under burning clouds, home past real graveyards with real cold people in them, your brother and sister, and you thinking of them suddenly and knowing the true, deep sense of Halloween.

The whole house had to be done over in a few short, 16 wildly laughing hours. All staircases must be eliminated by grabbing leaves out of dining-room tables and covering the steps so you could only scrabble and slip up and then slide, shrieking, down, down, down into night. The cellar must be mystified with sheets hung on lines in a ghostly maze through which giggling and screaming banshees must blunder and flee, children suddenly searching for mothers, and finding spiders. The icebox must be stashed with chicken viscera, beef hearts, ox tongues, tripe, chicken legs and gizzards, so that at the height of the party the participants, trapped in the coal cellar, might pass around the "parts" of the dead witch: "Here's her heart! . . . Here's her finger! . . . Here's her eyeball!"

Then, everything set and placed and ready, you run 17 out late from house to house to make certain-sure that each boy-ghost remembers, that each girl-become-witch will be there tomorrow night. Your gorilla fangs in your mouth, your winged cape flapping, you come home and stand in front of your grandparents' house and look at how great and spooky it has become, because your sappy aunt and your loony brother and you yourself have magicked it over, doused the lights, lit all the disemboweled pumpkins and got it ready like a dark beast to devour the children as they arrive through its open-mouth door tomorrow night.

You sneak up on the porch, tiptoe down the hall, 18 peer into the dim pumpkin-lit parlor and whisper: "Boo."

And that's *it*. 19

Oh, sure, Halloween arrived. Sure, the next night 20 was wild and lovely and fine. Apples swung in doorways to be nibbled by two dozen hungry mice-children. Apples and gargling kids almost drowned in water tubs while ducking for bites.

But the party was almost unimportant, wasn't it? 21 Preparation was 70 percent of the lovely, mad game. As with most holidays, the getting set, the gathering sulfur for the explosion, was sweeter, sadder, lovelier than the stampede itself.

That Halloween of 1928 came like the rusted moon 22 up in the sky—sailing, and then down like that same moon. And it was over. I stood in the middle of my grandma's living room and wept.

On the way home across the lawn to my house, I 23 saw the pile of leaves I had made just that afternoon. I ran and dived in, and vanished. I lay there under the leaves, thinking. This is what it's like to be dead. Under grass, under dirt, under leaves. The wind blew and stirred the grand pile. Way out in farm country, a train ran past, wailing its whistle. The sound cut my soul. I felt the tears start up again. I knew if I stayed I would never get out of the grass and leaves; I would truly be dead. I jumped up, yelling, and ran in the house.

Later, I went to bed. "Darn," I said in the middle of 24 the night.

"Darn what?" asked my brother, awake in bed beside 25 me.

"365 darn days until Halloween again. What if I die, 26 waiting?"

"Why, then," said my brother, after a long silence, 27 "you'll *be* Halloween. Dead people *are* Halloween."

"Hey," said I, "I never *thought* of that." 28

"Think," said my brother.   29

I thought: 365 days from now . . .   30

Gimme a pad, some paper. Neva, rev up that Model   31
A! Skip, hunch your back! Farmyards, grow pumpkins!
Graveyards, shiver your stones! Moon, rise! Wind, hit the
trees, blow up the leaves! Up, now, run! Tricks! Treats!
Gangway!

And a small boy in midnight Illinois, suddenly glad   32
to be alive, felt something on his face. Between the snail-
tracks of his tears . . . a smile.

And then he slept.   33

BUILDING VOCABULARY

1.   Bradbury has often used informal expressions
in this essay. First, explain the meaning of the words in
italics in each group below. Then suggest a word or phrase
that an author who wished to be more formal might have
used instead.

   a. *"Okay, kiddo"* (par. 7)
   b. When we picked the *spookiest* music (par. 9)
   c. Your *sappy* aunt and your *loony* brother and
      yourself have *magicked* it over (par. 17)
   d. *Gangway!* (par. 31)

2. A number of figurative expressions (see Glossary) spark this essay. In the list of examples of simile,
metaphor, and *personification* below, explain each figure.
(Personification is giving an object, thing, or idea lifelike or
human qualities.) What is being compared to what? What
other figures can you find in the essay?

   a. "Halloween, you see, didn't just stroll into our
yards. It had to be seized and shaped and made to happen"
(*personification*) (par. 9)
   b. "My grandparents' home was a caldron (*metaphor*) to which we might bring hickory sticks that looked
like witches' broken arms" (*simile*) (par. 10)

c. "Where *banshee* trains *ran* by at night" (*metaphor*) (par. 10)

d. "papier mâché masks that smelled *like* a *sour dog's fur*" (*simile*) (par. 10)

e. "The sun *furnaced* the Western sky (*personification*) and vanished, leaving *spilled blood* and *burnt pumpkin colors* behind" (*metaphor*) (par. 13)

UNDERSTANDING THE WRITER'S IDEAS

1. What part of the essay most clearly states the author's purpose?

2. What two things did autumn signify to Bradbury?

3. What were some of the various activities for the Bradburys before October 29?

4. Why were October 29 and 30 almost as great as October 31? What did Bradbury and Neva and Skip do?

5. What is the "true, deep sense of Halloween"?

6. How did the young Bradburys change the house into a Halloween place?

7. How do the activities before Halloween compare with the activities after it? Which activities did the narrator prefer?

8. Why does the author say "Darn" in the middle of the night after Halloween? Why is he unhappy?

9. How does his brother ease Bradbury's unhappiness?

10. Why does the author smile just before he goes to sleep?

UNDERSTANDING THE WRITER'S TECHNIQUES

1. How is this essay an example of *illustration?* What examples does Bradbury give to show he has been lucky to have Halloween-minded relatives? How does he illustrate that "1928 was one of the prime Halloween years"?

2.   The examples Bradbury offers to show the quality of the 1928 Halloween vary in their length and degree of development. Which examples are developed most fully?

3.   In any essay of illustration the writer will often provide a simple listing of examples to demonstrate a point he is trying to make. Paragraph 15 offers a listing of details, but none of the examples is fully developed. Why does Bradbury use this technique here? What other paragraphs offer a listing of details to illustrate a point?

4.   Check your responses to the question in Building Vocabulary 2. How do all the figurative expressions contribute to Bradbury's topic? How are most of the metaphors and similes related to the topic and to each other?

5.   Underline some sentences that you think have the best sensory details. Where does the author use color? action? sound? smell?

6.   Look at the last sentence in paragraph 9: "All of it had to be fetched, curried, touched, held, sniffed, crunched along the way." Why has Bradbury used so many verbs? What is the effect upon the reader?

7.   It is clear that the style here is simple, direct, and informal. Why has the writer chosen such a style? How is it related to the topic of the essay? to the character represented in it?

8.   What is the meaning of the title? Why do you think the author selected it? How does it reflect the personality of a young boy?

9.   To enrich the meaning of an essay, a writer will often use *allusion,* a reference to some other work in literature (see Glossary). The statement made by Aunt Neva, "Who gets bricked up in the cellar with the Amontillado?" is an allusion to a short story by Edgar Allan Poe, "The Cask of Amontillado." What is that brief story about? Why would Bradbury want to allude to Poe in this essay about Halloween? What other references to literature does the writer make (see paragraphs 2 and 8)? Explain them, or ask your instructor to if you are not familiar with them.

10.   In what sequence has Bradbury presented the events in this essay? How has he used the order he selects

to create a kind of suspense, a building up from minor events to major ones?

11. Before he states his purpose in this essay, Bradbury offers a couple of paragraphs of introduction. What information does he deal with in his introduction? How does that information set the stage for the real point of the essay?

EXPLORING THE WRITER'S IDEAS

1. It is a strong statement to make that Halloween is "wilder and richer and more important than Christmas morn." Does Bradbury support his point well? In your experience, is Halloween so wild, so rich, and so important a holiday? Why? In your family, is there a special holiday for which everyone makes grand preparations? Describe it.

2. Bradbury's wild view of Halloween was, to a large degree, encouraged by his relatives' reaction to the holiday, too. How do your views about some holiday—like the Fourth of July, Thanksgiving, even Halloween—compare with or differ from the views of your relatives? In what cases do your relatives enrich your appreciation? detract from it?

3. What is the real significance of Halloween (check the dictionary or encyclopedia)? Why does that holiday still have a hold on the imagination of children today? Bradbury says that passing by a graveyard, he knew from the dead the "true deep sense of Halloween." Do you agree? Is *that* the true sense of Halloween?

4. Bradbury says in paragraph 20 that the party was less important than the preparation for it. Would you agree, in general, that the *preparation* for an event—such as a holiday, a wedding, a party—is often more important than the event itself? Explain your answer by giving a specific example from your own life.

5. How are Bradbury's feelings after Halloween is over typical of feelings any young child would have? How is he able to overcome these feelings? Are children generally able to cope with disappointment in the way young Bradbury has?

Guided Writing

Write an essay of 500 words in which you *illustrate* the value to you of some holiday you celebrate.

    1. Write an introduction that builds up to your thesis, as Bradbury has. State in your thesis sentence just how you feel about the holiday. Is it a wild time, like Bradbury's Halloween, or deeply religious, or just a time of nonstop fun with marvelous meals and parties?

    2. Decide on an effective order for the illustrations you present. If you offer examples to support an idea about one particular holiday (the Christmas of 1982, for example) you might want to use chronology. If you present several examples (drawn over a number of years) to show why one holiday is important to you, you might again use chronology. But you might also want to tell the events according to their importance, saving the most important for last.

    3. Depending upon how many examples you offer, develop your illustrations with enough details. Some of your illustrations will require expanded treatment, others will not. In any case, offer at least three examples to support your point.

    4. Since you are drawing from your own experience, you will want to use sensory language—colors, smells, actions, sounds, images of touch. Try to use figurative expressions as effectively as Bradbury has.

    5. After you present and develop your illustrations, discuss in your conclusion how you feel after the holiday is over.

More Writing Projects

    1. In recent years, Halloween has become a rather dangerous holiday where innocent children often come to harm by thoughtless, mean adults. Write an essay of 350 to 500 words illustrating the dangers of Halloween. Or, write an essay in which you show by means of illustration what

steps your town or community takes to prevent Halloween accidents.

2.   Write an essay in which you show how one relative shared in the joys or pains of your childhood experiences. Select as illustration important moments that you can narrate clearly and in concrete, sensory language.

3.   Do some research about a local festival, the preparations for it, and the activities involved in its celebration. Or, you might choose to investigate a more remote festival in another part of the country, such as the chili contest in Texas, sausage festivals in Wisconsin, pie-eating contests associated with State Fairs. After you collect your research, write a four or five paragraph essay illustrating different features of this festival.

Lewis Thomas

DEATH IN THE OPEN

Dr. Lewis Thomas is president of the Memorial Sloan-Kettering Cancer Center in New York City. He has written numerous articles about science, medicine, and life structures and cycles geared for the lay reader. His observations often bring fascinating clarity to the cycles of life and death on our planet. The following essay, a brilliant inquiry into the "natural marvel" of death, appears in his book *Lives Of A Cell* (1974), which won the National Book Award for Arts and Letters in 1975.

Words to Watch

voles (par. 1): rodents
impropriety (par. 2): an improper action or remark
progeny (par. 4): descendants or offspring
mutation (par. 4): a sudden genetic change
amebocytes (par. 4): one-celled organisms
stipulated (par. 6): to make a special condition for
incongruity (par. 6): something which is not consistent with its environment
conspicuous (par. 7): very obvious
inexplicably (par. 7): unexplainably
anomalies (par. 10): irregularities
notion (par. 11): an idea
detestable (par. 11): hateful
synchrony (par. 11): simultaneous occurrence

Most of the dead animals you see on highways near 1
the cities are dogs, a few cats. Out in the countryside, the
forms and coloring of the dead are strange; these are the
wild creatures. Seen from a car window they appear as
fragments, evoking memories of woodchucks, badgers, skunks,
voles, snakes, sometimes the mysterious wreckage of a
deer.

It is always a queer shock, part a sudden upwelling 2
of grief, part unaccountable amazement. It is simply as-
tounding to see an animal dead on a highway. The outrage
is more than just the location; it is the impropriety of such
visible death, anywhere. You do not expect to see dead
animals in the open. It is the nature of animals to die alone,
off somewhere, hidden. It is wrong to see them lying out on
the highway; it is wrong to see them anywhere.

Everything in the world dies, but we only know 3
about it as a kind of abstraction. If you stand in a meadow,
at the edge of a hillside, and look around carefully, almost
everything you can catch sight of is in the process of dying,
and most things will be dead long before you are. If it were
not for the constant renewal and replacement going on
before your eyes, the whole place would turn to stone and
sand under your feet.

There are some creatures that do not seem to die at 4
all; they simply vanish totally into their own progeny. Single
cells do this. The cell becomes two, then four, and so on,
and after a while the last trace is gone. It cannot be seen
as death; barring mutation, the descendants are simply the
first cell, living all over again. The cycles of the slime mold
have episodes that seem as conclusive as death, but the
withered slug, with its stalk and fruiting body, is plainly
the transient tissue of a developing animal; the free-swim-
ming amebocytes use this organ collectively in order to
produce more of themselves.

There are said to be a billion billion insects on the 5
earth at any moment, most of them with very short life
expectancies by our standards. Someone has estimated that
there are 25 million assorted insects hanging in the air over
every temperate square mile, in a column extending upward
for thousands of feet, drifting through the layers of the

atmosphere like plankton. They are dying steadily, some by being eaten, some just dropping in their tracks, tons of them around the earth, disintegrating as they die, invisibly.

Who ever sees dead birds, in anything like the huge 6 numbers stipulated by the certainty of the death of all birds? A dead bird is an incongruity, more startling than an unexpected live bird, sure evidence to the human mind that something has gone wrong. Birds do their dying off somewhere, behind things, under things, never on the wing.

Animals seem to have an instinct for performing 7 death alone, hidden. Even the largest, most conspicuous ones find ways to conceal themselves in time. If an elephant missteps and dies in an open place, the herd will not leave him there; the others will pick him up and carry the body from place to place, finally putting it down in some inexplicably suitable location. When elephants encounter the skeleton of an elephant out in the open, they methodically take up each of the bones and distribute them, in a ponderous ceremony, over neighboring acres.

It is a natural marvel. All of the life of the earth 8 dies, all of the time, in the same volume as the new life that dazzles us each morning, each spring. All we see of this is the odd stump, the fly struggling on the porch floor of the summer house in October, the fragment on the highway. I have lived all my life with an embarrassment of squirrels in my backyard, they are all over the place, all year long, and I have never seen, anywhere, a dead squirrel.

I suppose it is just as well. If the earth were otherwise, 9 and all the dying were done in the open, with the dead there to be looked at, we would never have it out of our minds. We can forget about it much of the time, or think of it as an accident to be avoided, somehow. But it does make the process of dying seem more exceptional than it really is, and harder to engage in at the times when we must ourselves engage.

In our way, we conform as best we can to the rest of 10 nature. The obituary pages tell us of the news that we are dying away, while the birth announcements in finer print, off at the side of the page, inform us of our replacements, but we get no grasp from this of the enormity of scale. There are 3 billion of us on the earth, and all 3 billion must be dead, on a schedule, within this lifetime. The vast mortality, involving something over 50 million of us each year, takes place in relative secrecy. We can only really know of the deaths in our households, or among our friends. These, detached in our minds from all the rest, we take to be unnatural events, anomalies, outrages. We speak of our own dead in low voices; struck down, we say, as though visible death can only occur for cause, by disease or violence, avoidably. We send off for flowers, grieve, make ceremonies, scatter bones, unaware of the rest of the 3 billion on the same schedule. All of that immense mass of flesh and bone and consciousness will disappear by absorption into the earth, without recognition by the transient survivors.

Less than a half century from now, our replacements 11 will have more than doubled the numbers. It is hard to see how we can continue to keep the secret, with such multitudes doing the dying. We will have to give up the notion that death is catastrophe, or detestable, or avoidable, or even strange. We will need to learn more about the cycling of life in the rest of the system, and about our connection to the process. Everything that comes alive seems to be in trade for something that dies, cell for cell. There might be some comfort in the recognition of synchrony, in the information that we all go down together, in the best of company.

BUILDING VOCABULARY

1. Thomas uses *adjectives* freely throughout this essay to create vivid descriptions. Adjectives can be fairly obvious in their modification of nouns; for example: a *red* caboose, a *cold* winter, and a *slender* woman. However, Thomas makes imaginative and often unique use of adjectival expressions. Explain the meaning of each of the following:

   a. *queer* shock (par. 2)
   b. *unaccountable* amazement (par. 2)

c. *visible* death (pars. 2, 10)
d. *transient* tissue (par. 4)
e. *ponderous* ceremony (par. 7)
f. *neighboring* acres (par. 7)
g. *natural* marvel (par. 8)
h. *vast* majority (par. 10)
i. *relative* secrecy (par. 10)
j. *transient* survivors (par. 11)

2. An *idiom* is an expression that has a special meaning only when taken as a whole; taken separately, the words may not make sense.

What are the meanings of the following idioms?

a. upswelling of grief (par. 2)
b. catch sight of (par. 3)
c. on the wing (par. 6)
d. in time (par. 7)
e. no grasp on (par. 10)
f. for cause (par. 10)

UNDERSTANDING THE WRITER'S IDEAS

1. Why does Thomas feel that it is strange to see dead animals in the countryside? How are dead animals more varied in the country than in the city? According to Thomas, for what reason is it a shock to see a dead animal on the road?

2. In paragraph 3, Thomas suggests that death is often an "abstraction." What does he mean by this statement? How does he suggest we can make death something more real? In your own words, for what reasons does he suggest we accept the life-death cycle as a more concrete idea?

3. Why, according to Thomas, do single cells seem not to die?

4. What is the meaning of the question at the beginning of paragraph 6? How does it relate to the theme of the essay? To what does the author compare seeing a dead bird? Why does he call it an "incongruity"? How is it "sure evidence . . . that something has gone wrong"?

5. Explain the process of death among elephants as Thomas describes it.

6. Explain the meaning of "the old stump" in paragraph 8. What two examples of "the old stump" does Thomas offer?

7. What example from personal experience does Thomas give to show that dead animals seem "to disappear"?

8. Explain the meaning of the first sentence of paragraph 9. In your own words, tell why Thomas feels the way he does.

9. What is the "secret" in paragraph 11?

10. Thomas says, "In our own way, we conform as best we can to the rest of nature." What does he mean? What supporting examples does he offer? What is the result? What examples does Thomas give of our reactions to the death of other human beings?

11. Why does Thomas say we must change our attitude toward death? How does he suggest that we do so?

UNDERSTANDING THE WRITER'S TECHNIQUES

1. Study the introductory paragraphs. Why does the author offer several examples? Why is "the mysterious wreckage of a deer" an especially effective example?

2. Are there any clear illustrations in paragraph 2? Why or why not? What is the effect? Explain the connection between paragraphs 2 and 3.

3. Paragraphs 4 to 8 use illustrations to support a series of generalizations or topic sentences. Put a checkmark by the topic sentence in these paragraphs and identify the generalization. Then, analyze the illustrations used to support each one. Which examples are the most specific; the most visual; the most personal? Are there any extended examples?

4. How does paragraph 9 serve as a transition to the topic of paragraph 10? Why does Thomas use statistics in paragraph 10? How do they drive his point home?

5. What is Thomas's thesis in this essay? In what way is it reinforced by the concluding paragraph?

6. The author's use of pronouns in this essay is

interesting. First, trace the use of first-person pronouns ("I," "we," "my," "our"). Why does Thomas use such pronouns? Why is their use in paragraph 8 especially effective? Next, consider Thomas's frequent use of the pronoun *it*. (Beginning writers are often instructed to minimize their use of such pronouns as *it, this,* and *that* because they are not specific and may leave the reader confused). Explain what the word *it* stands for in paragraphs 2, 4, 8, and 9. Why does Thomas use a word whose meaning may be confusing?

7. Thomas uses *figurative language* (see Glossary) in this essay, particularly *similes* and *metaphors* (see Glossary). Explain in your own words the meanings of the following similes and metaphors:

    a. "*the mysterious wreckage* of a deer" (par. 1)
    b. "episodes that seem *as conclusive as death*" (par. 4)
    c. "drifting through the layers of the atmosphere *like plankton*" (par. 5)

8. We may say that the expression "dropping in their tracks" in paragraph 5 is a kind of pun. (A *pun* is a humorous use of a word or an expression that suggests two meanings.) What is the popular expression using the words *dropping* and *flies* that Thomas' phrase puns on?

9. Thomas makes use of a technique called "repetition with a difference," that is, saying *almost* the same thing for added emphasis. Explain how repetition with a difference adds effectiveness to the sentences in which each of the following expressions is used:

    a. "alone, hidden" (par. 7)
    b. "each morning, each spring" (par. 8)
    c. "unnatural events, anomalies, outrages" (par. 10)
    d. "catastrophe, or detestable, or avoidable, or even strange" (par. 11)

10. *Parallelism* is a type of sentence structure within a paragraph that creates a balance in the presentation of ideas and adds emphasis. It often uses a repeating pattern

of subjects and verbs, prepositional phrases, questions, and so on (see Glossary). How does Thomas use parallelism in paragraph 3? paragraph 10? paragraph 11?

EXPLORING THE WRITER'S IDEAS

1. We might say that Thomas's title, "Death in the Open," is a double entendre (that is, has a double meaning; see Glossary). In what two ways may we interpret the phrase "in the open" as it relates to the contents of the essay? How do the two meanings relate to the philosophical points Thomas makes, especially in the two opening paragraphs and in the conclusion? Do you feel it is important to be more "open" about death? Why?

2. In paragraph 10, Thomas writes, "We speak of our own dead in low voices; struck down, we . . ." "Struck down" is used here as a *euphemism* (a word or phrase used to replace others that are upsetting or distasteful; see Glossary). What other euphemisms do we have for death? Euphemisms for dying are often used to explain death to children. Do you think it is right, or necessary, to use such "guarded language" with youngsters? Why? For what other words or expressions do we commonly use euphemisms?

3. At the end of the essay, Thomas suggests that we might be less comfortable with death if we understood it more clearly as a natural, common occurrence. What are your feelings about this philosophy?

4. According to Thomas's views in paragraph 9, because we don't often see dead animals "in the open," we are less prepared when we do encounter death. Do you think this reasoning is correct? Why or why not?

5. In paragraph 7 Thomas explains the process of death among elephants. What is your impression of the elephant herd's behavior at the death of one of its members? Why does Thomas call it "a natural marvel"? Have you ever heard the expression "the elephant dying grounds"? What does it mean?

IDEAS FOR WRITING

Guided Writing

Write an essay in which you illustrate "_____ in the open." Fill the blank with a word of your choice, a word that reflects some phenomenon, emotion, or idea that has features often hard to understand. You might write about birth in the open, concerts in the open, love in the open, fear in the open, war in the open, for example.

1. Develop an introduction with general examples that are relevant to your topic.

2. Add one or two paragraphs in which you speculate or philosophize on the phenomenon you are writing about.

3. Point out how the topic is most common throughout nature, society, or the world.

4. Give at least three extended examples that illustrate your topic.

5. Use the first-person pronouns "I" and "we" to add emphasis.

6. Illustrate ways in which we are generally unaware of certain features of the topic or tend to hide these features.

7. Try to include at least one statistic in your essay.

8. Use some idiomatic expression in your essay.

9. Conclude your essay with some examples of how and why we can become more "open" about the topic.

More Writing Projects

1. Write an essay in which you use examples to tell of your first experiences with death. You may want to write about the death of a relative, a friend, an acquaintance, a celebrity, or a pet.

2. Visit a place in the countryside (or a park) for one hour. Make a written record as you walk around detailing all evidence of natural death that you come across. Then write an illustrative essay on natural death as you observed it.

3. In your library, explore various burial practices among different races, religions, or ethnic groups and write an essay in which you illustrate several of these practices.

4

Comparison and Contrast

Comparison and contrast is a method of analyzing likenesses and differences between two or more subjects. Writers use comparison and contrast simply because it is often the best way to explain something. An object or an idea is often better understood only when its features stand next to those of another object or idea. We appreciate soccer when we compare it with football; we understand communism when we see it in the light of capitalism.

In *comparison,* the likenesses or similarities appear in a carefully organized manner. In *contrast,* the approach centers on the differences between two items. Often you will employ only comparison or only contrast in an essay, but it is also possible to combine both methods in the same paper.

You frequently make comparisons and contrasts in the course of your daily life. If you have to select an accounting course during registration, you might find out about the instructors for the various sections before making a choice. If you want to buy a new car, you might locate comparative performance ratings for models that interest you most. If you are planning to buy ten packages of hot dogs for a barbecue, you might check prices, product quality, and other details before choosing one brand over another. In all cases, you employ a thought pattern that sorts out likenesses and differences and arrives at a decision based on a comparative analysis of items.

The pattern of comparison and contrast in writing is more carefully organized than the comparative pattern we employ in everyday situations. Yet both circumstances demand common sense. For one thing, any strong pattern of comparison and contrast treats items that are only in the same category or class. It makes little or no sense to compare an accounting teacher with a history teacher, a car with an ant, or a hot dog with a head of lettuce. Second, there always has to be a basis for your comparison; in other words, you compare or contrast two items in order to make a decision or choice about them. And third, you always try to deal with all important aspects of the things being compared before arriving at a final determination. These common-sense characteristics of comparison and contrast apply to our pattern of thought as well as to our pattern of writing.

When you write a comparison and contrast essay, you should begin by identifying clearly the subjects of your comparison and by establishing the basis of your comparison. The thesis sentence performs this function for you ("Professor Smith is a better accounting teacher than Professor Williams because he is more experienced, more structured, and more intelligent"). There are three main ways to present your points of comparison (block, alternating, and combination); each will be dealt with in detail in this chapter. It is necessary to note here, however, that in presenting your material you should maintain a balance in the treatment of the two subjects in your comparison. In other words you do not want to devote most of your essay to subject A, and only a small fraction to subject B. Proper arrangement and balance of items in a comparative essay is a major consideration.

Rachel Carson

A FABLE FOR TOMORROW

Rachel Carson wrote a number of books and articles in the 1950s and 1960s that alerted Americans to dangers facing our natural environment. In this section from *Silent Spring* (1962), look for the ways in which Carson establishes a series of contrasts for her imaginary American town.

Words to Watch

migrants (par. 2): people, animals, or birds that move from one place to another
blight (par. 3): a disease or condition that kills or checks growth
maladies (par. 3): illnesses
moribund (par. 4): dying
pollination (par. 5): the transfer of pollen (male sex cells) from one part of the flower to another
granular (par. 7): consisting of grains
specter (par. 9): a ghost; an object of fear or dread
stark (par. 9): bleak; barren; standing out in sharp outline

There was once a town in the heart of America 1 where all life seemed to live in harmony with its surroundings. The town lay in the midst of a checkerboard of prosperous farms, with fields of grain and hillsides of orchards where, in spring, white clouds of bloom drifted above the green fields. In autumn, oak and maple and birch set up a blaze of color that flamed and flickered across a backdrop of pines. Then foxes barked in the hills and deer silently crossed the fields, half hidden in the mists of the fall mornings.

Along the roads, laurel, viburnum and alder, great 2 ferns and wildflowers delighted the traveler's eye through much of the year. Even in winter the roadsides were places of beauty, where countless birds came to feed on the berries and on the seed heads of the dried weeds rising above the snow. The countryside was, in fact, famous for the abundance and variety of its bird life, and when the flood of migrants was pouring through in spring and fall people traveled from great distances to observe them. Others came to fish the streams, which flowed clear and cold out of the hills and contained shady pools where trout lay. So it had been from the days many years ago when the first settlers raised their houses, sank their wells, and built their barns.

Then a strange blight crept over the area and 3 everything began to change. Some evil spell had settled on the community: mysterious maladies swept the flocks of chickens; the cattle and sheep sickened and died. Every-where was a shadow of death. The farmers spoke of much illness among their families. In the town the doctors had become more and more puzzled by new kinds of sickness appearing among their patients. There had been several sudden and unexplained deaths not only among adults but even among children, who would be stricken suddenly while at play and die within a few hours.

There was a strange stillness. The birds, for exam- 4 ple—where had they gone? Many people spoke of them, puzzled and disturbed. The feeding stations in the backyards were deserted. The few birds seen anywhere were moribund; they trembled violently and could not fly. It was a spring without voices. On the mornings that had once throbbed with the dawn chorus of robins, catbirds, doves, jays, wrens, and scores of other bird voices there was now no sound; only silence lay over the fields and woods and marsh.

On the farms the hens brooded, but no chicks 5 hatched. The farmers complained that they were unable to raise any pigs—the litters were small and the young survived only a few days. The apple trees were coming into bloom but no bees droned among the blossoms, so there was no pollination and there would be no fruit.

The roadsides, once so attractive, were now lined 6 with browned and withered vegetation as though swept by fire. These, too, were silent, deserted by all living things. Even the streams were now lifeless. Anglers no longer visited them, for all the fish had died.

In the gutters under the eaves and between the 7 shingles of the roofs, a white granular powder still showed a few patches; some weeks before it had fallen like snow upon the roofs and the lawns, the fields and streams.

No witchcraft, no enemy action had silenced the 8 rebirth of new life in this stricken world. The people had done it themselves.

This town does not actually exist, but it might easily 9 have a thousand counterparts in America or elsewhere in the world. I know of no community that has experienced all the misfortunes I describe. Yet every one of these disasters has actually happened somewhere, and many real communities have already suffered a substantial number of them. A grim specter has crept upon us almost unnoticed, and this imagined tragedy may easily become a stark reality we all shall know.

BUILDING VOCABULARY

1. In the second paragraph, find at least five concrete words that relate to trees, birds, and vegetation. How many of these objects could you identify? Look in a dictionary for the meanings of those words you do not know.

2. Try to identify the italicized words through the

context clues (see Glossary) provided by the complete sentence.

    a. half-hidden in the *mists*. (par. 1)
    b. when the first settlers *raised* their houses. (par. 2)
    c. *stricken* suddenly at play. (par. 3)
    d. the hens *brooded,* but no chicks hatched. (par. 5)
    e. *Anglers* no longer visited them, for all the fish had died. (par. 6)

UNDERSTANDING THE WRITER'S IDEAS

1. What is the quality of the world that Carson describes in her opening paragraph? If you had to describe it in just one or two words, which would you use?

2. What are some of the natural objects that Carson describes in her first two paragraphs? Why does she not focus on simply one aspect of nature—like animals, trees, or flowers?

3. How does Carson describe the "evil spell" that settles over the countryside?

4. What does Carson mean when she declares, "It was a spring without voices?" (par. 4) Why does she show that the critical action takes place in the springtime?

5. What do you think is the "white granular powder" that Carson refers to in paragraph 7? Why does she not explain what it is or where it came from?

6. In paragraph 9, the author states her basic point. What is it? Does she offer a solution to the problem that she poses?

UNDERSTANDING THE WRITER'S TECHNIQUES

1. What is the purpose of the description in this essay? Why does the writer use such vivid and precise words?

2. A *fable* is a story with a moral; in other words, a fable is a form of teaching narrative. How does Carson structure her narrative in this essay?

3. Where in this essay does Carson begin to shift from an essentially optimistic tone to a negative one?

4. Does Carson rely on comparison or contrast in this essay?

5. In this selection Carson uses what we call *the block method* of comparison and contrast. The writer presents all information about one subject, and then all information about a second subject, as in the diagram below:

a. How does Carson use this pattern in her essay?

b. Are there actually two subjects in this essay, or two different aspects of one subject? How does chronology relate to the block structure?

c. Are the two major parts of Carson's essay equally weighted? Why or why not?

d. In the second part of the essay, does Carson ever lose sight of the objects introduced in the first part? What new terms does she introduce?

6. How can you explain paragraphs 8 and 9—which do not involve narration, description, or comparison and contrast—in relation to the rest of the essay? What is the nature of Carson's conclusion?

EXPLORING THE WRITER'S IDEAS

1. Today, chemicals are used to destroy crop insects, to color and preserve food, and to purify our water, among other things. Would Carson term this "progress"? Would you? Do you think that there are inadequate safeguards and

controls in the use of chemicals? What recent examples of chemical use have made the news?

2. Why would you agree or disagree that factories and corporations should protect the environment that they use? Should a company, for example, be forced to clean up an entire river that it polluted? What about oil spills?

3. Have there been any problems with the use of chemicals and the environment in your own area? Describe them. How do local citizens feel about these problems?

4. Do you think that it will be possible in the future for Americans "to live in harmony" with their natural surroundings? Why do you believe what you do?

IDEAS FOR WRITING

Guided Writing

Write a fable (an imaginary story with a moral) in which you contrast one aspect of the life of a person, community, or nation with another.

1. Begin with a phrase similar to Carson's "There was once. . . ." so that the reader knows you are writing a narrative fable.

2. Relate your story to an American problem.

3. Use the block method in order to establish your contrast. Write first about one aspect of the topic and then about the other.

4. Use sensory detail in order to make your narrative clear and interesting.

5. Make certain that you establish an effective transition as you move into the contrast.

6. In the second part of your essay, be sure to refer to the same points you raised in the first part.

7. Use the conclusion to establish the "moral" of your fable.

More Writing Projects

1. Write an essay that contrasts the behavior of a person you knew sometime ago with his or her current behavior.

2. Develop a contrastive essay on a place you know well, one that has changed for better or worse. Explain the place as it once was, and as it is now. Use concrete images that appeal to color, action, sound, smell, and touch.

3. Examine the two extremes of the ecology issue today.

4. Using the block method, compare and contrast Carson's fable with the fable you wrote in Guided Writing.

Russell Baker

THE TWO ISMO'S

Russell Baker's witty column "The Sunday Observer" runs each week in *The New York Times* and provides readers with numerous insights into modern life. In this 1982 piece, he treats us to a tongue-in-cheek comparison between two kinds of social behavior in American cities.

Words to Watch

doctrines (par. 1): beliefs that are taught as truths
adherents (par. 1): believers in a particular doctrine
dogma (par. 1): a tenet or code of beliefs
blitz (par. 2): a fast, intensive raid or campaign
recourse (par. 5): a source of aid or assistance
primp (par. 8): to dress in a careful or finicky manner
Ou sont les neiges d'antan? (par. 11): French for *Where are the snows of yesteryear?*

American city life is now torn by two violently 1 opposed doctrines of social conduct. One is machismo. Its adherents pride themselves on being "machos." The opposing dogma is quichismo (pronounced "key shizmo"), and its practitioners call themselves quiche-o's (pronounced "key shows").

A good study of a quichismo victory over machismo 2 in an urban war zone can be found in Philip Lopate's "Quiche

Blitz on Columbus avenue," included in his recent book, "Bachelorhood." Curiously, however, Mr. Lopate refers to the quichismo doctrine by its French name, *quichisme.*

In doing so he unwittingly reveals that he is himself 3 a quiche-o of the highest order, for no macho would dream of using a French word when discussing philosophy, and even the average quiche-o would avoid a word as difficult to pronounce as *quichisme* for fear of getting it wrong and being sneered at as unquiche-o.

For practitioners of quichismo there is no defense 4 against being sneered at, and they live in dread of it. The machismo adherent, on the other hand, positively enjoys being sneered at since it entitles him to punch the sneerer in the nose, a ritual act ceremonially confirming that he is truly macho.

When a quiche-o is sneered at, his only recourse is 5 to jog until he achieves a higher sense of total fulfillment. This is one reason behind the machismo slogan, "Machos have more fun."

Maybe so, quiche-o's say, but machos don't have 6 French dry cleaning or white bucks. Machos prefer no dry cleaning at all though they sometimes get their clothes pressed if they've slept in them all week and want to impress females during the weekend.

Machos impress females by taking them to bars 7 after opening the top four buttons on their shirts to show off the hair on their chests. Quiche-o women impress males by inviting them to dinner and serving salad from the carry-out gourmet shop, followed by a kiwi fruit. There are no macho women. If there were they would serve pigs' feet and beer because machos believe that real people don't eat salad, kiwi fruit or anything else that comes from gourmet shops.

Quiche-o people buy swedish toothpaste at gourmet 8 drugstores, Italian loafers at gourmet shoe shops, newspapers at gourmet newsstands and dogs at gourmet pet centers. Afterwards they have them wormed by gourmet veterinarians. They also go to the islands for a month or two, especially Bermuda, St. Bart's, Barbados and Trinidad. Machos also go to the islands—Coney and Long—usually for a Sunday afternoon. To primp for these vacations, machos first go to the barber.

No quiche-o has set foot in a barber shop for the last 9 20 years. He goes to a gourmet hairdresser for a styling, then, before jetting off to the islands, goes to the gourmet luggage shop for suitcases covered with the initials of gourmet designers. The macho packs a change of underwear and a drip-dry shirt in a zippered plastic briefcase his uncle brought back from a 1977 convention of T-shirt salesmen.

Quiche-o's are always redecorating. Machos are al- 10 ways repainting the room that has the TV set in it. When a macho's couch and chairs are finally ruined he goes to a department store and buys "a suit of furniture." Quich-o furniture is never ruined, but it goes out of style every two years, and when it does the quiche-o goes to an environmental systems boutique and buys a new environment.

No quiche-o would ever take a walk in his undershirt 11 unless it had something amusing printed on it, like *"Ou sont les neiges d'antan?"* No macho would ever appear on the beach in a male bikini. No quiche-o would every wear black U.S. Keds with white soles and laces. No macho would ever walk into a hardware store and ask for a wok spatula.

Machos don't see anything funny about New Jersey. 12 Quiche-o's never laugh at people who drive Volvos, people who pay $5.50 for a hamburger or quiche jokes, unless they're told by another quiche-o. Quiche-o's like a lot of butcher block and stainless steel. Machos like a lot of children.

Machos never bake carrot cake and don't go out with 13 women who do. Quiche-o's are proud of their cholesterol levels and never belch in public and never go out with women who do since they recognize them instantly as unquiche-o and unlikely ever to serve them a salad dinner that concludes with a kiwi fruit.

BUILDING VOCABULARY

1. In this essay Baker uses a number of *geographical* references in paragraph 8. Identify the following locations:

Bermuda, St. Bart's (St. Bartholomew's Island);
Barbados, Trinidad, Coney Island, Long Island

2. Define the following foods or cooking utensils mentioned in the essay:

quiche; kiwi fruit; pig's feet; wok spatula; butcher block; carrot cake

3. Match the words on the left (all from paragraph 4) with correct meanings on the right:

_____ practitioner	a. supporting
_____ sneered at	b. showed contempt
_____ ritual	c. one who engages in some
_____ ceremonially	technique
_____ confirming	d. praying
	e. system of rites
	f. showed great pleasure
	g. ritualistically

UNDERSTANDING THE WRITER'S IDEAS

1. What is quichisme? What is machismo?
2. What does Baker mean when he identifies Philip Lopate as "a quiche-o of the highest order"?
3. How do the two groups respond to sneering?
4. What is the attitude of each group toward clothing? How would you characterize the tasks of each group? Why are there are no macho women?
5. For what reasons do both machos and quiche-o's avoid saying the word "quichisme"?
6. In what ways do macho men and quiche-o men try to impress women? How does each group prepare for vacations?

UNDERSTANDING THE WRITER'S TECHNIQUES

1. What is the thesis statement of this essay? What two things are identified as the subjects for treatment? Is

the essay a *contrast* or a *comparison*? What key words does Baker use to indicate that he is dealing primarily with similarities or differences?

2. Along with the block method (see page 111), comparison and contrast essays can also be organized according to the *alternating method*. When using the alternating method, the writer gives a point-by-point treatment of both subjects A and B. The effect looks like this:

A
B

A
B

A
B

In other words, some discussion of both subjects A and B is presented in each paragraph. Something is said about one and then about the other subject as the writer discusses some specific feature of his topic.

a. How does the author use the alternating method in paragraph 1? How does he achieve *balance* between subjects A and B in the opening paragraph?

b. How is the one-sentence paragraph 3 ("In doing so . . .") a good example of the alternating method?

c. Identify sentences in paragraphs 10 and 11 that reflect Baker's use of the alternating method.

d. For each of paragraphs 3 to 13, identify the primary focus for contrast between each of the subjects.

e. What advantages does the alternating method have over the block method? What disadvantages does the alternating method have?

3. How does Baker use definition (see pages 141 to 142) in the opening paragraph of this essay? How does he use *illustration* (see pages 66 to 67) in the essay?

4. With the alternating method it is very important to use smooth-flowing and interesting *transitions* within and between paragraphs. In this essay, one of Baker's main transition techniques is the use of *repetition with a difference* (see page 102). How does he use this method in paragraphs 7, 8, 10, 11, and 12? What key word does he repeat to make the transition between paragraphs 8 and 9?

5. A satire (see Glossary) is a humorous treatment of a subject in order to expose the subject's vices, follies, or stupidities. Why may this essay be considered a satire on city dwellers? What follies does Baker point up for each of the two groups he is dealing with?

6. As one technique for humor, Baker uses repetition of the word "gourmet" in paragraphs 7 through 9. What does the word mean? How does the repetition achieve the humorous effects Baker wants? What other repetitions do you find here?

7. Baker plays on words as another technique to achieve humor. How does he achieve humorous effects in paragraph 8 by playing on the word "islands"? What word is he playing on within the phrase "a suit of furniture" in paragraph 10? Why does he place the phrase in quotation marks? Why does he use a question in French in paragraph 11?

8. Why does Baker refer to Philip Lopate's book? Might Baker have eliminated paragraphs 2 and 3? Why did he choose to include those paragraphs in the essay?

9. Whom do you think is the intended audience for this essay? Why?

EXPLORING THE WRITER'S IDEAS

1. Baker is implying that people's social behavior reflects the kind of status they want to achieve in society. Often that behavior makes them affected—that is, they pretend to certain tastes and preferences just because fashion dictates them. What affected people have you met? What kind of social behavior would you expect from someone who wanted to be thought of as an intellectual, as upper class, as radical, or as a great lover, for example?

2. In the last decade gourmet shops and boutiques have grown in numbers, and more and more people are interested in purchasing items there. How do you account for the popularity of such places? Why might you choose to purchase something at a gourmet shop or a boutique? Why is Baker poking fun at those people who buy at boutiques and gourmet shops?

3. A recent best-selling humor book was *Real Men Don't Eat Quiche* by Bruce Feirstein. The author's main premise was like Baker's but with a difference. Feirstein believes that not only are quiche-o's and machos at opposite ends of the social scale but also that machos are the much more desirable group to belong to. If you had to choose, would you choose to be macho or quiche-o? Why? Is it necessary to choose between the two, or is it possible to combine features from both groups?

4. Baker as a city dweller understandably focuses his essay on urban personalities. How could you expand the idea of quiche-o's and machos to suburban areas? Rural farm areas? Small towns?

IDEAS FOR WRITING

Guided Writing

Write an essay in which you contrast two types of people in the area where you live.

1. In your first paragraph, write a clear thesis statement that uses key words to indicate the contrast your essay will make.

2. Give the two types of people special names and define those names to help the reader understand your special use of them.

3. Use the alternating method of development in your essay.

4. Base your essay on personal observation of the two types of people.

5. Make sure each paragraph has a special point of contrast around which you organize your examples.

6. Use repetition with a difference as one device to accomplish smooth transitions between subjects in your discussions.

7. Give clear-cut examples of how each group would act in certain situations.

8. Try to cite at least one other writer who has discussed the same subject.

9. If possible, aim for some humorous effects by using satire, repetition, or plays on words.

More Writing Projects

1. Using the alternating method, write an essay in which your generation and your parents' generation did something such as dating, throwing a party, preparing for the future, or some such activity.

2. In one or two paragraphs, compare or contrast two teachers with distinctly different qualities.

Richard M. Restak

THE OTHER DIFFERENCE BETWEEN BOYS AND GIRLS

Richad M. Restak, a neurologist on the faculty of the Georgetown University School of Medicine, believes that men and women think differently, and in this essay he explores those differences. Although he admits that his position may not currently be a popular one, he combines personal observation, citation of authorities, and clear-cut examples to defend his opinion and to make the contrast clear to the reader.

Words to Watch

stereotype (par. 1): a standardized, often simplified attitude or judgment (as of a person, a race, an issue, or an event)
scholarship (par. 2): related to the qualities of learning
nonassertive (par. 4): not aggressive or forward in manner
repertoire (par. 4): a list of the skills or devices possessed by a person
corollary (par. 4): a deduction from a proposition already proved true
inherent (par. 5): established as an essential part of something
bias (par. 8): prejudice
proficiency (par. 13): ability or skill in an art, occupation, or branch of knowledge
deficiency (par. 13): a lack of something necessary for completeness
autonomy (par. 15): self-regulation
equity (par. 16): justness, impartiality
gross (par. 18): general; broad-based; large-scale

There is no denying it: Boys think differently from girls. Even though recent brain-research evidence is controversial, that conclusion seems inescapable. I know how offensive that will sound to feminists and others committed to overcoming sexual stereotypes. But social equality for men and women really depends on recognizing these differences in brain behavior.

At present, schooling and testing discriminate against both sexes, ignoring differences that have been observed by parents and educators for years. Boys suffer in elementary-school classrooms, which are ideally suited to the way girls think. Girls suffer later, when they must take scholarship tests that are geared for male performance.

Anyone who has spent time with children in a playground or school setting is aware of differences in the way boys and girls respond to similar situations. For example, at a birthday party for five-year-olds it's not usually the girls who pull hair, throw punches or smear each other with food.

Typically, such differences are explained on a cultural basis. Boys are expected to be more aggressive and play rough games, while girls are presumably encouraged to be gentle and nonassertive. After years of exposure to such expectations, the theory goes, men and women wind up with widely varying behavioral and intellectual repertoires. As a corollary, many people believe that if child-rearing practices could be equalized and sexual stereotypes eliminated, most of these differences would eventually disappear. The true state of affairs is not that simple.

Undoubtedly, many differences traditionally believed to exist between the sexes are based on stereotypes. But evidence from recent brain research indicates that some behavioral differences between men and women are based on differences in brain functioning that are biologically inherent and unlikely to be changed by cultural factors alone.

One clue to brain differences between the sexes came from observation of infants. One study found that from shortly after birth, females are more sensitive to certain types of sounds, particularly to a mother's voice. In a laboratory, if the sound of the mother's voice is displaced to another part of the room, female babies react while males usually seem oblivious to the displacement. Female babies are also more easily startled by loud noises.

Tests show girls have increased skin sensitivity, 7 particularly in the fingertips, and are more proficient at fine motor performance. Females are also generally more attentive to social contexts—faces, speech patterns, subtle vocal cues. By five months, a female can distinguish photographs of familiar people, a task rarely performed well by boys of that age. At five and eight months, girls will babble to a mother's face, seemingly recognizing her as a person, while boys fail to distinguish between a face and a dangling toy, babbling equally to both.

Female infants speak sooner, have larger vocabu- 8 laries and rarely demonstrate speech defects. (Stuttering, for instance, occurs almost exclusively among boys.) Girls exceed boys in language abilities, and this early linguistic bias often prevails throughout life. Girls read sooner, learn foreign languages more easily and, as a result, are more likely to enter occupations involving language mastery.

Boys, in contrast, show an early visual superiority. 9 They are also clumsier, performing poorly at something like arranging a row of beads, but excel at other activities calling on total body coordination. Their attentional mechanisms are also different. A boy will react to an inanimate object as quickly as he will to a person. A male baby will often ignore the mother and babble to a blinking light, fixate on a geometric figure and, at a later point, manipulate it and attempt to take it apart.

A study of preschool children by psychologist Diane 10 McGuinness of Stanford University found boys more curious, especially in regard to exploring their environment. Her studies also confirmed that males are better at manipulating three-dimensional space. When boys and girls are asked to mentally rotate or fold an object, boys overwhelmingly outperform girls. "I folded it in my mind" is a typical male response. Girls are likely to produce elaborate verbal descriptions which, because they are less appropriate to the task, result in frequent errors.

There is evidence that some of these differences in performance are differences in brain organization between boys and girls. Overall, verbal and spatial abilities in boys tend to be "packaged" into different hemispheres: the right hemisphere for nonverbal tasks, the left for verbal tasks. But in girls nonverbal and verbal skills are likely to be found on both sides of the brain. The hemispheres of women's brains may be less specialized for these functions.

These differences in brain organization and specialization are believed by some scientists to provide a partial explanation of why members of one sex or the other are underrepresented in certain professions. Architects, for example, require a highly developed spatial sense, a skill found more frequently among men. Thus, the preponderance of male architects may be partially caused by the more highly developed spatial sense that characterizes the male brain.

Psychological measurements of brain functioning between the sexes also show unmistakable differences. In 11 subtests of the most widely used general intelligence test, only two (digit span and picture arrangement) reveal similar mean scores for males and females. These sex differences are so consistent that the standard battery of this intelligence test now contains a masculinity-femininity index to offset sex-related proficiencies and deficiencies.

Most thought-provoking of all are findings by Eleanor Maccoby and Carol Nagy Jacklin of Stanford University on personality traits and intellectual achievement. They found that intellectual development in girls is fostered among individuals who are assertive and active, and have a sense that they can control, by their own actions, the events that affect their lives. These factors appear to be less important in the intellectual development of boys.

Recent studies even suggest that high levels of intellectual achievement are associated with cross-sex typing: the ability to express traits and interests associated with the opposite sex. Educational psychologist E. P. Torrance of the University of Georgia suggests that sexual stereotypes are a block to creativity, since creativity requires sensitivity— a female trait—as well as autonomy and independence— traits usually associated with males. M. P. Honzik and J. W.

Mcfarlane of the University of California at Berkeley support Torrance's speculation with a 20-year follow-up on subjects who demonstrated significant IQ gains. Those with the greatest gains displayed less dependency on traditional sex roles than those whose IQs remained substantially the same.

It's important to remember that we're not talking 16 about one sex being generally superior or inferior to another. In addition, the studies are statistical and don't tell us a lot about individuals. The findings are controversial, but they can help us establish true social equity.

One way of doing this might be to change such prac- 17 tices as nationwide competitive examinations. If boys, for instance, truly excel in right-hemisphere tasks, scholastic aptitude tests should be substantially redesigned to assure that both sexes have an equal chance. Some of the tests now are weighted with items that virtually guarantee superior male performance.

Attitude changes are also needed in our approach to 18 "hyperactive" or "learning disabled" children. The evidence for sex differences here is staggering: More than 90 percent of hyperactives are males. This is not surprising since the male brain is primarily visual, while classroom instruction demands attentive listening. The male brain learns by manipulating its environment, yet the typical student is forced to sit still for long hours in the classroom. There is little opportunity, other than during recess, for gross motor movements or rapid muscular responses. In essence, the classrooms in most of our nation's primary grades are geared to skills that come naturally to girls but develop very slowly in boys. The result shouldn't be surprising: a "learning disabled" child who is also frequently "hyperactive."

We now have the opportunity, based on emerging 19 evidence of sex differences in brain functioning, to restructure elementary grades so that boys find their initial educational contacts less stressful. At more advanced levels of instruction, teaching methods could incorporate verbal and linguistic approaches to physics, engineering and architecture (to mention only three fields where women are conspicuously underrepresented).

The alternative is to do nothing about brain differ- 20

ences. There is something to be said for this approach, too. In the recent past, enhanced social benefit has usually resulted from stressing the similarities between people rather than their differences. We ignore brain-sex differences, however, at the risk of confusing biology with sociology, and wishful thinking with scientific fact.

BUILDING VOCABULARY

1. As you know, *adjectives* add precision and vividness to writing. Many adjectives can be formed by adding a *suffix* to a root word. Two common suffixes of adjectives are *-al* ("relating to") and *-ic* ("characteristic of").

The following adjectives appear in Restak's essay. For each one, identify the root word; write a definition of the adjective; then use the adjective in a sentence of your own. (Sometimes you will be able to find the root simply by dropping the suffix; in other words, however, the root word will not be as obvious. Look up in a dictionary the derivations of words you are unsure about.)

a. controversial	f. visual
b. social	g. geometric
c. cultural	h. typical
d. behavioral	i. spatial
e. vocal	j. sexual

2. Find at least five additional adjectives in the selection and define them.

3. *Adverbs* are words that modify verbs, adjectives, or other adverbs. They typically indicate *how, why,* or *when* something is done. Adverbs are frequently formed by adding the suffixes *-ly, -ally,* or *-ically* to verbs or to adjectives. When these suffixes are added, they indicate that something is done *in a specified manner.*

Restak uses a great number of adverbs in this essay. List all the *-ly, -ally,* and *-ically* adverbs you can find. Write definitions for those you do not know. Then, write a short paragraph in which you use at least four of those adverbs.

UNDERSTANDING THE WRITER'S IDEAS

1. According to this article, what is the main "other" difference—aside from the obvious sexual differences—between boys and girls? Why does Restak call it the "other" difference? Is this difference stated in a thesis sentence?

2. Why does Restak think his conclusions about recent brain-research evidence may offend some people? If people overcame those feelings, what advantages might result, according to Restak?

3. What major difference in their responses to similar situations does Restak say exists between very young boys and very young girls? What specific examples does he cite to support his point?

4. Does Restak feel that all behavioral differences between the sexes are based on the particular values people are taught as they grow up? Why or why not?

5. According to Restak, which sex is more aware of social contexts earlier in life? In your own words, what evidence does he offer to support this claim?

6. What authority does Restak cite to support his point about boys' and girls' relative curiosity about their environments? Do you think this authority is a good source of information on the topic? Explain.

7. What are the major differences in brain organization between males and females? What are some of the major differences between the sexes caused by the contrasting brain organizations?

8. What is "cross-sex typing"?

9. What percentage of elementary school children labeled as hyperactive are male? What reasons does Restak offer for this figure?

10. Is it possible to say which sex Restak believes is better than the other? Why?

UNDERSTANDING THE WRITER'S TECHNIQUES

1. Among the purposes of a comparison or contrast essay are (a) to *explain* something unfamiliar in terms of

something already familiar, (b) to *understand* better two things already known by comparing them point for point (c) to *evaluate* the relative value of two things.

Which of the above most closely describes Restak's purpose in this essay? What key ideas from the essay support your choice?

2. In a comparison-contrast essay, there should be clear bases for comparison of the two items.

    a. Identify the two things being compared in this essay.

    b. Are they being compared mainly for their differences or for their similarities?

    c. What is the method of comparison or contrast in this essay? Does the author ever combine the *block* and *alternating* methods? (See pages 111 and 118).

    d. Identify the subtopics in the comparison. For each, determine whether the author uses the block or alternating method of development.

3. For what sort of audience is Restak writing in this essay? How do you know? Where does he use specialized language—language directed at experts in the field? Look up the meanings of the words with which you are familiar. Is the specialized language appropriate at these points? Did it ever confuse you? Could he not have used it and still have made his point clearly? Explain.

4. Writers achieve *coherence* and *unity* (see Glossary) in an essay through the use of *transitions* to link one idea to the next. Often, these transitions take the form of *connective words* that *add* one idea to another, that *compare* them, or that place them in a *time sequence* (see Glossary).

Beginning with the second paragraph, identify the transitions—words or phrases—that appear either in the first or second sentence of each paragraph. Tell how the word or phrase serves as a transition.

5. Where does the author name and refer to experts on the subject? Where does he use statistics? Why is

Restak providing details from these experts? In your judgment, how reliable are the authorities for statistics he uses?

6. Reexamine paragraph 19, where Restak talks about the possibility of restructuring elementary education. What difference does it make that he uses "could" instead of "should" in the second sentence?

7. A good *closing* for a comparison-contrast essay often will restate the main idea, will offer a solution, or will set a new frame of reference by generalizing from the thesis (see Glossary). Which approach or combination of approaches does Restak use? How effective is his conclusion? Explain.

8. Explain the title of this selection. How does the word "the" before "other" force us to consider only two alternatives? Why does Restak not want us to consider a range of differences?

EXPLORING THE WRITER'S IDEAS

1. In the very beginning of the essay, Restak says that he knows how offensive the remark "Boys think differently from girls" will sound to anyone who opposes stereotyping people because of sex. Do you feel that the evidence and conclusions presented in this essay would offend feminists? Why? Do you feel that most of our assumptions about the differences between men and women are based on cultural conditioning or reflect the existence of real biological differences? Explain your choice by referring to specific common stereotypes.

2. Do you believe that men and women should be considered totally equal?

3. In paragraph 4, Restak shows that boys are expected to be more aggressive and to grow up more aggressive, while girls are supposed to be "gentle and nonassertive." Should children be raised with these attitudes and goals? Did they influence the ways in which you or your friends were raised? How?

4. In paragraph 15, Restak cites E. P. Torrance's conclusion that "sexual stereotypes are a block to creativ-

ity." What is your opinion of this conclusion? Why do you feel as you do? Name some skills or activities that might be damaged by sexual stereotyping.

IDEAS FOR WRITING

Guided Writing

Write an essay in which you compare or contrast the ways of men and women. Focus your comparison or contrast on a single type of activity: performing a job, dealing with people, playing at sports, thinking—any activity that will allow you to highlight the similarities or differences (or both) between the sexes.

    1. Establish a clear attitude toward the subject in your first sentence. Make your first sentence your thesis statement. State whether you will concentrate on the differences or similarities.

    2. In the first paragraph, briefly mention what types of people might oppose your opinion and tell the probable reason for their opposition.

    3. Explain present-day attitudes toward men and women as they perform the activity you have named.

    4. Consult your library to read what others have written about your subject. In your essay cite authorities or statistics as supporting detail.

    5. Make use of a combination of the alternating and the block method if it is possible to do so.

    6. Use transition words or phrases to connect your ideas.

    7. Express some personal opinions throughout the essay, making sure you support them with clear and believable details.

    8. Deal with some common attitudes that reflect sexual stereotypes.

    9. In your conclusion propose various changes that could take place—for better or worse—in current attitudes toward the activity you are writing about.

More Writing Projects

1. Advertisements are often guilty of gross use of sexual stereotyping to sell products. Select two ads from newspapers or magazines that you feel rely heavily on sexual stereotyping. For each, list how and why these stereotypes are used. Then write an essay in which you compare or contrast them.

2. Select a popular television series that you think makes excessive use of sexual stereotypes and write a point-by-point comparison of that show with one you feel is careful to avoid such stereotyping.

3. Use the combined block and alternating method to write an essay of comparison or contrast (or both) for one of these:

    a. train travel and bus travel
    b. disco dancing and ballroom dancing
    c. a college English class and a high school English class
    d. working mothers and mothers who stay at home
    e. mothers without husbands and fathers without wives

Bruno Bettelheim

FAIRY TALES AND MODERN STORIES

Bruno Bettelheim was born in Austria in 1903 and came
to the United States in 1939. For many years he has been
one of the major child psychologists in the world. In this
selection, taken from *The Uses of Enchantment* (1976),
Bettelheim compares fairy tales and realistic stories,
analyzing the effect that they have on both children and
adults. As you read this essay, keep in mind the various
stories he is comparing.

Words to Watch

realistic (par. 1): having to do with real things
props (par. 1): supports
elaboration (par. 1): a thing worked out carefully
rankled (par. 1): caused pain or resentment
idyllic (par. 2): pleasing and simple
protracted (par. 2): drawn out
gratifications (par. 2): things that cause satisfaction
sustained (par. 3): maintained; supported; comforted
effected (par. 4): brought to pass; accomplished
consolation (par. 5): comfort
vagaries (par. 5): odd notions; unexpected actions
extricating (par. 5): setting free; getting out of; releasing
prevail (par. 5): to triumph; to gain the advantage
asocial (par. 5): unsocial

The shortcomings of the realistic stories with which 1
many parents have replaced fairy tales is suggested by a
comparison of two such stories—"The Little Engine That
Could" and "The Swiss Family Robinson"—with the fairy
tale of "Rapunzel." "The Little Engine That Could" encour-
ages the child to believe that if he tries hard and does not
give up, he will finally succeed. A young adult has recalled
how much impressed she was at the age of seven when her
mother read her this story. She became convinced that one's
attitude indeed affects one's achievements—that if she would
now approach a task with the conviction that she could
conquer it, she would succeed. A few days later, this child
encountered in first grade a challenging situation: she was
trying to make a house out of paper, gluing various sheets
together. But her house continually collapsed. Frustrated,
she began to seriously doubt whether her idea of building
such a paper house could be realized. But then the story of
"The Little Engine That Could" came to her mind; twenty
years later, she recalled how at that moment she began to
sing to herself the magic formula "I think I can, I think I
can, I think I can . . ." So she continued to work on her paper
house, and it continued to collapse. The project ended in
complete defeat, with this little girl convinced that she had
failed where anybody else could have succeeded, as the Little
Engine had. Since "The Little Engine That Could" was a story
set in the present, using such common props as engines that
pulled trains, this girl had tried to apply its lesson directly in
her daily life, without any fantasy elaboration, and had experienced a defeat that still rankled twenty years later.

Very different was the impact of "The Swiss Family 2
Robinson" on another little girl. The story tells how a
shipwrecked family manages to live an adventurous, idyllic,
constructive, and pleasurable life—a life very different from
this child's own existence. Her father had to be away from
home a great deal, and her mother was mentally ill and
spent protracted periods in institutions. So the girl was
shuttled from her home to that of an aunt, then to that of
a grandmother, and back home again, as the need arose.
During these years, the girl read over and over again the

story of this happy family who lived on a desert island, where no member could be away from the rest of the family. Many years later, she recalled what a warm, cozy feeling she had when, propped up by a few large pillows, she forgot all about her present predicament as she read this story. As soon as she had finished it, she started to read it over again. The happy hours she spent with the Family Robinson in that fantasy land permitted her not to be defeated by the difficulties that reality presented to her. She was able to counteract the impact of harsh reality by imaginary gratifications. But since the story was not a fairy tale, it merely gave her a temporary escape from her problems; it did not hold out any promise to her that her life would take a turn for the better.

Consider the effect that "Rapunzel" had on a third 3 girl. This girl's mother had died in a car accident. The girl's father, deeply upset by what had happened to his wife (he had been driving the car), withdrew entirely into himself and handed the care of his daughter over to a nursemaid, who was little interested in the girl and gave her complete freedom to do as she liked. When the girl was seven, her father remarried, and, as she recalled it, it was around that time that "Rapunzel" became so important to her. Her stepmother was clearly the witch of the story, and she was the girl locked away in the tower. The girl recalled that she felt akin to Rapunzel because the witch had "forcibly" taken possession of her, as her stepmother had forcibly worked her way into the girl's life. The girl felt imprisoned in her new home, in contrast to her life of freedom with the nursemaid. She felt as victimized as Rapunzel, who, in her tower, had so little control over her life. Rapunzel's long hair was the key to the story. The girl wanted her hair to grow long, but her stepmother cut it short; long hair in itself became the symbol of freedom and happiness to her. The story convinced her that a prince (her father) would come someday and rescue her, and this conviction sustained her. If life became too difficult, all she needed was to imagine herself as Rapunzel, her hair grown long, and the prince loving and rescuing her.

"Rapunzel" suggests why fairy tales can offer more 4
to the child than even such a very nice children's story as
"The Swiss Family Robinson." In "The Swiss Family Robinson," there is no witch against whom the child can discharge
her anger in fantasy and on whom she can blame the father's
lack of interest. "The Swiss Family Robinson" offers escape
fantasies, and it did help the girl who read it over and over
to forget temporarily how difficult life was for her. But it
offered no specific hope for the future. "Rapunzel," on the
other hand, offered the girl a chance to see the witch of the
story as so evil that by comparison even the "witch" stepmother at home was not really so bad. "Rapunzel" also
promised the girl that her rescue would be effected by her
own body, when her hair grew long. Most important of all,
it promised that the "prince" was only temporarily blinded—
that he would regain his sight and rescue his princess. This
fantasy continued to sustain the girl, though to a less intense
degree, until she fell in love and married, and then she no
longer needed it. We can understand why at first glance the
stepmother, if she had known the meaning of "Rapunzel" to
her stepdaughter, would have felt that fairy tales are bad
for children. What she would not have known was that
unless the stepdaughter had been able to find that fantasy
satisfaction through "Rapunzel," she would have tried to
break up her father's marriage and that without the hope
for the future which the story gave her she might have gone
badly astray in life.

It seems quite understandable that when children 5
are asked to name their favorite fairy tales, hardly any
modern tales are among their choices. Many of the new tales
have sad endings, which fail to provide the escape and
consolation that the fearsome events in the fairy tale require
if the child is to be strengthened for meeting the vagaries
of his life. Without such encouraging conclusions, the child,
after listening to the story, feels that there is indeed no
hope for extricating himself from his despairs. In the traditional fairy tale, the hero is rewarded and the evil person
meets his well-deserved fate, thus satisfying the child's deep
need for justice to prevail. How else can a child hope that
justice will be done to him, who so often feels unfairly

treated? And how else can he convince himself that he must act correctly, when he is so sorely tempted to give in to the asocial proddings of his desires?

BUILDING VOCABULARY

1.   *Jargon* is specialized vocabulary that appears in a certain profession or discipline. Bettelheim might be expected to use a certain amount of jargon from psychology. (Fortunately, he keeps it to a minimum.) Try to figure out what Bettelheim means by the following terms:

    a. fantasy elaboration (par. 1)
    b. imaginary gratifications (par. 2)
    c. escape fantasies (par. 4)
    d. fantasy satisfaction (par. 4)
    e. asocial proddings (par. 5)

2.   Write sentences in which you use the following words correctly:

    a. *impressed* (par. 1)
    b. *conviction* (par. 1)
    c. *impact* (par. 2)
    d. *predicament* (par. 2)
    e. *victimized* (par. 3)
    f. *astray* (par. 4)
    g. *sorely* (par. 5)

3.   Would you say that the level of vocabulary in this essay is concrete or abstract? Why?

UNDERSTANDING THE WRITER'S IDEAS

1.   Check in the children's book section of your library to summarize the stories and fairy tales Bettelheim discusses. How many stories is he examining in this essay?

2.   What is the most important similarity between *The Little Engine That Could* and *The Swiss Family Robinson?*

3. What is the effect on children of *The Little Engine That Could*? How does it influence the adult whom Bettelheim introduces in paragraph 1?

4. How does Bettelheim summarize the story of *The Swiss Family Robinson*? Does this story, according to the author, have a beneficial effect on adults with problems?

5. Explain why "Rapunzel" was so important to the girl who had lost her mother in the car accident.

6. Why do fairy tales benefit readers more than modern fairy tales and realistic stories do? What do traditional fairy tales provide?

7. What does Bettelheim mean by his last sentence, "And how else can he convince himself that he must act correctly, when he is so sorely tempted to give in to the asocial proddings of his desires?"

UNDERSTANDING THE WRITER'S TECHNIQUES

1. Where does Bettelheim state his main point? How clear is his statement of it? Does he indicate in his thesis sentence his plan of development for the essay?

2. How does Bettelheim order his essay in terms of comparison and contrast? What is interesting about the pattern he chooses?

3. Where does the writer use narration? Why does he use it? How does it support the technique of comparison and contrast?

4. What is the function of paragraph 1? of paragraph 2? of paragraph 3?

5. How does the writer organize paragraph 4?

6. Is the same amount of emphasis given to "Rapunzel" as to the two "realistic" tales? Why or why not?

7. In concluding paragraphs of comparison and contrast papers, it is common to bring the two subjects together for a final observation. Does Bettelheim follow this strategy? How does he organize his subjects in the last paragraph?

8. How does Bettelheim achieve clear transitions from paragraph to paragraph? Discuss some of the words he uses so that his ideas are connected together clearly.

EXPLORING THE WRITER'S IDEAS

1. Bettelheim suggests that certain types of fairy tales help us to cope with problems. Do you agree or disagree? What particular fairy tale do you remember that might help a child deal with his or her problems?

2. Why do most children clearly take delight from traditional fairy tales?

3. Look again at Bettelheim's psychoanalysis of the three children whom he uses as examples in his essay. Do you accept his explanations of their behavior? How might his ideas be criticized by other psychologists?

4. Which fairy tales—traditional or modern—appealed to you as a child? Why were you so fond of them?

5. If exposure to certain types of fairy tales can affect us seriously, then what can we conclude about our exposure to stories on television, film, and other types of media? Is it fair to generalize about television from Bettelheim's argument?

IDEAS FOR WRITING

Guided Writing

Write an essay in which you compare and/or contrast two or three fairy tales or stories that you remember from early childhood. Or, do the same for two films, two television programs, two newspapers, or two subjects from another media form.

1. State the purpose of your comparison as soon as you can.

2. Decide on the best pattern of development (block, alternating, or a combination of both) for your purposes.

3. List the point of comparison or contrast that you plan to cover for each subject.

4. Be certain to support each point with substantial detail. Summarize parts of stories that bear out your point. Quote where you have to.

5. Make certain that, in the closing paragraph, you draw conclusions about all the subjects treated.

More Writing Projects

1. Write an essay in which you compare or contrast two newspapers or magazines. Be prepared to compare and contrast their contents, and also to indicate the type of audience at which they are aimed. Write a comparative paper on your findings.

2. Compare and contrast the style of writing of any two writers in this section.

3. Select two heroes or heroines from popular children's stories or fairy tales; compare and contrast the two characters in regard to personality and behavior.

5

Definition

Definition is a way of explaining an important word so that the reader knows, as exactly as possible, what you mean by it. You probably have written essays requiring short "dictionary definitions" of words that were not clear to the reader. However, there are terms that require longer definitions because they may be central to the writer's thought. When an entire essay focuses on the meaning of a key word or group of related words, you will need to employ "extended definition" as a method of organization.

Words requiring extended definition tend to be abstract, controversial, or complex. Terms like "freedom," "pornography," and "communism" reflect the need for extended definition. Such words depend on extended definition because they are often confused with some other word or term; because they are easily misunderstood; or because they are of special importance to the writer, who chooses to redefine the term for his or her own purposes. We can, of course, simply offer an extended definition of a word for the sake of definition itself; this is valid. But we usually have strong opinions about complex and controversial words, and, consequently, we try to provide an extended definition for the purpose of illuminating a thesis. The word "abortion" could be defined objectively, with the writer tracing its history, explaining its techniques, and describing its effects on the patient. Yet many writers asked to provide an extended definition of "abortion" would have strong personal opinions about the term. They would want to develop a thesis about it, perhaps covering much of the same ground as the objective account, but taking care that the reader understands the word as they do. It is normal for us to have our own opinions about any word, but in all instances we must make the reader understand fully what we mean by it.

Writers use several techniques to develop extended definitions. One common strategy is to define some general group to which the subject belongs (for instance, the mallard is a member of a larger group of ducks), and to show how the word differs from all other words in that general group. A second technique is to give the etymology of a word—its origin and history in the language—to help the reader. Yet another method of extended definition is to deal with what you do *not* mean by the term—a technique called "negation." Finally, many methods that you already learned can be used profitably in extended definition. You can define a word by narrating an event that reveals its meaning; you can provide specific examples, even a simple listing, to illustrate what you mean by a term; you can compare and contrast related terms; you can describe details that help to establish meaning.

Extended definition involves no single pattern of essay organization, but rather a group of available strategies that you use depending on your purpose and on the word itself. The word selected may be ordinary and relatively concrete, or it may be abstract and complex like "immobilization." Often, as in the essays here on the "international insult" and on "fun," the definition is never directly stated, but is understood or put together from the information a writer gives. Because so many methods can be applied effectively in an essay of extended definition, you should be able to organize and develop this type of composition easily.

Wayne W. Dyer

IMMOBILIZATION

Dr. Wayne W. Dyer, a therapist and counselor, believes that people *can* realize their own potential if they learn to change any emotional behavior that defeats happiness. Here in a chapter from his book *Your Erroneous Zones* he explains through definition a key word in his approach to understanding feelings. Notice how he uses illustration to strengthen his definition.

Words to Watch

brood (par. 3): think about unhappily; sulk
gnawing (par. 3): eating away at; irritating
abusive (par. 3): insulting
twitching (par. 3): moving jerkily and suddenly
cut a wide swath (par. 4): create a great impression
virtually (par. 4): essentially; practically
strategy (par. 4): plan of action

  As you consider your potential for choosing happi- 1
ness, keep in mind the word *immobilization* as the indicator
of negative emotions in your life. You might believe that
anger, hostility, shyness and other similar feelings are worth
having at times, and so you want to hang on to them. Your

guide should be the extent to which you are in any way immobilized by the feeling.

Immobilization can range from total inaction to mild 2 indecision and hesitancy. Does your anger keep you from saying, feeling, or doing something? If so, then you are immobilized. Does your shyness prevent you from meeting people you want to know? If so, you are immobilized and missing out on experiences that are rightfully yours. Is your hate and jealousy helping you to grow an ulcer or to raise your blood pressure? Does it keep you from working effectively on the job? Are you unable to sleep or make love because of a negative present-moment feeling? These are all signs of immobilization. *Immobilization:* A state, however mild or serious, in which you are not functioning at the level that you would like to. If feelings lead to such a state, you need to look no further for a reason to get rid of them.

Here is a brief checklist of some instances in which 3 you may be immobilized. They range from minor to major states of immobility.

You are immobilized when . . .

You can't talk lovingly to your spouse and children though you want to.

You can't work on a project that interests you.

You don't make love and would like to.

You sit in the house all day and brood.

You don't play golf, tennis, or other enjoyable activities, because of a leftover gnawing feeling.

You can't introduce yourself to someone who appeals to you.

You avoid talking to someone when you realize that a simple gesture would improve your relationship.

You can't sleep because something is bothering you.

Your anger keeps you from thinking clearly.

You say something abusive to someone that you love.

Your face is twitching, or you are so nervous that you don't function the way you would prefer.

Immobilization cuts a wide swath. Virtually all 4 negative emotions result in some degree of self-immobility, and this alone is a solid reason for eliminating them entirely from your life. Perhaps you are thinking of occasions when a negative emotion has a payoff, such as yelling at a young child in an angry voice to emphasize that you do not want him to play in the street. If the angry voice is simply a device for emphasis and it works, then you've adopted a healthy strategy. However, if you yell at others not to make a point, but because you are internally upset, then you've immobilized yourself, and it's time to begin working at new choices that will help you to reach your goal of keeping your child out of the street without experiencing feelings that are hurtful to you.

BUILDING VOCABULARY

1. You have already seen how prefixes and suffixes affect the meanings of words. Each of these words from the essay you just read begins with *in*. After you check a dictionary, explain whether or not the element *in* has the same meaning or use in each word:

> indicator (par. 1)
> inaction (par. 2)
> indecision (par. 2)
> instance (par. 3)
> internally (par. 4)

2. Examine the definitions in the Words to Watch section on page 143. Write an original sentence that uses each word correctly.

UNDERSTANDING THE WRITER'S IDEAS

1. What negative feelings might be worth having at times according to Dyer?

2. How can immobilization "range from total in-action to mild indecision and hesitancy"?

3. What is Dyer's definition of *immobilization?* Quote exactly the sentence that states the definition in the essay. Which part of the definition gives the general group into which *immobilization* fits? Which part of the definition gives the special qualities that distinguish the word from others in the general group?

4. What specific examples of immobility does the writer offer?

5. How may the use of a negative emotion be a healthy strategy in dealing with people? How may the use of a negative emotion immobilize someone, according to the writer?

UNDERSTANDING THE WRITER'S TECHNIQUES

1. How does the opening paragraph serve as an introduction to Dyer's purpose in this brief selection? Which sentence serves as a thesis sentence?

2. Why does Dyer offer a definition of the word "immobilization" at the end of paragraph 2? Why does he ask a series of questions just before providing the definition? Do the questions lead effectively to that definition? Is it a good technique to build in this way to the word Dyer wishes to define?

3. Check the word "immobilization" in a dictionary. How does Dyer's definition contrast with the dictionary definition? How do the differences in meaning explain why Dyer wrote this chapter? If he could define the word in one sentence, why does he need four paragraphs to extend that definition?

4. Why has the writer offered a simple listing to explain states of immobility? What effect does the repetition of the word "you" have upon the reader?

5. Does the final paragraph serve as an effective conclusion? How does the discussion of the effects of negative emotion contribute to our understanding of immobilization as Dyer uses that word?

EXPLORING THE WRITER'S IDEAS

1. Do you believe that people have the potential for choosing happiness? Or, do you believe that circumstances in life (more than individual choice) create states of happiness or sadness?

2. Do you agree that there are negative feelings that are worth having at times? Give an example from your own life of how anger, hostility, or shyness may be healthy or unhealthy strategies in dealing with people.

3. Have you ever been immobilized in the sense that Dyer means? When?

4. Which items in the checklist of instances in which immobilization occurs do you think most people have experienced? Would you agree that the examples do indeed suggest immobilization?

5. In the last paragraph Dyer shows how the expression of a negative emotion "has a payoff." Do you agree that, if an angry voice is simply a device for emphasis, it is a healthy strategy? In the instance of a child playing in the street, does an angry voice serve its purpose? Would it matter, do you think, if the reasons for yelling at that moment stemmed from the person's internal feelings?

6. In general, are people's expressions of anger more a result of healthy strategies for emphasis or more a result of hurtful internal feelings? Explain your response with an example.

IDEAS FOR WRITING

Guided Writing

Write an extended definition of some negative emotion, like *fear, shyness, anger, hate, loneliness, depression,* or some other that you think needs defining.

1. In your first paragraph write an introduction which names the emotion with which you will be dealing.

2. Build up to a one-sentence definition of the word. You might want to ask a series of questions which will point out situations in which the emotion works negatively.

3. In your one-sentence definition, explain exactly and clearly your definition of the emotion. And you should also, in that sentence, be sure to name the general group to which the word belongs, and also the special qualities which distinguish the word from others in the general group. Later in the paragraph, you might want to compare your definition of the word with a definition you took from a dictionary. Although Dyer does not do this, comparison is often very helpful in the writing of an extended definition.

4. As Dyer has done, include in your essay a simple listing illustrating some feature of your definition. You might want to list different ways people express the emotion; or you might want to list ways they deal with the emotion.

5. In your final paragraph explain how negative emotion can be a healthy strategy. If you think the emotion is never a healthy strategy in dealing with people, explain *that*. But in either case, give a specific example of a situation in which the emotion might appear, in order to make your point. (Dyer discusses the example of a parent raising a voice in anger to a child playing in the street.)

More Writing Projects

1. Take any important term or concept in psychology today and write an extended definition of it. You might choose *neurosis, paranoia, therapy, guilt, Freudian, complex,* or some other word.

2. Write your own extended definition of immobilization. In this essay narrate a specific instance from your own life in which you show how you were immobilized.

Suzanne Britt Jordan

FUN, OH BOY. FUN. YOU COULD DIE FROM IT.

Most of us never really consider exactly what it means to have a good time. Suzanne Britt Jordan, a writer who claims she "tries to have fun, but often fails," offers an extended definition of the word "fun" by pointing out what it is *not*.

Words to Watch

puritan (par. 3): one who practices or preaches a more strict moral code than that which exists

selfless (par. 4): unselfish; having no concern for oneself

fetish (par. 5): something regarded with extravagant trust or respect

licentiousness (par. 9): a lack of moral restraints

consumption (par. 9): to take in or to use up a substance; eating or drinking

epitome (par. 11): an ideal; a typical representation

capacity (par. 12): the ability to hold something

damper (par. 13): something that regulates or that stops something from flowing

reverently (par. 13): respectfully; worshipfully

blaspheme (par. 13): to speak of without respect

weary (par. 14): tired; worn-out

horizon (par. 14): the apparent line where the earth meets the sky

scan (par. 14): to examine something carefully

Fun is hard to have.

Fun is a rare jewel.

Somewhere along the line people got the modern 1
idea that fun was there for the asking, that people deserved 2
fun, that if we didn't have a little fun every day we would 3
turn into (sakes alive!) puritans.

"Was it fun?" became the question that overshad- 4
owed all other questions: good questions like: Was it moral?
Was it kind? Was it honest? Was it beneficial? Was it generous? Was it necessary? And (my favorite) was it selfless?

When the pleasure got to be the main thing, the fun 5
fetish was sure to follow. Everything was supposed to be fun.
If it wasn't fun, then by Jove, we were going to make it fun,
or else.

Think of all the things that got the reputation of be- 6
ing fun. Family outings were supposed to be fun. Sex was
supposed to be fun. Education was supposed to be fun. Work
was supposed to be fun. Walt Disney was supposed to be fun.
Church was supposed to be fun. Staying fit was supposed to
be fun.

Just to make sure that everybody knew how much 7
fun we were having, we put happy faces on flunking test
papers, dirty bumpers, sticky refrigerator doors, bathroom
mirrors.

If a kid, looking at his very happy parents traipsing 8
through that very happy Disney World, said, "This ain't fun,
ma," his ma's heart sank. She wondered where she had
gone wrong. Everybody told her what fun family outings to
Disney World would be. Golly gee, what was the matter?

Fun got to be such a big thing that everybody started 9
to look for more and more thrilling ways to supply it. One way
was to step up the level of danger or licentiousness or alcohol
or drug consumption so that you could be sure that, no matter
what, you would manage to have a little fun.

Television commercials brought a lot of fun and fun- 10
loving folks into the picture. Everything that people in those
commercials did looked like fun: taking Polaroid snapshots,
swilling beer, buying insurance, mopping the floor, bowling,

taking aspirin. We all wished, I'm sure, that we could have half as much fun as those rough-and-ready guys around the locker room, flicking each other with towels and pouring champagne. The more commercials people watched, the more they wondered when the fun would start in their own lives. It was pretty depressing.

Big occasions were supposed to be fun. Christmas, 11 Thanksgiving and Easter were obviously supposed to be fun. Your wedding day was supposed to be fun. Your wedding night was supposed to be a whole lot of fun. Your honeymoon was supposed to be the epitome of fundom. And so we ended up going through every Big Event we ever celebrated, waiting for the fun to start.

It occurred to me, while I was sitting around waiting 12 for the fun to start, that not much is, and that I should tell you just in case you're worried about your fun capacity.

I don't mean to put a damper on things. I just mean 13 we ought to treat fun reverently. It is a mystery. It cannot be caught like a virus. It cannot be trapped like an animal. The god of mirth is paying us back for all those years of thinking fun was everywhere by refusing to come to our party. I don't want to blaspheme fun anymore. When fun comes in on little dancing feet, you probably won't be expecting it. In fact, I bet it comes when you're doing your duty, your job, or your work. It may even come on a Tuesday.

I remember one day, long ago, on which I had an es- 14 pecially good time. Pam Davis and I walked to the College Village drug store one Saturday morning to buy some candy. We were about 12 years old (fun ages). She got her Bit-O-Honey. I got my malted milk balls, chocolate stars, Chunkys, and a small bag of M & M's. We started back to her house. I was going to spend the night. We had the whole day to look forward to. We had plenty of candy. It was a long way to Pam's house but every time we got weary Pam would put her hand over her eyes, scan the horizon like a sailor and say, "Oughta reach home by nightfall," at which point the two of us would laugh until we thought we couldn't stand it another minute. Then after we got calm, she'd say it again. You should have been there. It was the kind of day and friendship and occasion that made me deeply regretful that I had to grow up.

It was fun. 15

BUILDING VOCABULARY

1. *Trite language* refers to words and expressions that have been overused, and, consequently, have lost much of their effectiveness. People do rely on trite language in their conversations, but writers usually avoid overused expressions. However, a good writer will be able to introduce such vocabulary at strategic points. Examples of trite language in Jordan's essay appear below. Explain in your own words what they mean:

   a. "a rare jewel" (par. 2)
   b. "by Jove" (par. 5)
   c. "golly gee" (par. 8)
   d. "his ma's heart sank" (par. 8)

2. For each of the following words drawn from Jordan's essay, write a denotative definition. Then list four connotations (see pages 363–64) each word has for you.

   a. overshadow (par. 4)
   b. flunking (par. 7)
   c. traipsing (par. 8)
   d. swilling (par. 10)
   e. mirth (par. 13)

3. Select five words from the Words to Watch section and use them in sentences of your own.

UNDERSTANDING THE WRITER'S IDEAS

1. What are some of the things Jordan says fun is not?

2. What does Jordan suggest we did to something

if it wasn't already fun? Identify some of the things she says are "supposed" to be fun.

3.   In paragraph 7, Jordan lists some common things that certainly aren't any fun. How does she say people made them fun anyway?

4.   What are some of the ways people make fun even more thrilling?

5.   What does Jordan list as looking like fun on television commercials?

6.   Discuss the relationship between big occasions and the experience of fun. Explain the meaning of the statement, "It may even come on a Tuesday."

7.   Describe Jordan's attitude concerning how much in life really is fun. According to Jordan, how should we treat fun? Why? Is it something she says can only be experienced at special times?

8.   How old was Jordan at the time she remembers having an especially good time with her friend Pam? Describe in your own words why she had such a good time that day. What are some of the candies she remembers buying? Why was it especially funny when Pam would say, "Oughta reach home by nightfall"?

9.   For what reason does Jordan feel regretful at the end of the essay? Although she is regretful, do you think she is actually sad? Why?

UNDERSTANDING THE WRITER'S TECHNIQUES

1.   Does Jordan ever offer a single-sentence definition of "fun"? Where? Is that sentence sufficient to define the concept? Why?

2.   Jordan employs the technique of *negation*— defining a term through showing what it is *not*—so strongly in this essay that the writing verges on *irony*. Irony is using language to suggest the opposite of what is said (see Glossary). Explain the irony in paragraphs 7, 8, and 9.

3.   Why does the author continually point out things that are supposed to be fun? What is she trying to tell us about these things?

4. Writers usually avoid vague words such as "everything" or "everybody" in their writing, yet Jordan uses these words frequently in this essay. Explain her purpose in deliberately avoiding concrete terms.

5. What is the *tone* (see Glossary) of this essay? Is it fun? How does Jordan create this tone? Much of the writing in this essay has a very conversational quality to it, as though the author were speaking directly to the reader. Locate five words or phrases that have this quality.

6. Why does Jordan use so many examples and illustrations in this essay? Which paragraphs use multiple illustrations with special effectiveness?

7. There is a definite turning point in this essay where Jordan switches from an ironic to an affirmative point of view in which she begins to explain what fun *can be* rather than what is *is not*. One paragraph in particular serves as the transition between the two attitudes. Which one is it? Which is the first paragraph to be mostly affirmative? What is the result of this switch?

8. Jordan uses specific brand names in the essay. Locate at least four of them. Why do you think she uses these brand names instead of names that simply identify the object?

9. What is the function of narration in the development of this essay? Where does the author *narrate* an imagined incident? Where does she use a real incident? Why does Jordan use narration in this paper?

10. Compare the effects of the two simple, direct statements that begin and end the essay. Why does Jordan not develop a more elaborate introduction and conclusion?

EXPLORING THE WRITER'S IDEAS

1. Jordan begins her essay by stating, "Fun is hard to have." At one point she indicates that "Fun got to be such a big thing that everybody started looking for more and more thrilling ways to supply it" (par. 9). Do you think that fun is hard to have? Why or why not? What relationship does the epidemic use of drugs and alcohol have to our difficulties in having fun today?

2. The author raises the question of how at big events we are sometimes left "waiting for the fun to start" (par. 11). What functions do events or occasions such as holidays, weddings, or birthdays play in our society? Why is there an emphasis placed on having fun at those events? Do you think there should be such an emphasis? Why?

3. This essay appeared as a guest editorial in the *New York Times*. We do not usually think of the *New York Times* as a "fun" newspaper, but rather as one that deals with serious issues of international significance. Jordan's article might be considered popular writing or light reading. Do you feel there is a place in the media—newspapers, magazines, radio, television—for a mixture of "heavy" and "light" attitudes? What well-respected newspapers or magazines that you know include articles on popular topics? What subjects do you think would currently be most appealing to popular audiences?

4. At the end of the essay, Jordan seems to imply that it is easier for children to have fun than it is for grown-ups. Do you agree? Is the basic experience of fun any different for kids or for adults? Do you feel it was any easier for people to have fun in days past than it is now? Why?

IDEAS FOR WRITING

Guided Writing

Select one of the following highly connotative terms for various types of experiences and write an extended definition about it: love, creativity, alienation, prejudice, fidelity.

1. Prepare for your essay by consulting a good dictionary for the lexical definition of the term. However, instead of beginning with this definition, start with some catchy, interesting opening statements related to the definition.

2. Write a thesis sentence that names the word you will define and that tells the special opinion, attitude, or point of view you have about the word.

3. Attempt to establish the importance of your sub-

ject by considering it in terms of our current understanding of fun.

4. Use the technique of negation (see page 146) by providing various examples and illustrations of what your topic *is not* in order to establish your own viewpoint of what it *is*.

5. Use other strategies—description, narration, comparison and contrast, and so forth—to aid in clearly establishing an extended definition of your topic.

6. At the end of your essay dramatize through narration at least one personal experience that relates the importance of the topic to your life.

More Writing Projects

1. From a book of popular quotations (*Bartlett's Familiar Quotations, The Oxford Dictionary of Quotations*) check under the heading "fun" and select a number of statements about fun by professional writers. Then write an essay in which you expand one of those definitions. Draw upon your own experiences or readings to support the definition you choose to expand.

2. Write an extended definition of "triumph," using the main techniques seen in the Jordan essay.

Gregg Easterbrook

ESCAPE VALVE

A contemporary journalist, Gregg Easterbrook tries here to define a phrase that he has coined to identify a phenomenon of modern life. Take note of the way he develops his definition by means of personal anecdote, history, and causal analysis. As you read, think about whether or not you know anyone guilty of "automatic-out."

Words to Watch

deep-rooted (par. 3): firmly planted
foundations (par. 4): underlying supports
stints (par. 5): fixed share of work to be performed within a given time period
truism (par. 5): statement of a very obvious truth
hierarchies (par. 6): body of people organized or classified according to rank
integrity (par. 7): adherence to a code of behavior: honesty; uprightness
perpetuate (par. 9): prolong the existence of

A man and woman I know moved in together 1 recently. It was, as such occasions are, a moment of sentiment and celebration. It was also a limited engagement. Before moving in, they had already set a fixed date when they would break up.

They explained their reasons to one and all. In a 2
year, the woman planned to change jobs and cities; the man
did not plan to follow. An eventual split is unfortunate, they
said, but also inevitable, so why not plan on it? Yet, far
from being a sad twist of fate, my woman friend's scheduled
departure, I fear, was a liberating force, making possible
whatever short-term romance the couple will enjoy. Without
the escape clause of a pre-set termination of their affair,
they might never have lived together at all.

This situation is not unique. More and more, people 3
are ordering their lives along a principle I call the "automatic-out." In love, friendship, work, and the community,
people increasingly prefer arrangements that automatically
end at some pre-set date. Automatic-out is not a phenomenon
confined to my still-unsettled generation (the late 20's), with
its flair for "flexible" styles of life. It is a force in society as
a whole, as more of us hunger for lives that appear stable
and deep-rooted but lack the complications of commitment.

Automatic-out may have its foundations in the pre- 4
set cycles of academic life. In recent decades, an ever-higher
percentage of the population has been able to attend college
and postgraduate schools. That's a good thing for the cause
of education but perhaps not so good for society's spirit.
Longtime students learn to view institutions as places where
people briefly come to rest, and from which they will be
automatically removed on a date known years in advance.
They also tend to see institutions as a means by which to
take things for themselves, instead of adding things for
others.

So it may be no surprise that professionals—usually 5
the beneficiaries of advanced schooling—seem increasingly
uninterested in staying put. Or, if they remain with one
organization, lean toward fellowships, temporary assign-
ments, and other stints with automatic-outs. For some time,
this has been a troubling truism of Washington. A Brookings
Institution study shows that Government-agency managers
immediately below the rank of Presidential appointees turn
over, on average, every 21 months. Now it is becoming true
of private enterprise as well. According to the Conference

Board, a business research organization, top corporate executives now switch jobs every 4.5 years on average—an all-time high.

The job-switching mania, it is sometimes suggested, 6 stems from a combination of boredom and expectations of promotion. But most switches among Government agencies and corporate hierarchies do not involve dramatic changes of life; they are changes from one job to another fairly similar to it, in a fairly similar organization. The number of top-level positions available doesn't increase just because the switching rate is increasing.

The switch mania is, I think, motivated by the desire 7 for automatic-outs. When you know in advance that you will soon be changing jobs, you are relieved of concern for the overall integrity of your institution—whether the quality of its products, the fairness of its service, the odds of its survival. You have a built-in excuse for selfishness ("I'll be leaving in a year anyway") and can concentrate on advancing yourself, secure in the knowledge that if you fail to improve your organization—or, as in the case of so many business and Government managers, actively damage it—you personally won't suffer. You'll be one step ahead of the crumbling walls.

It seems to be the same way in love. If a romance 8 operates under some pre-set restriction, neither partner feels obliged to sacrifice his interests for joint interests. Why sacrifice for something not expected to last anyway? Thus, the short-term benefits of marriage and living together (companionship, warmth, convenience) remain popular. But long-term obligation to the institution of marriage has fallen into disrepute among many young people. Children and family life are especially in disrepute today, for whenever children are present there is no easy out, emotionally or legally. The weekend romance is especially desirable today, not because "people move around more now" but because distance guarantees an automatic-out. Just step back on the plane Sunday night.

Many troublesome aspects of life perpetuate themselves through downward-drawing spirals. As corporate and 9 public institutions fall deeper into disrepair, as men and women becoming increasingly small-minded and cool to the touch, there seems all the more reason to opt for automatic-outs. Who wants to be committed to the kinds of people and organizations at loose in the world today? This, of course, helps only to accelerate the decay. Many people capable of helping right what's wrong with society seek instead mainly to exempt themselves from responsibility for its condition. Why should I care? I'll be leaving in a year anyway.

BUILDING VOCABULARY

Match each term at the left below with an appropriate definition among those appearing at the right. There are two more definitions than you need.

1. inevitable (par. 2)
2. stable (par. 3)
3. beneficiaries (par. 5)
4. mania (par. 6)
5. motivated (par. 7)
6. disrepute (par. 8)
7. disrepair (par. 9)
8. opt (par. 9)
9. accelerate (par. 9)
10. exempt (par. 9)

a. disgrace
b. attractive
c. stimulated to action
d. speed up
e. intense, abnormal desire for something
f. automatic
g. resistant to change
h. free from obligation
i. choose
j. unavoidable
k. state of neglect
l. those who receive advantages

UNDERSTANDING THE WRITER'S IDEAS

1. What arrangement does the couple the author knows make? What reasons do they offer for this arrangement?

2. What is the "automatic-out" principle? Why does the author believe that it appeals to society as a whole and not just to his own generation of men and women in their late twenties?

3. What, according to Easterbrook, are the foundations for automatic-out?

4. What does the Brookings Institution study demonstrate? How does the Conference Board reinforce that study in a business setting?

5. What are the reasons generally offered for what Easterbrook calls "the job-switching mania"? Why are top-level positions not increasing in number? How does Easterbrook explain the switch mania?

6. For what reason does the desire to switch operate for love as well as for jobs? What are the short-term benefits of marriage and living together? Why, according to the author, has the long-term obligation to marriage fallen into disrepute? Why is the weekend romance attractive?

7. How does the automatic-out serve to accelerate the decay of people and institutions today?

UNDERSTANDING THE WRITER'S TECHNIQUE

1. Which sentence of this essay is the thesis sentence? Why does Easterbrook not place it in the opening paragraph?

2. What is your opinion of the introduction in paragraphs 1 and 2? What is the value to the essay of the incident about the author's acquaintances? What rhetorical technique appears?

3. Where does the writer use negation (see page 142)?

4. In paragraph 4 why does he give backgrounds to the concept "automatic-out"?

5. Why does Easterbrook present findings of the Brookings Institution and the Conference Board? How do the findings enhance his point?

6. Where does the writer use causal analysis (see pages 246–248)? Why does he use it?

7. What transitions serve to connect one paragraph to the next? Look especially at the first sentence in paragraphs 3, 4, 5, 6, 7, and 8.

8. In paragraphs 3, 7, and 8 Easterbrook uses

parenthetical expressions. Why does he choose to place information in parentheses?

9. The writer frames a number of questions in the essay. For example, in paragraph 8, he says, "Why sacrifice for something not expected to last anyway?" What is the value of the question? Why doesn't Easterbrook answer it? What other unanswered questions appear?

10. What is your opinion of the conclusion? How does Easterbrook establish a new, broader context for the term "automatic-out"? Why does he choose that context to close the essay?

11. Why do you think that the essay is called "Escape Valve" instead of "Automatic-Out"? What is an escape valve? Used here, of course, the title is metaphorical (see Glossary). What value is there in using the metaphorical title in this case?

12. What is your reaction to the conclusion? Why does Easterbrook end by condemning the automatic-out philosophy? Do you find the last two sentences effective? Why?

EXPLORING THE WRITER'S IDEAS

1. Has Easterbrook defined clearly a recognizable principle in today's society as you view it? Why do you feel as you do? What evidence of the automatic-out do you find among your family, friends, or acquaintances? Have you yourself ever entered into a relationship based upon automatic-out?

2. Easterbrook blames in part the academic institution—our public and private schools and colleges—for our acceptance of the value in short-term commitments. Why might you agree or disagree with him? What other forces or institutions may encourage short-term commitments?

3. Do you agree that the high level of job switching apparent today is related more to the desire for escaping commitments than to "boredom and expectations of promotion"? Defend your answer.

4. Why might you agree or disagree that "marriage

has fallen into disrepute among many young people"? Is automatic-out a real threat to marriage as a basic institution of our culture? Why? (Look ahead to the essay "I Wish They'd Do It Right" for another perspective on marriage.)

5. Answer the question in paragraph 9: "Who wants to be committed to the kinds of people and organizations at loose in the world today?"

6. The writer states that "many people capable of helping right what's wrong with society" try "to exempt themselves from responsibility for its condition." What are some of the things wrong with society today? How might people right those wrongs?

IDEAS FOR WRITING

Guided Writing

Choose a word or term that you think is opposite in meaning to "automatic-out" and write an essay of 500 to 750 words in which you define that term. You may choose a word or term like *commitment, staying in, holding on, hanging in,* or some such expression. You may even want to coin your own phrase.

1. Start with an anecdote about friends or acquaintances and explain it. Your anecdote should demonstrate the word or phrase that you are trying to define.

2. In your thesis statement name the term and give an expanded definition of it in a paragraph or two.

3. Explain the foundations or the history of the situation your term is naming as Easterbrook does in paragraph 4 of his essay.

4. If possible, present data to support your interpretation of the term.

5. Give examples to expand your meanings further. Draw your examples from people at work or from personal relationships with other people.

6. Use an occasional unanswered question to challenge the reader.

7. If you can, use negation to help you define the term.

8. Connect your paragraphs with transitions that relate one idea thoughtfully to the next.

9. In your conclusion, place the term in a broader perspective, one that goes beyond the specific conditions you are explaining.

10. Try to give your essay a metaphorical title.

More Writing Projects

1. Easterbrook uses the term "switch mania" when he writes about jobs. Think about the term and then write a definition of it as it pertains to our culture today.

2. An "escapist" is someone who looks to break loose from unpleasant realities through self-deceiving fantasy or entertainment. In an essay write an extended definition of the word "escapist." Draw upon your own experiences and (or) your readings to support your definition.

Charles F. Berlitz

THE ETYMOLOGY OF THE INTERNATIONAL INSULT

In this essay, Charles Berlitz uses a variety of examples
to define the insult related to a person's race or religion,
and the insult related to country of birth. The author, who
founded the internationally known Berlitz School of Languages, analyzes words that have highly charged meanings and connotations for all of us. He does not use such
words to insult any readers, but rather to aid us in
understanding how "international insults" have developed.

Words to Watch

etymology (title): the origin and development of a word
derived (par. 2): traced from a source
perjorative (par. 2): showing disrespect for
appellation (par. 3): a name
opprobrious (par. 3): abusive; disrespecful
inversion (par. 3): a reversal
swarthy (par. 5): dark
epithets (par. 6): words or phrases that describe a particular
   characteristic of a person or thing
semantic (par. 7): relating to meaning in language
diminutive (par. 11): shortening (in this case, of a word)
contraction (par. 11): shortening
physiognomy (par. 12): features (of the face) thought to reveal
   character
reciprocated (par 12): given or done in return
sanctified (par 15): made holy

"**W**hat is a kike?" Disraeli once asked a small 1
group of fellow politicians. Then, as his audience shifted
nervously, Queen Victoria's great Jewish Prime Minister
supplied the answer himself. "A kike" he observed, "is a
Jewish gentleman who has just left the room."

The word kike is thought to have derived from the 2
ending -*ki* or -*ky* found in many names borne by the Jews
of Eastern Europe. Or, as Leo Rosten suggests, it may come
from *kikel,* Yiddish for a circle, the preferred mark for name
signing by Jewish immigrants who could not write. This
was used instead of an X, which resembles a cross. Kikel
was not originally pejorative, but has become so through
use.

Yid, another word for Jew has a distinguished 3
historic origin, coming from the German *Jude* (through the
Russian *zhid*). *Jude* itself derives from the tribe of Judah,
a most honorable and ancient appellation. The vulgar and
opprobrious word "Sheeny" for Jew is a real inversion, as it
derives from *shaine* (Yiddish) or *schön* (German), meaning
"beautiful." How could beautiful be an insult? The answer
is that it all depends on the manner, tone or facial expression
or sneer (as our own Vice President* has trenchantly observed) with which something is said. The opprobrious
Mexican word for an American—*gringo,* for example, is
essentially simply a sound echo of a song the American
troops used to sing when the Americans were invading
Mexico—"Green Grow the Lilacs." Therefore the Mexicans
began to call the Americans something equivalent to "los
green-grows" which became Hispanized to *gringo.* But from
this innocent beginning to the unfriendly emphasis with
which many Mexicans say *gringo* today there is a world of
difference—almost a call to arms, with unforgettable memories of past real or fancied wrongs, including "lost" Texas
and California.

The pejorative American word for Mexicans, Puerto 4
Ricans, Cubans and other Spanish-speaking nationals is
simply *spik,* excerpted from the useful expression "No esspick
Englitch." Italians, whether in America or abroad, have

---

* A reference to Spiro Agnew who served as Vice President to Richard
Nixon.

been given other more picturesque appellations. *Wop,* an all-time pejorative favorite, is curiously not insulting at all by origin, as it means, in Neapolitan dialect, "handsome," "strong" or "good looking." Among the young Italian immigrants some of the stronger and more active—sometimes to the point of combat—were called *guappi,* from which the first syllable, "wop," attained an "immediate insult" status for all Italians.

"Guinea" comes from the days of the slave trade and is derived from the African word for West Africa. This "guinea" is the same word as the British unit of 21 shillings, somehow connected with African gold profits as well as New Guinea, which resembled Africa to its discoverers. Dark or swarthy Italians and sometimes Portuguese were called *Guineas* and this apparently spread to Italians of light complexion as well.

One of the epithets for Negroes has a curious and tragic historic origin, the memory of which is still haunting us. The word is "coons." It comes from *baracoes* (the o gives a nasal *n* sound in Portuguese), and refers to the slave pens or barracks (*"baracoons"*) in which the victims of the slave trade were kept while awaiting transshipment. Their descendants, in their present emphasizing of the term "black" over "Negro," may be in the process of upgrading the very word "black," so often used pejoratively, as in "black-hearted," "black day," "black arts," "black hand," etc. Even some African languages use "black" in a negative sense. In Hausa "to have a black stomach" means to be angry or unhappy.

The sub-Sahara African peoples, incidentally, do not think that they are black (which they are not, anyway). They consider themselves a healthy and attractive "people color," while whites to them look rather unhealthy and somewhat frightening. In any case, the efforts of African Americans to dignify the word "black" may eventually represent a semantic as well as a socio-racial triumph.

A common type of national insult is that of referring to nationalities by their food habits. Thus "Frogs" for the French and "Krauts" for the Germans are easily understandable, reflecting on the French addiction to *cuisses de gren-*

ouilles (literally "thighs of frogs") and that of the Germans for various kinds of cabbage, hot or cold. The French call the Italians *"les macaronis"* while the German insult word for Italians is *Katzenfresser* (cateaters), an unjust accusation considering the hordes of cats among the Roman ruins fed by individual cat lovers—unless they are fattening them up? The insult word for an English person is "limey," referring to the limes distributed to seafaring Englishmen as an antiscurvy precaution in the days of sailing ships and long periods at sea.

At least one of these food descriptive appellations 9 has attained a permanent status in English. The word "Eskimo" is not an Eskimo word at all but an Algonquin word unit meaning "eaters-of-flesh." The Eskimos naturally do not call themselves this in their own language but, with simple directness, use the word *Inuit*—"the men" or "the people."

Why is it an insult to call Chinese "Chinks"? Chink 10 is most probably a contraction of the first syllables of *Chung-Kuo-Ren*—"Middle Country Person." In Chinese there is no special word for China, as the Chinese, being racially somewhat snobbish themselves (although *not* effete, according to recent reports), have for thousands of years considered their land to be the center or middle of the world. The key character for China is therefore the word *chung* of "middle" which, added to *kuo,* becomes "middle country" or "middle kingdom"—the complete Chinese expression for "China" being *Chung Hwa Min Kuo* ("Middle Flowery People's Country"). No matter how inoffensive the origin of "Chink" is, however, it is no longer advisable for everyday or any-day use now.

Jap, an insulting diminutive that figured in the last 11 national U.S. election (though its use in the expression "fat Jap" was apparently meant to have an endearing quality by our Vice President) is a simple contraction of "Japan," which derives from the Chinese word for "sun." In fact the words "Jap" and "Nip" both mean the same thing. "Jap" comes from Chinese and "Nip" from Japanese in the following fashion: *Jihpen* means "sun origin" in Chinese, while *Ni-*

hon (Nippon) gives a like meaning in Japanese, both indicating that Japan was where the sun rose. Europeans were first in contact with China, and so originally chose the Chinese name for Japan instead of the Japanese one.

The Chinese "insult" words for whites are based on 12 the observations that they are *too* white and therefore look like ghosts or devils, *fan kuei* (ocean ghosts), or that their features are too sharp instead of being pleasantly flat, and that they have enormous noses, hence *ta-bee-tsu* (great-nosed ones). Differences in facial physiognomy have been fully reciprocated by whites in referring to Asians as "Slants" or "Slopes."

Greeks in ancient times had an insult word for 13 foreigners too, but one based on the sound of their language. This word is still with us, though its original meaning has changed. The ancient Greeks divided the world into Greeks and "Barbarians"—the latter word coming from a description of the ridiculous language the stranger was speaking. To the Greeks it sounded like the "baa-baa" of a sheep—hence "Barbarians!"

The black peoples of South Africa are not today 14 referred to as Negro or Black but as Bantu—not in itself an insult but having somewhat the same effect when you are the lowest man on the totem pole. But the word means simply "the men," *ntu* signifying "man" and *ba* being the plural prefix. This may have come from an early encounter with explorers or missionaries when Central or South Africans on being asked by whites who they were may have replied simply "men"—with the implied though probably unspoken follow-up question, "And who are you?"

This basic and ancient idea that one's group are the 15 only people—at least the only friendly or non-dangerous ones—is found among many tribes throughout the world. The Navajo Indians call themselves *Diné*—"the people"—and qualify other tribes generally as "the enemy." Therefore an Indian tribe to the north would simply be called "the northern enemy," one to the east "the eastern enemy," etc., and that would be the *only* name used for them. These ancient customs, sanctified by time, of considering people who differ in color, customs, physical characteristics and habits—and by enlargement all strangers—as potential enemies is something mankind can no longer afford, even linguistically. Will man ever be able to rise above using insult as a weapon? It may not be possible to love your neighbor, but by understanding him one may be able eventually to tolerate him. Meanwhile, if you stop calling him names, he too may eventually learn to dislike *you* less.

BUILDING VOCABULARY

1. Use any five words from the Words to Watch section (page 165) in sentences of your own.

2. Many of the words that Berlitz defines in this essay (like *kike, wop, coon*) are not appropriate to formal writing or normal conversation. They are *vulgarisms*—words that exist at a level below conventional vocabulary. List five vulgarisms or slang terms from your vocabulary and try to define them on your own or by consulting a specialized dictionary of slang.

3. Define the following words from Berlitz's essay. If you are not sure of the meanings, use the dictionary:

    a. *shifted* (par. 1)
    b. *facial* (par. 2)
    c. *excerpted* (par. 3)
    d. *transshipment* (par. 5)
    e. *scurvy* (par. 8)
    f. *Algonquin* (par. 9)
    g. *effete* (par. 10)

UNDERSTANDING THE WRITER'S IDEAS

1. Who was Disraeli? Explain in your own words the meaning of Disraeli's definition of "kike."

2. Find original meanings in Berlitz's essay for the following words: *Jude; Wop; Schon; Guappi; Chung-Kuo-Ren.* What are the similarities among these five terms?

3. How does Berlitz explain the way in which something beautiful can be turned into an insult?

4.   What does Berlitz mean when he says that "the efforts of African Americans to dignify the word 'black' may eventually represent a semantic as well as socio-racial triumph"?

5.   What is the relationship between national eating habits and the national insult?

6.   Why do white people look frightening to both sub-Sahara Africans and to Chinese?

7.   Why do we find so many tribes who refer to themselves as "the men" or "the people"?

8.   What attitude toward the national insult does Berlitz suggest in the last paragraph?

UNDERSTANDING THE WRITER'S TECHNIQUES

1.   There are many ways to develop introductory paragraphs in essays. One useful strategy is to tell a brief story or *anecdote,* as Berlitz does in this essay. Do you find Berlitz's anecdote effective? Why or why not? Why is there no thesis sentence? How does the anecdote relate to the rest of the essay?

2.   How does Berlitz create a smooth transition (see Glossary) between paragraphs 2 and 3? between 3 and 4? Find other examples of skillful transitions between paragraphs.

3.   Does Berlitz ever offer a single-sentence definition of the "national insult"? Why or why not? What strategy does he employ to make the meaning of his extended definition clear? What is the relationship of the many definitions of specific national insults to the large definition that Berlitz presents?

4.   Berlitz tries hard to select examples from many races, nationalities, and geographic areas. Why does he do this? Is there any geographic pattern that you detect in the organization of the essay?

5.   Why does Berlitz withhold his thesis until the last paragraph? Do you find the last paragraph effective? Why or why not?

6.   What is the tone of the essay? Is it appropriate to the subject? Why or why not?

EXPLORING THE WRITER'S IDEAS

1. Do you think that all national and ethnic insults develop in as clear a manner as Berlitz describes it?

2. Does understanding a national insult make it any easier to accept? Why? Why not?

3. Why is it that we have so many ethnic and national insults in the English language? Why do so many individuals use these insults from time to time? Is it ever possible to use them in a joking manner? Is it possible to use them with positive rather than negative connotations? For instance, if one black person called another "nigger," what would the effect be? How would the effect differ if a white person were to use the word?

4. Do you think that ethnic insults are a form of violence with language? Why? Do you feel that all types of insults have some form of aggression behind them? How do music, film, and television contribute to the growth of ethnic insults? List some songs or films that do this.

5. Try to answer the question Berlitz raises in the last paragraph. Do you agree with the last sentence?

IDEAS FOR WRITING

Guided Writing

Write an extended definition of an insult you find especially ugly or vulgar.

1. Start with a brief anecdote that might be drawn from personal experience.

2. Try to discuss insults related to the one you have singled out. Compare or contrast them to your word.

3. Use a number of examples to support your general ideas. Be certain to define what each insult means.

4. Pay attention to transitions as you move from one example to another.

5. Reserve your thesis for the concluding paragraph of your essay.

More Writing Projects

   1.   Select a racial, a religious, or a national insult and define it by showing what negative qualities about the race are suggested by the insult. Then, show what positive contributions the people labeled by the "insult" have made to American society.

   2.   Some comedians—Groucho Marx, W. C. Fields, Don Rickels, Richard Pryor—made their fame with insults that make audiences laugh. Write an essay in which you define an insult or insults used for humorous effects. Be sure to treat this question in your essay: Is it possible *not* to offend someone with a racial or ethnic insult?

6

Classification

Classification is the arrangement of information into groups or categories in order to make clear the relationships among members of the group. Writers need to classify, because it helps them present a mass of material by means of some orderly system. Related bits of information seem clearer when presented together as parts of a group. We are always classifying things in our daily lives: We put all our text books on one shelf or in one corner of the desk; we count on similar items in the supermarket being grouped together so we can buy all our canned vegetables or snacks in a single area; we make categories in our minds of the teachers we like, of the relatives who annoy us, and of the cars that look sleekest on the road. In classifying, we show how things within a large body of information relate to each other; we organize those things into groups so that they make sense to us and to anybody else who is interested in what we are thinking, or saying, or doing.

Classification helps writers explain relationships to their readers. First, a writer will *analyze* a body of material in order to divide some large subject into categories. Called *division* or *analysis*, this first task helps split an idea or an object into parts. Then, some of the parts can serve as categories into which the writer can fit individual pieces that share some common qualities. So, if you wanted to write about sports, for example, you might first break the topic down—*divide* it—into *team sports* and *individual sports* (although there are many other ways you might have made the division). Then you could group together (*classify*) baseball, soccer, and football in the first category; and, perhaps, boxing, wrestling and tennis in the second. Your purpose in dividing or analyzing is to determine the parts of a whole (team sports and individual sports *are* very different).

Division does not always require that classification follow it. Your purpose in classifying, however, is to show how things in a group are similar. (Baseball, soccer, and football have interesting similarities as team sports; boxing, wrestling, and tennis—stressing individual achievement—are related, too.) Yet division and classification do work together. If you emptied the contents of a pocketbook onto a table, you would begin to divide those contents into groups. Through division, you would identify objects relating to finances, objects relating to personal care, objects relating to school work. Once you had the divisions clear, you would place objects in each category: money, checks, and credit cards in the first; cosmetics, a comb, perfume in the second; pens, pencils, a notebook in the third.

When you divide and classify for writing, you have to keep several things in mind. You have to think carefully about the division of the topic so that you limit the overlap from group to group. That is best achieved by creating categories different enough from each other so there is no blending. Since you, the writer, have to establish the groups (and sometimes there are many different ways to set up groups for the same topic), you need to use a principle of classification that is sensible, accurate, and complete. Do not force categories just for the sake of making groups. You have to show how things in a group relate to each other, and this you must do without ignoring their differences and without making them stereotypes. If you stereotype objects in a group (whether the objects are people, things, or ideas), you will be oversimplifying them, taking away their individuality, and forcing them to fit your categories.

Classification resembles outlining. It provides the writer with a plan of organization. Whether the subject is personal, technical, simple, complex, or abstract, the writer can organize material about it into categories, and can move carefully from one category to another in developing an essay.

Judith Viorst

FRIENDS, GOOD FRIENDS— AND SUCH GOOD FRIENDS

In this essay Judith Viorst, who writes for numerous popular magazines, examines types of friends in her life. Her pattern of development is easy to follow, because she tends to stay on one level in the process of classification. As you read this essay, try to keep in mind the similarities and distinctions that Viorst makes among types of friends, as well as the principles of classification that she uses.

Words to Watch

nonchalant (par. 3): showing lack of interest or concern
endodontist (par. 14): a dentist specializing in diseases of dental pulp and root canals.
sibling (par. 16): brother or sister
dormant (par. 19): as if asleep; inactive
self-revelation (par. 22): self-discovery; self-disclosure
calibrated (par. 29): measured; fixed; checked carefully

Women are friends, I once would have said, when 1 they totally love and support and trust each other, and bare to each other the secrets of their souls, and run—no questions asked—to help each other, and tell harsh truths to each other (no, you can't wear that dress unless you lose ten pounds first) when harsh truths must be told.

Women are friends, I once would have said, when 2 they share the same affection for Ingmar Bergman, plus train rides, cats, warm rain, charades, Camus, and hate with equal ardor Newark and Brussels sprouts and Lawrence Welk and camping.

In other words, I once would have said that a friend 3 is a friend all the way, but now I believe that's a narrow point of view. For the friendships I have and the friendships I see are conducted at many levels of intensity, serve many different functions, meet different needs and range from those as all-the-way as the friendship of the soul sisters mentioned above to that of the most nonchalant and casual playmates.

Consider these varieties of friendship: 4

1. Convenience friends. These are the women with 5 whom, if our paths weren't crossing all the time, we'd have no particular reason to be friends: a next-door neighbor, a woman in our car pool, the mother of one of our children's closest friends or maybe some mommy with whom we serve juice and cookies each week at the Glenwood Co-op Nursery.

Convenience friends are convenient indeed. They'll 6 lend us their cups and silverware for a party. They'll drive our kids to soccer when we're sick. They'll take us to pick up our car when we need a lift to the garage. They'll even take our cats when we go on vacation. As we will for them.

But we don't, with convenience friends, ever come 7 too close or tell too much; we maintain our public face and emotional distance. "Which means," says Elaine, "that I'll talk about being overweight but not about being depressed. Which means I'll admit being mad but not blind with rage. Which means I might say that we're pinched this month but never that I'm worried sick over money."

But which doesn't mean that there isn't sufficient 8 value to be found in these friendships of mutual aid, in convenience friends.

2. Special-interest friends. These friendships aren't 9 intimate, and they needn't involve kids or silverware or

cats. Their value lies in some interest jointly shared. And so we may have an office friend or a yoga friend or a tennis friend or a friend from the Women's Democratic Club.

"I've got one woman friend," says Joyce, "who likes, 10 as I do, to take psychology courses. Which makes it nice for me—and nice for her. It's fun to go with someone you know and it's fun to discuss what you've learned, driving back from the classes." And for the most part, she says, that's all they discuss.

"I'd say that what we're doing is *doing* together, not 11 being together," Suzanne says of her Tuesday-doubles friends. "It's mainly a tennis relationship, but we play together well. And I guess we all need to have a couple of playmates."

I agree. 12

My playmate is a shopping friend, a woman of 13 marvelous taste, a woman who knows exactly *where* to buy *what*, and furthermore is a woman who always knows beyond a doubt what one ought to be buying. I don't have the time to keep up with what's new in eyeshadow, hemlines and shoes and whether the smock look is in or finished already. But since (oh, shame!) I care a lot about eyeshadow, hemlines and shoes, and since I don't *want* to wear smocks if the smock look is finished, I'm very glad to have a shopping friend.

3. Historical friends. We all have a friend who knew 14 us when . . . maybe way back in Miss Meltzer's second grade, when our family lived in that three-room flat in Brooklyn, when our dad was out of work for seven months, when our brother Allie got in that fight where they had to call the police, when our sister married the endodontist from Yonkers and when, the morning after we lost our virginity, she was the first, the only, friend we told.

The years have gone by and we've gone separate 15 ways and we've little in common now, but we're still an intimate part of each other's past. And so whenever we go to Detroit we always go to visit this friend of our girlhood. Who knows how we looked before our teeth were straightened. Who knows how we talked before our voice got un-Brooklyned. Who knows what we ate before we learned about artichokes. And who, by her presence, puts us in touch with an earlier part of ourself, a part of ourself it's important never to lose.

"What this friend means to me and what I mean to her," says Grace, "is having a sister without sibling rivalry. We know the texture of each other's lives. She remembers my grandmother's cabbage soup. I remember the way her uncle played the piano. There's simply no other friend who remembers those things." 16

4. Crossroads friends. Like historical friends, our crossroads friends are important for *what was*—for the friendship we shared at a crucial, now past, time of life. A time, perhaps, when we roomed in college together; or worked as eager young singles in the Big City together; or went together, as my friend Elizabeth and I did through pregnancy, birth and that scary first year of new motherhood. 17

Crossroads friends forge powerful links, links strong enough to endure with not much more contact than once-a-year letters at Christmas. And out of respect for those crossroads years, for those dramas and dreams we once shared, we will always be friends. 18

5. Cross-generational friends. Historical friends and crossroads friends seem to maintain a special kind of intimacy—dormant but always ready to be revived—and though we may rarely meet, whenever we do connect, it's personal and intense. Another kind of intimacy exists in the friendships that form across generations in what one woman calls her daughter-mother and her mother-daughter relationships. 19

Evelyn's friend is her mother's age—"but I share so much more than I ever could with my mother"—a woman she talks to of music, of books and of life. "What I get from her is the benefit of her experience. What she gets—and enjoys—from me is a youthful perspective. It's a pleasure for both of us." 20

I have in my own life a precious friend, a woman of 65 who has lived very hard, who is wise, who listens well; who has been where I am and can help me understand it; 21

and who represents not only an ultimate ideal mother to me but also the person I'd like to be when I grow up.

In our daughter role we tend to do more than our 22 share of self-revelation; in our mother role we tend to receive what's revealed. It's another kind of pleasure—playing wise mother to a questing younger person. It's another very lovely kind of friendship.

6. Part-of-a-couple friends. Some of the women we 23 call our friends we never see alone—we see them as part of a couple at couples' parties. And though we share interests in many things and respect each other's views, we aren't moved to deepen the relationship. Whatever the reason, a lack of time or—and this is more likely—a lack of chemistry, our friendship remains in the context of a group. But the fact that our feeling on seeing each other is always, "I'm *so* glad she's here" and the fact that we spend half the evening talking together says that this too, in its own way, counts as a friendship.

(Other part-of-a-couple friends are the friends that 24 came with the marriage, and some of these are friends we could live without. But sometimes, alas, she married our husband's best friend; and sometimes, alas, she *is* our husband's best friend. And so we find ourself dealing with her, somewhat against our will, in a spirit of what I'll call *reluctant* friendship.)

7. Men who are friends. I wanted to write just of 25 women friends, but the women I've talked to won't let me— they say I must mention man-woman friendships too. For these friendships can be just as close and as dear as those that we form with women. Listen to Lucy's description of one such friendship:

"We've found we have things to talk about that are 26 different from what he talks about with my husband and different from what I talk about with his wife. So sometimes we call on the phone or meet for lunch. There are similar intellectual interests—we always pass on to each other the books that we love—but there's also something tender and caring too."

In a couple of crises, Lucy says, "he offered himself, 27 for talking and for helping. And when someone died in his family he wanted me there. The sexual, flirty part of our friendship is very small, but *some*—just enough to make it fun and different." She thinks—and I agree—that the sexual part, though small is always *some,* is always there when a man and a woman are friends.

It's only in the past few years that I've made friends 28 with men, in the sense of a friendship that's *mine,* not just part of two couples. And achieving with them the ease and the trust I've found with women friends has value indeed. Under the dryer at home last week, putting on mascara and rouge, I comfortably sat and talked with a fellow named Peter. Peter, I finally decided, could handle the shock of me minus mascara under the dryer. Because we care for each other. Because we're friends.

8. There are medium friends, and pretty good friends, 29 and very good friends indeed, and these friendships are defined by their level of intimacy. And what we'll reveal at each of these levels of intimacy is calibrated with care. We might tell a medium friend, for example, that yesterday we had a fight with our husband. And we might tell a pretty good friend that this fight with our husband made us so mad that we slept on the couch. And we might tell a very good friend that the reason we got so mad in that fight that we slept on the couch had something to do with that girl who works in his office. But it's only to our very best friends that we're willing to tell all, to tell what's going on with that girl in his office.

The best of friends, I still believe, totally love and 30 support and trust each other, and bare to each other the secrets of their souls, and run—no questions asked—to help each other, and tell harsh truths to each other when they must be told.

But we needn't agree about everything (only 12- 31 year-old girl friends agree about *everything*) to tolerate each other's point of view. To accept without judgment. To give and to take without ever keeping score. And to *be* there, as

I am for them and as they are for me, to comfort our sorrows, to celebrate our joys.

BUILDING VOCABULARY

1. Find antonyms (words that mean the opposite of given words) for the following entries:

a. harsh (par. 1)
b. mutual (par. 8)
c. crucial (par. 17)
d. intimacy (par. 29)
e. tolerate (par. 31)

2. The *derivation* of a word—how it originated and where it came from—can make you more aware of meanings. Your dictionary normally lists abbreviations (for instance, L. for Latin, Fr. for French) for word origins, and sometimes explains fully the way a word came into use. Look up the following words to determine their origins:

a. psychology (par. 10)
b. historical (par. 14)
c. sibling (par. 16)
d. Christmas (par. 18)
e. sexual (par. 27)

UNDERSTANDING THE WRITER'S IDEAS

1. What is Viorst's definition of friendship in the first two paragraphs? Does she accept this definition? Why or why not?

2. Name and describe in your own words the types of friends that Viorst mentions in her essay.

3. In what way are "convenience friends" and "special interest friends" alike? How are "historical friends" and "crossroads friends" alike?

4. What does Viorst mean when she writes, "In our daughter role we tend to do more than our share of self-

revelation; in our mother role we tend to receive what's revealed" (par. 22)?

5. How do part-of-a-couple friends who came with the marriage differ from primary part-of-a-couple friends?

6. Does Viorst think that men can be friends for women? Why or why not? What complicates such friendships?

7. For Viorst, who are the best friends?

UNDERSTANDING THE WRITER'S TECHNIQUES

1. Which paragraphs make up the introduction in this essay? How does Viorst organize these paragraphs? Where does she place her thesis sentence?

2. How does the thesis sentence reveal the principles of classification (the questions Viorst asks to produce the various categories) that the author employs in the essay?

3. Does Viorst seem to emphasize each of her categories equally? Is she effective in handling each category? Why or why not? Do you think that men belong in the article as a category? For what reasons?

4. Analyze the importance of illustration in this essay. From what sources does Viorst tend to draw her examples?

5. How do definition and comparison and contrast operate in the essay? Cite specific examples of these techniques.

6. The level of language in this essay tends to be informal at times, reflecting patterns that are as close to conversation as to formal writing. Identify some sentences that seem to resemble informal speech. Why does Viorst try to achieve a conversational style?

7. Which main group in the essay is further broken down into categories?

8. Analyze Viorst's conclusion. How many paragraphs are involved? What strategies does she use? How does she achieve balanced sentence structure (parallelism) in her last lines?

EXPLORING THE WRITER'S IDEAS

1. Do you accept all of Viorst's categories of friendship? Which categories seem the most meaningful to you?

2. Try to think of people you know who fit into the various categories established by Viorst. Can you think of people who might exist in more than one category? How do you explain this fact? What are the dangers in trying to stereotype people in terms of categories, roles, backgrounds, or functions?

3. Viorst maintains that you can define friends in terms of functions and needs (see paragraph 3 and paragraphs 29 to 31). Would you agree? Why or why not? What principle or principles do you use to classify friends? In fact, *do* you classify friends? For what reasons?

IDEAS FOR WRITING

Guided Writing

Using the classification method, write an essay on a specific group of individuals—for instance, *types of friends, types of enemies, types of students, types of teachers, types of politicians, types of dates*—and so forth.

1. Establish your subject in the first paragraph. Also indicate to the reader the principle(s) of classification that you plan to use. (For guidelines look again at the second sentence in paragraph 3 of Viorst's essay.)

2. Start the body of the essay with a single short sentence that introduces categories (see paragraph 4). In the body, use numbers and category headings ("Convenience friends" . . . "Special interest friends") to separate groups.

3. Try to achieve a balance in the presentation of information on each category. Define each type and provide appropriate examples.

4. If helpful, use comparison and contrast to indicate from time to time the similarities and differences among groups. Try to avoid too much overlapping of groups, since this is harmful to the classification process.

5. Employ the personal "I" and other conversational techniques to achieve an informal style.

6. Return to your principle(s) of classification and amplify this feature in your conclusion. If you want, make a value judgement, as Viorst does, about which type of person in your classification scheme is the most significant.

More Writing Projects

1. Write an essay classifying the varieties of love.

2. Classify varieties of show business comedians, singers, talk show hosts, star athletes, or the like.

E. B. White

THE THREE NEW YORKS

E. B. White, whose frequently used book *The Elements of Style* is well known to college composition students, here classifies "The Three New Yorks." Although the selection is an excerpt from his book *Here Is New York* (1949), the descriptive illustrations remain remarkably fresh after more than thirty years. Look closely at the way White clearly defines his categories of classification, then skillfully blends them to create a vivid sense of the whole city.

Words to Watch

turbulence (par. 1): wild commotion
locusts (par. 1): migratory grasshoppers that travel in swarms, stripping vegetation as they pass over the land
quest (par. 1): pursuit; search
disposition (par. 1): temperament; way of acting
deportment (par. 1): the way in which a person carries himself or herself
tidal (par. 1): coming in wave-like motions
continuity (par. 1): uninterrupted flow of events
slum (par. 1): a highly congested residential area marked by insanitary buildings, poverty, and social disorder
indignity (par. 1): humiliating treatment
vitality (par. 2): lively and animated character
gloaming (par. 2): a poetic term for *twilight.*
ramparts (par. 2): high broad structures guarding a building
negligently (par. 2): nonchalantly; neglectfully
loiterer (par. 2): a person who hangs around aimlessly
spewing (par. 2): coming in a flood or gush
rover (par. 2): wanderer; roamer

There are roughly three New Yorks. There is, first, 1
the New York of the man or woman who was born here, who
takes the city for granted and accepts its size and its turbulence as natural and inevitable. Second, there is the New
York of the commuter—the city that is devoured by locusts
each day and spat out each night. Third, there is the New
York of the person who was born somewhere else and came
to New York in quest of something. Of these three trembling
cities the greatest is the last—the city of final destination,
the city that is a goal. It is this third city that accounts for
New York's high-strung disposition, its poetical deportment,
its dedication to the arts, and its incomparable achievements. Commuters give the city its tidal restlessness; natives
give it solidity and continuity; but the settlers give it passion. And whether it is a farmer arriving from Italy to set up
a small grocery store in a slum, or a young girl arriving from
a small town in Mississippi to escape the indignity of being
observed by her neighbors, or a boy arriving from the Corn
Belt with a manuscript in his suitcase and a pain in his
heart, it makes no difference; each embraces New York with
the intense excitement of first love, each absorbs New York
with the fresh eyes of an adventurer, each generates heat
and light to dwarf the Consolidated Edison Company.

The commuter is the queerest bird of all. The suburb 2
he inhabits has no essential vitality of its own and is a mere
roost where he comes at day's end to go to sleep. Except in
rare cases, the man who lives in Mamaroneck or Little Neck
or Teaneck, and works in New York, discovers nothing much
about the city except the time of arrival and departure of
trains and buses, and the path to a quick lunch. He is desk-
bound, and has never, idly roaming in the gloaming, stum-
bled suddenly on Belvedere Tower in the Park, seen the ramparts rise sheer from the water of the pond, and the boys
along the shore fishing for minnows, girls stretched out negligently on the shelves of the rocks; he has never come suddenly on anything at all in New York as a loiterer, because
he has had no time between trains. He has fished in Manhattan's wallet and dug out coins, but has never listened to
Manhattan's breathing, never awakened to its morning,

never dropped off to sleep in its night. About 400,000 men and women come charging onto the Island each week-day morning, out of the mouths of tubes and tunnels. Not many among them have ever spent a drowsy afternoon in the great rustling oaken silence of the reading room of the Public Library, with the book elevator (like an old water wheel) spewing out books onto the trays. They tend their furnaces in Westchester and in Jersey, but have never seen the furnaces of the Bowery, the fires that burn in oil drums on zero winter nights. They may work in the financial district downtown and never see the extravagant plantings of Rockefeller Center—the daffodils and grape hyacinths and birches of the flags trimmed to the wind on a fine morning in spring. Or they may work in a midtown office and may let a whole year swing round without sighting Governor's Island from the sea wall. The commuter dies with tremendous mileage to his credit, but he is no rover. His entrances and exits are more devious than those in a prairie-dog village; and he calmly plays bridge while his train is buried in the mud at the bottom of the East River. The Long Island Rail Road alone carried forty million commuters last year; but many of them were the same fellow retracing his steps.

The terrain of New York is such that a resident some- 3 times travels farther, in the end, than a commuter. The journey of the composer Irving Berlin from Cherry Street in the lower East Side to an apartment uptown was through an alley and was only three or four miles in length; but it was like going three times around the world.

BUILDING VOCABULARY

1. One very important aspect of vocabulary development is an ability to understand specific place or name references in whatever you are reading. Underline the numerous references in this essay to buildings, people, and areas in and around New York City and be prepared to identify them. If necessary, consult a guidebook, map, or history of New York City for help.

2. White divides the inhabitants of New York into

three categories: commuters, natives, settlers. Write a literal definition for the word that labels each category; then write at least one figurative meaning for each (see Glossary).

3. Write a *synonym* (a word that means the same) for each of these adjectives in the essay:

    a. inevitable (par. 1)
    b. high-strung (par. 1)
    c. essential (par. 2)
    d. drowsy (par. 2)
    e. devious (par. 2)

UNDERSTANDING THE WRITER'S IDEAS

1. What are the three New Yorks?

2. What single-word designation does E. B. White assign to each of the three types of New Yorkers? Match up each of the three New Yorks you identified in the first question with each of the three types of New Yorkers.

3. For what reasons do people born elsewhere come to New York to live? What three illustrations of such people does White describe? What is the young girl's indignity? What is the occupation or hope of the boy from the Corn Belt? Why might he have "a pain in his heart"?

4. What does each type of New Yorker give to the city?

5. What is White's attitude toward the suburbs? What key phrases reveal this attitude?

6. What are some of the things commuters miss about New York by dashing in and out of the city? What does White ironically suggest will be the commuter's final fate?

7. Are we to take literally White's conclusion that "many of them are the same fellow retracing his steps"? Why or why not?

8. Explain the sentence "The terrain of New York is such that a resident sometimes travels farther, in the end, than a commuter." Be aware that White is using language figuratively.

9. The author tells of composer Irving Berlin's jour-

ney through an alley. He is referring to "Tin Pan Alley."
Identify this place.

UNDERSTANDING THE WRITER'S TECHNIQUES

   1.   In this essay what is the thesis? Where is it? Is it
developed fully?
   2.   What is the purpose of classification in this essay? What is the basis of the classification White uses? What
key words at the beginning of paragraph 1 direct your attention to each category discussed? How do these key words
contrast in tone with the descriptions in the first few sentences? What sort of rhythm is established?
   3.   White vividly *personifies* (see Glossary) New
York City in paragraph 1. List and explain the effects of
these personifications. Where else does he personify?
   4.   Refer to your answer to question 2 in the Building Vocabulary section. Are the literal meanings of those
words appropriate to White's three types of New Yorkers?
Defend your answer. Figuratively, what does each term
make you think of? How do the figurative meanings enhance the essay?
   5.   How does White use *illustration* in this essay?
Where does he use it most effectively?
   6.   What is the function of *negation* (see page 142)
in the first part of paragraph 2? What is the *implied contrast*
in this paragraph?
   7.   How is White's attitude toward New York re-
flected in the tone of this essay?
   8.   White makes widespread use of *metaphor* (see
Glossary) in this essay. How does his use of metaphor affect
the *tone* of the essay? State in your own words the meaning
of each of the following metaphors:

      a. ". . . the city that is devoured by locusts each day
          and spat out each night." (par. 1)
      b. "The commuter is the queerest bird of all." (par. 2)
      c. "a mere roost" (par. 2)
      d. "idly roaming in the gloaming" (par. 2)

e. "He has fished in Manhattan's wallet and dug out coins, but he has never listened to Manhattan's breathing." (par. 2)

f. "the great rustling oaken silence" (par. 2)

9. Among all the metaphors, White uses just one *simile* (see Glossary). What is it? What is the effect of placing it where he did?

EXPLORING THE WRITER'S IDEAS

1. At the beginning of the essay, E. B. White states that New York's "turbulence" is considered "natural and inevitable" by its native residents. But such a condition is true for any large city. If you live in a large city, or if you have ever visited one, what are some examples of its turbulence? Do you think it is always a good idea to accept the disorder of the place where you live? How can such acceptance be a positive attitude? How can it be negative? How do you deal with disruptions in your environment?

2. White writes of "a young girl arriving from a small town in Mississippi to escape the indignity of being observed by her neighbors." Tell in your own words what might cause her indignity. How can neighbors bring about such a condition?

3. Some people feel the anonymity of a big city like New York makes it easier just to "be yourself" without having to worry about what others might say. Others feel such anonymity creates a terrible feeling of impersonality. Discuss the advantages and disadvantages of each attitude.

4. Do you agree that the suburbs have "no essential vitality"? Explain your response by referring to suburbs you have visited, have read about, or have inhabited.

5. White claims that those who choose to leave their homes and who come to live in New York give the place a special vitality. Do you know any people who chose to leave their places of birth to live in a large city like New York? Why did they move? How have things gone for them since

they began living in the city? Have you noticed any changes? For what reasons do people leave one place to live in another? When have you moved from place to place? Why?

IDEAS FOR WRITING

Guided Writing

Organize a classification essay around the city or town in which you live.

1.   Begin with a simple direct thesis statement that tells the reader how many categories of classification you will consider.

2.   Briefly outline the different categories. Indicate each with a key organizational word or phrase.

3.   Indicate which category is the most important. Tell why.

4.   Develop this category with at least three vivid illustrations.

5.   Define one of the categories through both negation and an implied contrast to another category.

6.   Use figurative language (metaphors, similes, personification) throughout your essay.

7.   Use specific name or place references.

8.   End your essay with a brief factual narrative that gives the reader a feel for your town or city.

More Writing Projects

1.   Write an essay that classifies three main categories of jobs and the people who work at each.

2.   Write a classification essay on the suburbs, or the country.

3.   Select a cultural group and classify various characteristics common to that group. Be careful to avoid stereotyping.

Noel Perrin

COUNTRY CODES

Noel Perrin, "town-bred" in the East, now lives the country life as a college teacher. In this essay, he classifies the codes for speaking and interacting in the countryside. He relates the sometimes embarrassing ways in which he and others have learned the detailed structures of country codes.

Words to Watch

town-bred (par. 1): raised in the city, not in the country
haycocks (par. 1): small, cone-shaped piles of hay
rural (par. 3): of the countryside, not the city
exposition (par. 4): a detailed explanation
peremptory (par. 5): imperative; domineering
culvert (par. 6): a drain crossing under a road
to scythe (par. 10): to cut grass or grain by a hand implement
motive (par. 14): a reason for doing something
budge (par. 18): to move slightly
fervency (par. 18): intense feeling
stoic (par. 19): someone unaffected by joy, grief, pleasure, or pain
cordwood (par. 22): firewood that has been cut and stacked
B.O. (par. 29): slang for "body odor"

Robert Frost once wrote a poem about a 'townbred' 1
farmer who was getting his hay in with the help of two

hired men, both locals. As they're working, the sky clouds over, and it begins to look like rain. The farmer instructs the two hired men to start making the haycocks especially carefully, so that they'll shed water. About half an hour later (it still isn't raining), one of them abruptly shoves his pitchfork in the ground and walks off. He has quit.

The farmer is utterly baffled. The hired man who 2 stays explains to him that what he said was a major insult.

> 'He thought you meant to find fault with his work,
> That's what the average farmer would have meant.'

This hired man goes on to say that he would have quit, too—if the order had been issued by a regular farmer. But seeing as it was a city fellow, he made allowances.

> 'I know you don't understand our ways.
> You were just talking what was in your mind,
> What was in all our minds, and you weren't hinting.'

Frost called that poem 'The Code.' He published it in 1914.

Sixty-four years later, the country code is still going 3 strong, and it is still making trouble for town-bred people who live in rural areas. Only I think the code is even more complicated than Frost had room to describe in his poem. In fact, there isn't just one country code, there are at least three. What they all have in common is that instead of saying things out plainly, the way you do in the city, you approach them indirectly. You hint.

I am going to call these three the Power Code, the 4 Non-Reciprocity Code, and the Stoic's Code. These are not their recognized names; they don't *have* recognized names. Part of the code is that you never speak of the code, and I am showing my own town-bredness in writing this exposition. (As Frost showed his in writing the poem. He was a city kid in San Francisco before he was a farmer in New Hampshire.)

In Frost's poem, it was the Power Code that the 5 townie violated. Under the rules of the Power Code, you *never* give peremptory orders, and you ordinarily don't even make demands. You make requests. What the code says is that everybody is to be treated as an equal, even when financially or educationally, or whatever, they're not. Treat them as either inferiors or superiors, and you can expect trouble.

Just recently, for example, a young city doctor moved 6 to our town, and began violating the Power Code right and left. Take the way he treated the boss of the town road crew. The house the doctor was renting has a gravel driveway that tends to wash out after storms. It washed out maybe a month after he had moved in. He is said to have called the road commissioner and given him a brisk order. 'I want a culvert installed, and I want it done by this weekend.'

Now in the city that would be a quite sensible 7 approach. You're calling some faceless bureaucrat, and you use standard negotiating technique. You make an outrageous demand; you throw your weight around, if you have any; and you figure on getting part of what you ask for. You're not surprised when the bureaucrat screams, *'This week!* Listen, we got a hunnert and sixty-two jobs aheada you right now. If you're lucky, we'll get to you in October.' You scream back and threaten to call the mayor's office. Then you finally compromise on August.

But it doesn't work that way in the country. The 8 code doesn't encourage throwing your weight around. Our road commissioner had been given an order, and he instantly rejected it. ' 'Tain't the town's job to look after folks' driveways. If you want a culvert, you can buy one down to Write River Junction.'

I happened to hear what the road commissioner told 9 some friends later. The doctor had actually called at a good time. The town had several used culverts lying around— road culverts they had replaced, which were still good enough to go at the end of a driveway. 'If he'd asked decent, we'd have been glad to put one in for him, some day when work was slack.' If he'd used the code, that is.

That's nothing, though, compared with the way the 10 young doctor handled one of our retired farmers. When the doctor decided to live in our town—it meant a fifteen-mile drive to the hospital where he worked—it was because he had gotten interested in country things. He wanted to have a garden, burn wood, learn how to scythe a patch of grass, all those things. During his first spring and summer in town, he probably asked the old farmer a hundred questions. He got free lessons in scything. He consulted on fencing problems. Learned how thick to plant peas.

11   Then one day the farmer asked *him* a question. 'I understand you know suthin' about arthritis,' the farmer said. 'Well, my wife's is actin' up.' And he went on to ask a question about medication.

12   The young doctor's answer was quick and smooth. 'I'll be glad to see her in office hours,' he said.

13   Again, normal city practice. You've got to protect yourself against all the people at cocktail parties who want free medical advice. Furthermore, you probably really should examine a patient before you do any prescribing. All the same, what he was saying loud and clear in the country code was, 'My time is worth more than yours; I am more important than you are. So I can ask you free questions, but you must pay for any you ask me.' Not very polite. What he should have done was put down the scythe and say, 'Let's go have a look at her.'

14   Actually, if he had done that, he probably would have muffed it anyway. Because then he would have come up against the Non-Reciprocity Code, and he didn't understand that, either. The Non-Reciprocity Code says that you never take any favors for granted (or call in your debts, as city politicians say). Instead, you always pretend that each favor done you is a brand-new one. In the case of the young doctor, suppose he *had* stopped his free scythe lesson and gone to examine the farmer's wife. When he was ready to leave, the farmer would have said to him, 'What do I owe you?' And then one of two things would have happened. Old habits would have asserted themselves, and he would have said smoothly, 'That will be twenty-five dollars, please.' Or else, a little cross with the farmer for not recognizing his generous motive (does the old fool think I make *house calls?*),

he would have said that it was free, in a sort of huffy, look-what-a-favor-I'm-doing-you voice.

Both answers would have been wrong. The correct 15 response would be to act as if the farmer was doing *you* a favor in letting you not charge. Something like, 'Come on, if you can teach me to scythe, and how to plant peas, I guess there's no harm in my taking a look at your wife.'

One of the funniest instances in which you see the 16 Non-Reciprocity Code operating is after people get their trucks stuck, which during mud season in Vermont is constantly. You're driving along in your pickup, and there's your neighbor with two wheels in the ditch, unable to budge. You stop, get out your logging chain, hook on, and pull him out. 'How much will that be?' he asks, as if his cousin Donald hadn't just pulled you out the week before. In a way it's a ritual question. He would be surprised out of his mind if you thought a minute and said, 'Oh, I guess five dollars would be about right.'

But it's not entirely ritual. He would be surprised. 17 But he would hand over the five dollars. The point of the question is to establish that you don't *have* to pull him out just because he's a friend and will someday pull you out. It's treated as an act of free will, a part of New England independence.

The third code, the Stoic's Code, is sometimes con- 18 fused with machismo, but really has no connection with it. Country people of both sexes practice it with equal fervency. Basically, it consists of seeing who can go without complaining longest.

I first became aware of the Stoic's Code when I was 19 helping two people put hay bales into a barn loft about fifteen years ago. It was a hot day in late June, with the humidity running at least ninety percent. I function badly in hot weather. Within ten minutes I was pouring sweat— as were my coworkers. The difference was that I kept bitching about it. Finally, after three-quarters of an hour, I flopped down and announced I'd have to cool off before I touched another bale.

To me this just seemed common sense. We had no 20

special deadline to meet in loading that hay. What I really thought was that all three of us should go take a dip in the river.

But the Stoic's Code doesn't stress common sense. It stresses endurance. Maybe that's because to survive at all as a farmer in New England you need endurance. In any case, the other two flicked me one quick scornful look and kept on working. One of them has never really respected me again to this day. The other, like the second hired man in Frost's poem, made allowances for my background and forgave me. We have since become fast friends. I have never dared to ask, but I think he thinks I have made real progress in learning to shut my mouth and keep working. 21

I could never be a stoic on the true native level, though. Consider the story of Hayden Clark and Rodney Palmer, as Rodney tells it. A good many years ago, before there were any paved roads in town. Hayden ran a garage. (Rodney runs it now.) He also sold cordwood. 22

One day when there wasn't much doing at the garage, Hayden was sawing cordwood just across the road, where he could keep an eye on the gas pumps. If you saw with a circular saw, and do it right, it takes three men. One person lifts up the logs, one does the actual cutting, and one throws the cut pieces into a pile. The three jobs are called putting on, sawing, and taking off. In all three you are doing dangerous work at very high speed. 23

On this day a man named Charlie Raynes was putting on, Hayden was sawing, and young Rodney was taking off. Hayden kept the wood coming so fast that Rodney was always a beat behind. He never paused a second to let Rodney catch up, and this torture went on for nearly an hour. No one spoke. (Not that you could hear over a buzz saw, anyway.) 24

Then finally a customer pulled in for gas. Hayden left the other two sawing, and went over to pump it. Charlie continued to put on, and Rodney sawed in Hayden's place. 25

Rather than interrupt their rhythm when he came back, Hayden began to take off. Rodney and Charlie exchanged a quick glance, and began putting the wood to Hayden so fast that *he* was off balance the whole time, and 26 not infrequently in some danger of getting an arm cut off. At this speed and in this way they finished the entire pile. It was Rodney's revenge, and as he told me about it, his eyes gleamed.

It was only a year or two ago that Rodney told me 27 the story. In the very act of telling it, he included me as one who knew the code. But I instantly betrayed it. My city background is too strong. I'm too verbal, too used to crowing over triumphs.

'After you were done sawing, Hayden never said 28 anything about it?' I asked.

'Oh, *no*,' Rodney answered, looking really shocked. 29 'Any more than I'd have said anything to him.'

So, next time you're in a country store and you get a sense 30 that the locals are avoiding you as if you had the worst case of B.O. in the county, you can be pretty sure of the reason. You've probably just said some dreadful thing in code.

BUILDING VOCABULARY

1. Using context clues from the story, explain the figurative meanings of these phrases (see Glossary):

    a. "had room to describe" (par. 3)
    b. "throw your weight around" (par. 7)
    c. "call in your debts" (par. 14)
    d. "surprised out of his mind" (par. 16)
    e. "to cool off" (par. 19)
    f. "flicked me one quick scornful look" (par. 21)

2. Match the words and expressions in Column A with their meanings in Column B.

Column A	Column B
a. utterly baffled (par. 2)	1. complaining
b. muffed it (par. 14)	2. confused
c. take . . . for granted (par. 14)	3. made a mistake
d. bitching (par. 19)	4. to consider as true or already accepted
e. made allowances (par. 21)	5. accepted for special reasons

3. Explain the meanings of the following adjective-noun combinations:

    a. city fellow (par. 2)
    b. brisk order (par. 6)
    c. faceless bureaucrat (par. 7)
    d. outrageous demand (par. 7)
    e. free will (par. 17)
    f. fast friends (par. 21)

UNDERSTANDING THE WRITER'S IDEAS

1. What is a "code"?

2. Perrin opens his essay with a *paraphrase* (a rewording of something that had been written before) and some direct quotations from a Robert Frost poem, "The Code." What is the story line of "The Code"? What is the theme or "message" of the poem? What do Frost and Perrin have in common?

3. How do town-bred people respond to country codes?

4. Name the three country codes that Perrin discusses. Briefly outline the conditions of each code. What is the most important feature of each?

5. What codes does the doctor violate, and how?

6. Describe in your own words the "standard negotiating technique" used in the city. Why doesn't that technique work in the country?

7. What does Perrin say about "rituals"? Explain the meaning of the statement: "In a way it's a ritual question." (par. 16)

8. Name the three jobs involved in cutting cordwood. Describe the actions involved in each activity. In your own words, explain the "torture" mentioned in paragraph 23.

9. How does the author break the code when he talks to Rodney? To what reason does he attribute his error?

10. Explain the meaning of the last sentence of the essay. How is Perrin's use of the expression "in code" different from his use of the word "code" throughout the essay?

UNDERSTANDING THE WRITER'S TECHNIQUES

1. What is the purpose of the Frost poem? What is its connection to the thesis of the essay? Where does Perrin place his thesis?

2. What distinct classifications does the author establish for this essay? How does he *order* his classification (by type, class, chronology, or climactic order?) Why did he choose that order? How does he achieve balance among his groups? What transitional devices does he use to connect his groups?

3. How does Perrin use the young city doctor as an *extended example* (see page 66) in this essay? What parts of the country code does the doctor illustrate?

4. What are the uses of *narration* in this essay; of *definition*?

5. The author makes frequent use of a variety of punctuation in this essay, including *parentheses, dashes,* and *italics.* In general, what is the use of each of these three types of punctuation? In what ways does Perrin use each in this essay?

6. In his use of dialogue, Perrin attempts to copy the speech patterns of "city-talk" and "country-talk." What are the differences between the city speech patterns of paragraphs 6 and 7 and the country patterns of paragraphs 8 and 9? Where else does he use the two types of speech? Do you think his imitations are effective? Why?

7. What is the *tone* of this essay? Do you think that the author slants his tone toward country life or city life? Explain your response.

8. Why does Perrin set off the concluding paragraph from the rest of the essay? What is the effect on the meaning of the essay?

EXPLORING THE WRITER'S IDEAS

1. Do you agree with the basic premise of this essay: that codes of behavior exist and that those codes are related to geographical regions? Why? What codes have you observed in other places: farms, ranches, towns by the sea, mountain villages, and so on?

2. What conditions other than geographical ones might be responsible for codes of behavior? Consider with the class these as possible sources of behavioral codes: religion, economic status, ethnic background.

3. One of the codes says that country people always make requests and not demands and that "everybody is to be treated as an equal." Do you agree with those premises? Why? Could they—should they—apply to city people as well as country people? Why? Is it possible or desirable at all times to make requests instead of demands? to treat everybody equally?

4. Very often children will use "code languages" to speak, supposedly so that adults or other children won't understand. A common code language is called "pig Latin," in which you drop the first consonant sound and add it to the end of the word joined to the syllable "-ay." For example, the word "bicycle" would become "icycle-bay." The word "China" would become "ina-Chay." What code languages are you familiar with?

IDEAS FOR WRITING

Guided Writing

Write an essay in which you classify three or more codes or categories of acceptable behavior within a group that you know well. Such groups as your family, your team, your fraternity or sorority, your high school "clique," or your parents' social friends would serve as a basis for this classification essay.

1. Begin with an extended reference to something you have read about the social behavior you are describing, and paraphrase or summarize the contents of that reference. Or, as an alternative, provide an anecdote that relates to your thesis.

2. Establish your thesis in a paragraph that comes *after* your paraphrase or your anecdote.

3. Name the typical modes of behavior that you will be classifying.

4. Throughout the essay be sure to remind the reader of your own relationship to the groups you establish.

5. Make use of narratives to illustrate how each category of behavior works. Show how people within the group conform to the code, and how people outside the group can come into conflict with it.

6. Include some "authentic" ways of speaking.

7. Keep the tone of the essay somewhat light and humorous.

8. Try to use figurative language and vivid sensory language throughout the essay.

9. End with an explanation of your difficulty (or ease) in accepting these modes of behavior.

More Writing Projects

1. Different people will approach the same task in different ways. Select a task—such as doing homework, going shopping, planning a vacation, and so on—and write an essay that classifies at least three different approaches to the same task.

2. Write an essay that classifies the different ways in which people express happiness or sadness.

3. Study the students in one of your larger lecture classes. Write a classification essay analyzing their different codes of behavior.

Adam Smith

A VERY SHORT HISTORY OF SOME AMERICAN DRUGS FAMILIAR TO EVERYBODY

The widespread use of drugs is an ever-increasing problem that confronts our society daily. In this article, Adam Smith classifies some of the more commonly used drugs (some *surprisingly* common!) and discusses the extent and effects of their use. Notice how he blends objective presentation of information with a wry personal commentary to produce a perceptive and entertaining study.

Words to Watch

unabridged (par. 1): complete; unedited
placebo (par. 1): a substance containing no medication but given to a patient for its psychological rather than for its physiological effects
toxic (par. 3): poisonous
pharmacology (par. 4): the science of drugs
intoxication (par. 4): feeling of elation or drunkenness
stimuli (par. 5): plural of stimulus, something that brings about a reaction in something else
bronchi (par. 7): the two windpipes leading to the lungs
chromosome (par. 7): the part of the cell nucleus containing the genes, which determine various hereditary and physical characteristics
stimulant (par. 8): a drug that temporarily increases the activity of an organism
domesticated (par. 10): adapted for human use
buffered (par. 10): protected against shock or full impact
genteel (par. 11): politely refined

verbena (par. 11): bright, long-lasting flowers, spiked-petalled and fragrant

meditation (par. 16): disciplined thought, often religious or spiritual in nature

biofeedback (par. 16): the technique of making the senses aware of the body's processes (such as heartbeat or brainwaves) in order to manipulate them through conscious mental control

sobriety (par. 17): solemnity; earnestness

Our attitude toward the word "drug" depends on 1 whether we are talking about penicillin or heroin or something in-between. The unabridged three-volume Webster's says a drug is "a chemical substance administered to prevent or cure disease or enhance physical and mental welfare" or "a substance affecting the structure or function of the body." Webster's should have added "mind," but they probably thought that was part of the body. Some substances that aren't drugs, like placebos, affect "the structure or function of the body," but they work because we *think* they're drugs.

We are a drug-using society. We take, for example, 2 twenty thousand tons of aspirin a day, almost one aspirin per person in the whole country. Aspirin is a familiar drug from a family called salicylates, specifically, acetylsalicylic acid. It lowers body temperature, alleviates some types of pain, and stimulates respiration.

Nicotine is a familiar and widely recognized drug, 3 a stimulant to the central nervous system. It is addictive. The toxic effects of nicotine have been detailed at great length by the Surgeon General. Americans smoke 600 billion cigarettes a year.

Alcohol is also a widely recognized drug. In the 4 United States 70 million users spend $10 billion a year. Five million of the 70 million alcohol users are said to be addicts, that is, they have a physical dependence on the drug. Alcohol is unique, says the pharmacology textbook, because it is "the only potent pharmacological agent with which self-induced intoxication is socially acceptable." Alcohol is so much a part of everyday life we do not think of it, on the rocks or straight up, as a drug or a potent pharmacological agent.

Then there is the family of drugs called the xan- 5 thines. Americans take xanthines at the rate of 100 *billion* doses per year. Xanthines are alkaloids which stimulate portions of the cerebral cortex. They give you "a more rapid and clearer flow of thought, allay drowsinesss . . . motor activity is increased. There is a keener appreciation of sensory stimuli, and reaction time to them is diminished." This description, again from the pharmacology textbook, is similar to descriptions of cocaine and amphetamine. Of course, the xanthine addict pays a price. He is, says Sir Clifford Allbutt, Regius Professor of Medicine at Cambridge, "subject to fits of agitation and depression; he loses color and has a haggard appearance. The appetite falls off; the heart suffers; it palpitates, or it intermits. As with other such agents, a renewed dose of the poison gives temporary relief, but at the cost of the misery."

Xanthines are generally taken orally through "aque- 6 ous extracts" of the plants that produce these alkaloids, either in seeds or leaves. In the United States the three most common methylated xanthines taken are called caffeine, theophylline and theobromine. The seeds of *Coffea arabica* contain caffeine, the leaves of *Thea sinensis* contain caffeine and theophylline, and the seeds of *Theobroma cacao* contain caffeine and theobromine. In America the three are known as "coffee," "tea" and "cocoa," and they are consumed daily, at the rate of billions of pounds a year. They are generally drunk as hot drinks, but Americans also drink cold drinks containing caffeine from the nuts of the tree *Cola acuminata*. The original drinks ended in the word "cola," but now there are many "colas" which do not bear that name in the title. The early ads for Coca-Cola said it gave you a lift.

Coffee, tea, cocoa and cola drinks are all drugs. Caf- 7 feine is a central nervous system stimulant, theophylline less so, and theobromine hardly at all. All xanthines increase the production of urine. Xanthines act on smooth muscles—relaxing, for example, especially in the case of theophylline, bronchi that may have been constricted. Like the salicylates—aspirin—xanthines can cause stomach irritation. Caffeine can cause sleeplessness, and researchers have found that it causes chromosome breaks.

Maxwell House, meet the Regius Professor of Medicine. Is the stuff good to the last drop, or another dose of the poison? Is it a food, to be sold in supermarkets, or a stimulant to the central nervous system like the amphetamines? "The popularity of the xanthine beverages depends on their stimulant action, although most people are unaware of any stimulation," says the giant pharmacology text. 8

It is surprising to find substances we think of so cheerfully, perkin' in the pot, listed as drugs. That's the point. In our society, there are some drugs we think of as okay drugs, and other drugs make us gasp. A coffee drinker who drinks coffee all day and cannot function without it is just a heavy coffee drinker, but someone using a non-okay drug is a "drug user" or an "addict." 9

Consumer Reports asked: how did drugs with such potential hazard spread without arousing the legal repression and social condemnation aroused by other drugs? They were domesticated, it said. There was no illegal black market, the dosages were relatively small, and some people buffered the drug effect with cream and sugar. 10

The worst of what our society thinks of as "hard drugs" comes from the unripe capsule of the opium poppy. In the nineteenth-century United States, you could buy opiates at grocery stores and drugstores, and by mail. Godfrey's Cordial—a molasses, sassafras and opium combination—was especially popular. Genteel Southern ladies in lace and ruffles, smelling of verbena and other sweet things, sounding like Scarlett O'Hara, were slugging down daily a combination of opium and alcohol called laudanum. The first surveys of narcotics showed that women outnumbered men three to one, because "the husbands drank alcohol at the saloon, and the wives took opium at home." 11

The point of this capsule history is not to warn peo- 12

ple from the perilous xanthines. (I drink them all, *Coffea arabica* and *Thea sinensis,* sweetened, no cream, please, and *Theobroma cacao* on cold winter days, and *Cola acuminata* on warm summer ones, and I have to be paying attention to be aware of the stimulant action.)

13   Nor is it to diminish the danger of illegal narcotics. (Legal narcotics are part of legitimate medicine.) There is no comparison between legal, domesticated, mild, buffered drugs and illegal and undomesticated ones, but it is society that has produced the legalities and the domestication. Illegal narcotics, producing huge profits and employing the worst criminal elements, are merchandised to the least stable elements of society, producing tremendous social problems.

14   A Coke at snack time, a drink before dinner, a cup of coffee after dinner, a cigarette with the coffee—very relaxing. Four shots of drugs. Domesticated ones. It would be rather comic to have addicts sneaking down dark alleys for a shot of coffee, but nicotine is so strong that when currencies fail—Germany right after World War II, for example—cigarettes become currency.

15   In some Muslim countries, you can sit and smoke hashish all day at a café, but possession of alcohol will land you in jail; in the United States, you can sit in a saloon ingesting alcohol all day, but possession of hashish will land you in jail.

16   The drug taken by the astronauts of inner space was, at that time, legal. It was also nonnarcotic and nonaddictive. It crops up in the story not only because it was used in the exploration of the mind, but because so many explorers in meditation, biofeedback and other disciplines went through a stage with it.

17   Lysergic acid diethylamide was invented by the Swiss. Curious to think of the Swiss, the symbol of sobriety and industry, watch-making and cuckoo clocks, as having invented LSD, Librium and Valium, psychedelics and tranquilizers, the turn-ons and the turn-offs; but then the Swiss have been in the drug business since Paracelsus of Basle, roughly a contemporary of Columbus.

BUILDING VOCABULARY

1. Explain these *colloquialisms* (see Glossary) found in Smith's essay:

a. "the stuff" (par. 8)
b. "perkin' in the pot" (par. 9)
c. "that's the point" (par. 9)
d. "okay"; "non-okay" (par. 9)
e. "make us gasp" (par. 9)
f. "slugging down" (par. 11)

2. Identify these references:

a. the Surgeon General (par. 3)
b. Coca-Cola (par. 6)
c. Maxwell House (par. 8)
d. *Consumer Reports* (par. 10)
e. black market (par. 10)
f. Scarlett O'Hara (par. 11)
g. Paracelsus of Basle (par. 17)

3. Identify these drugs mentioned in the essay:

a. cocaine
b. amphetamines
c. hashish

UNDERSTANDING THE WRITER'S IDEAS

1. According to the author, on what does our attitude towards the word *drug* depend? Why is *drug* placed in quotation marks in the first sentence?

2. What does the author mean by "Webster's"? Why does he quote from it?

3. What is Webster's definition of a drug? What does Adam Smith think is missing from that definition? Why does he think that that element is left out?

4. What main groups of drugs does Smith identify in this essay? Which is identified as the worst by society? Why?

5. Why is alcohol unique among drugs?

6. What are commonly used examples of the *xanthine* family of drugs? Approximately how many doses per year of xanthines do Americans use? What are the Latin names for these examples? What are the common names?

7. Outline some of the positive effects of using certain xanthines. What are the negative effects? What does the popularity of xanthine beverages depend on? What is the apparent contradiction in this basis for popularity?

8. Why did early Coca-Cola ads claim it would give the drinker a lift?

9. According to *Consumer Reports,* how did many xanthine drugs escape being banned or being deemed socially unacceptable?

10. What is laudanum? How is it used? What are the effects of its use?

11. How could cigarettes come to be used as currency in Germany right after World War II?

12. Explain the metaphor, "The astronauts of inner space" (par. 16).

13. What is "the story" Smith refers to in paragraph 16?

14. In what century were the Swiss first involved in the drug business?

UNDERSTANDING THE WRITER'S TECHNIQUES

1. What is Smith's thesis in this essay? Where does he state it? What, in your own words, is his purpose?

2. Why is definition an important rhetorical device in this essay? Where is it used? How do comparison and contrast operate in the selection? Where does Smith use *illustration*?

3. Smith uses a variety of tones in this essay. What is the tone of the title? What function do paragraphs 8 and 9 have in determining tone in this selection?

4. Why does Smith use the word *history* in his title? How is this essay a history?

5. In the first sentence two examples imply two large categories of drugs. What are the examples? What are

the implied categories? Where are these categories summarized later in the essay?

6. For paragraphs 2 through 7, prepare a paragraph-by-paragraph outline of the main groups of drugs classified. For each, include the following:

    a. examples discussed
    b. effects described
    c. statistics on usage

7. Where does Smith cite an authority? Would you trust that authority's conclusions? Why or why not?

8. Throughout the selection, Smith refers to "the" pharmacological textbook. What do you think of his identification of the source for so many of the quotations he uses? Why? Can you think of any reason he might have made his identification in this way?

9. Writers use *parentheses* for material that is not strictly a part of the development of the main point, but rather that explains or modifies the main thought. What is the purpose of the parentheses in paragraph 12? What pronoun is used there that is not used in any other part of the essay? Why do you think Smith uses it?

10. What paragraphs constitute the conclusion of this essay? Analyze the connection between each paragraph in the concluding section.

EXPLORING THE WRITER'S IDEAS

1. It is sometimes said that America is a nation of "soft drug" addicts—that we cannot get through the day without our coffee, cigarettes, martinis, tranquilizers, aspirins, sleeping pills, and so on. How does Smith's essay support this conclusion? What evidence do you see that Americans are too dependent on drugs? Can you propose any remedies for this situation?

2. As Smith points out, there are both positive and negative effects of using various types of drugs. List a few commonly used drugs and compare the positive and negative effects of their usage.

3.   When we speak of an addiction, we usually mean a daily physical dependence on a hard drug like heroin. Yet, as Smith points out, we may also be addicted to soft drinks like aspirin or coffee. There is, however, another type of addiction—psychological addiction. What types of psychological addictions can you think of? Describe any circumstances under which you or someone you know has been addicted to something other than a drug. You might want to refer to Clifton Fadiman's definition of pop culture. What does he suggest about possible addictions to items like television?

4.   In his discussion of society's attitudes toward drugs in paragraph 9, Smith tells us that we cheerfully accept users of "okay" drugs, although users of "non-okay" drugs are branded as addicts. He thus implies that we have a double standard in our attitudes toward drug use. For what other important issues does our society seem to have a double standard? Discuss one of them at length.

IDEAS FOR WRITING

Guided Writing

Write an essay of classification around the topic "A Very Short History of _____ Familiar to Everybody." Fill in the blank with a word or phrase like "victimless crimes," "automobiles," "schools," "home appliances," "newspapers," "beverages," "fast food restaurants," "soap operas," "entertainment"—in short, with an expression that lends itself to a historical discussion within a framework of classification.

1.   Begin by introducing the reader to the extremes of opinions on your topic.

2.   Use a definition as the basis for your categorization. Try to cite an objective definition (perhaps from a textbook, an encyclopedia, or a dictionary) and then comment on the completeness of that definition.

3.   Establish at least three or four categories.

4.   Develop your classification using examples, statistics, and authorities.

5.   Devote at least one paragraph to each category

and deal with both positive and negative features of each category.

6. In the first half of the essay try to be as objective as possible. Use a transitional paragraph to help you switch to a more subjective tone for the second half of your essay.

7. Draw on and discuss some popular ideas—both past and present—about your topic.

8. Devote a few paragraphs to your conclusion. In it, contrast society's various attitudes toward your subject. Begin the conclusion by stating its purpose clearly.

More Writing Projects

1. Write an essay in which you classify various illegal nonaddictive drugs, such as marijuana or cocaine, that are used commonly. Try to gear your essay toward supporting an opinion for or against the illegal status of such drugs, but make sure to base your decision on the *facts presented,* not just on personal preferences or general opinions.

2. Look in old newspapers or magazines, or in the reprints available of old mail-order catalogs, for early advertisements of popular goods and services. Write an essay in which you classify those advertisements according to some logical scheme.

3. In paragraph 8, when Smith asks, "Is the stuff good to the last drop?" he is referring to an advertising *slogan* used by Maxwell House Coffee. A slogan was originally thought of as a word or phrase expressing the spirit or aim of a political party, group, or cause. Today, slogans are often used as advertising devices.

In an essay of 750 to 1,000 words, classify the various slogans that surround us today, slogans drawn perhaps from the following: political campaigns, floor care products, automobiles, television networks, radio stations, fast food chains, or some others you can think of.

7

Process Analysis

Process analysis concentrates on *how* something is done, how something works, or how something occurs. If writing aims essentially to explain things, you can see why writers need to use process analysis. Often, the major point that will impress a reader depends on his or her ability to understand the logical steps in some plan of procedure. As a method of paragraph or essay development, process analysis traces all important steps, from beginning to end, in an activity or event. The amount of detail provided for each step in the process will depend on how much the audience knows about the subject.

Whether you are dealing with such subjects as how Columbus discovered America, how a carburetor works, how to deliver a good speech, or how to can fruit at home, you must present all essential information to your audience. Frequently, other methods of essay development help reinforce your analysis of process. (For example, writers often use *definition* to explain terms in a technical process that might not be familiar to readers; and to relate in clear order the steps in a process, an essay might require *narrative* techniques.) These methods will serve your main objective of explaining the process from beginning to end.

Although the purpose of process analysis is to provide your audience with a step-by-step explanation of a procedure, process analysis can also inform readers about the *significance* of the process; that is, it will instruct and inform. A typical problem in explanations of process is that a writer often assumes that readers know more than they do. You can avoid this problem by defining your audience carefully. Certainly, you would use one approach to explain how to make a perfect cheese omelet to newlyweds; and you would use a completely different approach to explain it to students in advanced cooking class. Although both groups might have to follow the same sequence of steps, the kind of information you provide and the range of your explanations would be significantly different. No matter what approach you take to process analysis, remember to present material in a clear and lively manner. In reading about how something is done, or how something works, no reader wants to be bored; make an effort to keep your writing interesting.

Sam Negri

LOAFING MADE EASY

Sam Negri takes a light-hearted look at a topic that seems
funny but is serious business to all those who work hard
constantly. He tells us how to do nothing. A self-proclaimed
expert in the art of loafing, Negri gives a few step-by-step
how to's when it comes to goofing off. Notice how his essay
blends narration, classification, and contrast into the
analysis of process.

Words to Watch

mediocre (par. 3): ordinary
damper (par. 5): fireplace valve to regulate the air flow
lexicon (par. 11): dictionary; word list
debilitating (par. 12): impairing the strength of something
coax (par. 15): to convince by gentle urging or flattery
lush (par. 15): covered with abundant natural growth

The fabled season of the sun is upon us and it is once 1
again time to hook our thumbs in our suspenders and talk
about America's most treasured art form, loafing.

The purest form of loafing is practiced in Arizona, 2
where summertime temperatures will often exceed 110 degrees. If we regard the Arizona loafer as a natural resource,
as I've been doing for the last eight years, we will see that the

art form has applications that go far beyond the business of surviving in hot weather.

When I came to Arizona, I was a mediocre loafer, dis- 3 playing a definite need for a degree of mental reconditioning. I'd moved here from Connecticut, where people relax by putting aside their copy of Gray's "Anatomy" and picking up a novel by Dostoevsky. In Arizona, this is referred to as insanity.

Here is a better method: 4

To begin with, shut the damper on your fireplace, if 5 you have one, and turn on your air-conditioner, if you have one. Otherwise, hang a wet sheet in the window and pray for a breeze.

Now you are ready to memorize a handful of impor- 6 tant and useful phrases. Try these: "I don't know"; "I don't care"; "no"; and the old standby, "well . . ."

These phrases are extremely valuable when your 7 jaws are sagging like deflated bicycle tubes and your mind has turned to wax.

For example, it is 106 degrees in the shade and your 8 son comes racing in the house, shouting, "Hey, you seen those long-handled pliers anywhere?" With a minimum of effort you are free to say, "no."

His anger may mount and he'll insist: "But you were 9 using them yesterday! Where'd you leave 'em?"

If you haven't passed out from the strain of this con- 10 versation, you can then reply, "I don't know."

"But I need those pliers to fix my skateboard," he 11 will cry. Then you break out the ultimate weapon in the loafer's lexicon. Without any inflection whatsoever, you declare, "Well . . ."

You can now get back to some serious loafing, which 12 means that you will try to prove that Benjamin Franklin was correct when he observed: "It is hard for an empty sack to stand upright." In short, empty your mind. Learn to ask questions like these: "Mail come yet?" and "Anything doin'?" The responses to these questions usually involve one word, and often they aren't debilitating.

There are a few additional rules to keep in mind for 13
successful loafing.

First, never loaf near a pool or a lake because you 14
might be tempted to go for a swim. Swimming frequently
leaves a body feeling refreshed and may lead to a desire to
do something.

Second, under no circumstances should you allow 15
anyone to coax you into a camping trip in the mountains.
Mountains tend to be lush, green and cool, and next thing
you know you'll be wanting to split logs for a fire, go for a
hike, or pump up your Coleman stove. Resist. "Patience is a
necessary ingredient of genius," said Disraeli. If you want to
be a fine loafer you have to make enemies.

Of course, it is impossible to get by in life if you don't 16
do something, even in the summer. Household jobs are the
easiest for a loafer to contend with, if he is selective and
deliberate.

One satisfying and undemanding job involves a ball 17
of twine. Find a ball of twine that a cat has unraveled so
badly that you can't find the end. Get scissors and slowly cut
it into small pieces, scrunch it into a smaller ball, and throw
it away. Now look at all the extra space you have in your
junk drawer.

Another relatively simple and useful job for summer- 18
time loafing centers on light bulbs. Limp through your house
or apartment, removing the light bulbs from every lamp.
Coat the very bottom of each bulb with petroleum jelly and
put it back in the lampsocket. This will clean some of the
crud off the contact point and solve the problems with flicker-
ing lightbulbs. For variety you can take the bulb that was in
a living-room lamp and put it in a bedroom lamp. It helps to
sigh and gaze wistfully at the base of the lightbulb as you
are performing this function.

Last, if you have a dog, sit in your most comfortable 19
chair and stare at your dog's eyes for five of 10 minutes.
Every so often, mutter something incomprehensible. Your
dog is certain to understand, and your family will not come
near you for the rest of the afternoon.

BUILDING VOCABULARY

1. Though some synonyms can be used interchangeably within a given piece of writing, often substituting one word for another will change the *tone* or *shades of meaning* of a sentence or phrase. Rewrite the following phrases substituting your own word(s) for those in italics. Then discuss how your substitution changes the meaning or tone.

    a. "America's *most treasured* art form" (par. 1)
    b. "the *business* of surviving in hot weather" (par. 2)
    c. "a definite need for *mental reconditioning*" (par. 3)
    d. "your jaws are sagging like *deflated* bicycle tires" (par. 7)
    e. "If you haven't *passed out* from the *strain* of this conversation" (par. 10)
    f. "the *ultimate* weapon" (par. 11)
    g. "*gaze wistfully*" (par. 18)
    h. "*mutter* something *incomprehensible*" (par. 19)

2. Identify:

    a. Gray's "Anatomy"
    b. Dostoevsky
    c. Benjamin Franklin
    d. Benjamin Disraeli

UNDERSTANDING THE WRITER'S IDEAS

1. Why is loafing such an important activity in Arizona?

2. What is the purpose of this essay? Where does the author announce it?

3. According to the author, how do people in Connecticut relax? Why do people in Arizona consider this method insanity?

4. What alternative to air conditioning does Negri offer for relaxing in 110° weather?

5. What is the author's attitude toward making conversation while relaxing? What ways does he suggest to avoid undue strain?

6. When loafing seriously, why should you never be near a place to swim? Why should you never let anyone convince you to go camping?

7. Why are household jobs good activities for loafers? What three relatively painless household jobs does Negri describe? Trace the suggested process for performing each.

UNDERSTANDING THE WRITER'S TECHNIQUES

1. Which paragraphs make up the introduction for this essay? How do they serve as an effective beginning?

2. What is the connection between narration and process analysis in paragraphs 6 through 11?

3. Would you say that Negri is ever ironic (see Glossary) in this essay? Is he ever sarcastic? Point to places in the essay that demonstrate irony or sarcasm or both.

4. In any process analysis, it is important to tailor the depth and range of your explanations to your audience. For whom is Negri writing this essay? How does his language and tone reflect his audience?

5. An *aphorism* is a short, often ingenious saying that states a simple truth, usually in one sentence. Negri uses aphorisms by Benjamin Franklin (par. 12) and Benjamin Disraeli (par. 15). What are they? Explain in your own words what you think the original messages of those aphorisms were. Does Negri use them for their original meanings? If not, how does he adapt the aphorisms to the tone of his essay?

6. Explain Negri's use of transitional devices throughout the essay. Compare Negri's use of transitions with E. B. White's use of them in "The Three New Yorks" (pages 187–188).

7. Where does Negri use a one-word sentence? What is your reaction to it? Why does he use it, do you think?

8. How do paragraphs 16 through 19 make use of classification? How do the same paragraphs contribute to the process analysis?

EXPLORING THE WRITER'S IDEAS

1. In paragraph 3, Negri contrasts loafers in Connecticut with loafers in Arizona. What are some of the contrasting ways that people relax in two places you know about? What are some of your favorite ways of goofing off?

2. At the beginning of paragraph 16, Negri writes: "Of course, it is impossible to get by in life if you don't do something." Although the essay is written in a humorous vein, there are certainly many serious implications to the above statement. Discuss what the statement means to you.

3. Negri's point is that loafing is an art and that loafing is good for us. Do you agree? Why? What dangers exist for loafers?

IDEAS FOR WRITING

Guided Writing

Write an essay in which you analyze the best ways to succeed in the art of _____. (Fill in the blank with a word or phrase of your own choice.)

1. Begin by letting the reader know why and how you are intimately familiar with the fine points of this art.

2. State the purpose of your essay at the end of the second paragraph.

3. Contrast a bad way of doing this activity with a good way of doing it.

4. In a tone suited to the activity you are analyzing, describe the best way to avoid letting someone get in the way of your goal. Use narration to illustrate this method.

5. Use an aphorism or two—adapting it to the tone and purpose of your process analysis.

6. Point out two special rules for the reader to keep in mind in order to be successful in this art.

7. Use clear, simple transitions throughout the essay (see Glossary).

8. Somewhere in the essay, use a one-word sentence for a special effect.

9. For your concluding section, consider activities that might be necessary to offset the effects of the art described. Through process analysis, develop examples of the best ways to perform those activities.

More Writing Projects

1. Explain the process you use to *avoid* loafing too much.

2. Give a step-by-step account of what you did the last time you had an unexpected day off from work, school, or other responsibilities.

3. Explain how you keep a balance between working, studying, and relaxing.

George Plimpton

HOW TO MAKE A SPEECH

George Plimpton is an author, television personality, editor of the *Paris Review* literary magazine, and speech-maker. Here he makes the process of speechmaking easy and enjoyable.

Words to Watch

the uninitiated (par. 1): those who have never tried a particular activity
articulate (par. 5): to state clearly
convulses (par. 11): shakes violently and uncontrollably
exhortation (par. 12): a forceful urging or warning
dismayed (par. 14): saddened; unhappy
sheaf (par. 14): a group of things bound together
ad-lib (par. 15): improvise
allotted (par. 17): assigned; apportioned
brevity (par. 18): shortness of duration
dais (par. 20): a raised platform usually reserved for important guests at a meeting or social affair
sectors (par. 21): definite parts of a whole
notion (par. 22): idea; concept
stage fright (par. 24): fear of speaking or performing before an audience

One of life's terrors for the uninitiated is to be 1 asked to make a speech.

"Why me?" will probably be your first reaction. "I 2
don't have anything to say." It should be reassuring (though
it rarely is) that since you were asked, somebody must think
you do. The fact is that each one of us has a store of material
which should be of interest to others. There is no reason
why it should not be adapted to a speech.

Scary as it is, it's important for anyone to be able 3
to speak in front of others, whether twenty around a
conference table or a hall filled with a thousand faces.

Being able to speak can mean better grades in any 4
class. It can mean talking the town council out of increasing
your property taxes. It can mean talking top management
into buying your plan.

You were probably asked to speak in the first place 5
in the hope that you would be able to articulate a topic that
you know something about. Still, it helps to find out about
your audience first. Who are they? Why are they there?
What are they interested in? How much do they already
know about your subject? One kind of talk would be appropriate for the Women's Club of Columbus, Ohio, and quite
another for the guests at the Vince Lombardi dinner.

Here is where you must do your homework. 6

The more you sweat in advance, the less you'll have 7
to sweat once you appear on stage. Research your topic
thoroughly. Check the library for facts, quotes, books and
timely magazine and newspaper articles on your subject.
Get in touch with experts. Write to them, make phone calls,
get interviews to help round out your material.

In short, gather—and learn—far more than you'll 8
ever use. You can't imagine how much confidence that
knowledge will inspire.

Now start organizing and writing. Most authorities 9
suggest that a good speech breaks down into three basic
parts—an introduction, the body of the speech, and the
summation.

Introduction: An audience makes up its mind very 10
quickly. Once the mood of an audience is set, it is difficult
to change it, which is why introductions are important. If
the speech is to be lighthearted in tone, the speaker can

start off by telling a good-natured story about the subject or himself.

But be careful of jokes, especially the shaggy-dog variety. For some reason, the joke that convulses guests in a living room tends to suffer as it emerges through the amplifying system into a public gathering place.

Main body: There are four main intents in the body of the well-made speech. These are 1) to entertain, which is probably the hardest; 2) to instruct, which is the easiest if the speaker has done the research and knows the subject; 3) to persuade, which one does at a sales presentation, a political rally, or a town meeting; and finally, 4) to inspire, which is what the speaker emphasizes at a sales meeting, in a sermon, or at a pep rally. (Hurry-Up Yost, the onetime Michigan football coach, gave such an inspiration-filled half-time talk that he got carried away and at the final exhortation led his team on the run through the wrong locker-room door into the swimming pool.)

Summation: This is where you should "ask for the order." An ending should probably incorporate a sentence or two which sounds like an ending—a short summary of the main points of the speech, perhaps, or the repeat of a phrase that most embodies what the speaker has hoped to convey. It is valuable to think of the last sentence or two as something which might produce applause. Phrases which are perfectly appropriate to signal this are "In closing . . ." or "I have one last thing to say . . ."

Once done—fully written, or the main points set down on 3″ × 5″ index cards—the next problem is the actual presentation of the speech. Ideally, a speech should not be read. At least it should never appear or sound as if you are reading it. An audience is dismayed to see a speaker peering down at a thick sheaf of papers on the lectern, wetting his thumb to turn to the next page.

The best speakers are those who make their words sound spontaneous even if memorized. I've found it's best to learn a speech point by point, not word for word. Careful preparation and a great deal of practicing are required to make it come together smoothly and easily. Mark Twain

11

12

13

14

15

once said, "It takes three weeks to prepare a good ad-lib speech."

Don't be fooled when you rehearse. It takes longer 16 to deliver a speech than to read it. Most speakers peg along at about 100 words a minute.

A sensible plan, if you have been asked to speak to 17 an exact limit, is to talk your speech into a mirror, and stop at your alloted time; then cut the speech accordingly. The more familiar you become with your speech, the more confidently you can deliver it.

As anyone who listens to speeches knows, brevity is 18 an asset. Twenty minutes are ideal. An hour is the limit an audience can listen comfortably.

In mentioning brevity, it is worth mentioning that 19 the shortest inaugural address was George Washington's— just 135 words. The longest was William Henry Harrison's in 1841. He delivered a two-hour 9,000-word speech into the teeth of a freezing northeast wind. He came down with a cold the following day, and a month later he died of pneumonia.

Consult a dictionary for proper meanings and pro- 20 nunciations. Your audience won't know if you're a bad speller, but they will know if you use or pronounce a word improperly. In my first remarks on the dais, I used to thank people for their "fulsome introduction," until I discovered to my dismay that "fulsome" means *offensive* and *insincere*.

It helps one's nerves to pick out three or four people 21 in the audience—preferably in different sectors so that the speaker is apparently giving his attention to the entire room—on whom to focus. Pick out people who seem to be having a good time.

A question period at the end of a speech is a good 22 notion. One would not ask questions following a tribute to the company treasurer on his retirement, say, but a technical talk or an informative speech can be enlivened with a question period.

The larger the crowd, the easier it is to speak, 23 because the response is multiplied and increased. Most people do not believe this. They peek out from behind the curtain and if the auditorium is filled to the rafters they begin to moan softly in the back of their throats.

Very few speakers escape the so-called "butterflies." 24 There does not seem to be any cure for them, except to realize that they are beneficial rather than harmful, and never fatal. The tension usually means that the speaker, being keyed up, will do a better job. Edward R. Murrow called stage fright "the sweat of perfection." Mark Twain once comforted a fright-frozen friend about to speak: "Just remember they don't expect much." My own feeling is that with thought, preparation and faith in your ideas, *you* can go out there and expect a pleasant surprise.

And what a sensation it is—to hear applause. In- 25 variably after it dies away, the speaker searches out the program chairman—just to make it known that he's available for next month's meeting.

BUILDING VOCABULARY

1. In this essay Plimpton uses a number of *figurative expressions* (see Glossary) which use specific words for other than their usual meanings. Be sure you first understand the usual meaning of each of the italicized words, then explain each of the following phrases:

    a. "each one of us has a *store* of material" (par. 2)
    b. "to help *round* out your material" (par. 7)
    c. "*incorporate* a sentence or two" (par. 13)
    d. "*peg* along at about 100 words a minute" (par. 16)
    e. "filled to the *rafters*" (par. 23)
    f. "a fright-frozen friend" (par. 24)

2. Use any five words from the Words to Watch section in sentences of your own.

UNDERSTANDING THE WRITER'S IDEAS

1. For what reasons does Plimpton say it is important to be able to make an effective speech?

2. Why is it important to identify the audience when you make a speech? What things does Plimpton suggest you find out?

3. How does Plimpton suggest you gather information on your topic? Why is complete research crucial to the success of a speech? Explain the meaning of the sentence "The more you sweat in advance the less you'll have to sweat once you appear on stage." (par. 7)

4. What are the basic parts of a good speech? Briefly outline the most important aspects of each.

5. What two methods of actually writing the text of a speech does Plimpton suggest? Which method do you think Plimpton prefers? Why?

6. In his discussion of speechmaking, the author touches on a number of important techniques. What are they? Name each and state the most important aspect of each.

7. Explain the reference to Hurry-Up Yost in paragraph 12.

8. What does Plimpton feel is the ideal time span of a speech? What is the outer limit?

9. According to the writer, why is it important to use three or four people in the audience as focal points? By what process does he suggest you select those people. Why?

10. For what reason is a large audience better than a small one?

11. Identify Vince Lombardi, Mark Twain, and Edward R. Murrow. Why is each a good person to mention in an article about making speeches?

UNDERSTANDING THE WRITER'S TECHNIQUES

1. What paragraphs constitute an overview or introduction to the process? Is there a thesis statement and if so, where?

2. What is the tone and effect of the opening sentence? In what way is this short opening paragraph like the "lead" in a newspaper article?

3. Explain Plimpton's relationship to his audience

in this essay. Why does he use the pronoun "you" throughout? What is his purpose: to give instructions or to provide information? Cite evidence to support your response.

4. How does Plimpton organize his presentation of the speechmaking process? Which sentences signal the start of new steps in the process? Which steps receive more emphasis, and why?

5. Plimpton uses both subheadings and numbering in paragraphs 11 to 14. How does he still manage to achieve *coherence*, that is, a smooth and logical connection between parts?

6. Plimpton uses personal examples and anecdotes (an *anecdote* is a brief story of an interesting incident). Where does he use them, and why are they effective?

7. Where does Plimpton use classification, and why?

8. Why does the author rely on relatively short paragraphs in this essay? Are they a strength or a weakness in analyzing the process? Why?

9. What is the relationship between the last paragraph and the first one?

EXPLORING THE WRITER'S IDEAS

1. In paragraph 12 Plimpton indicates that one of the main purposes of a good speech is to instruct. If this article were delivered as a speech, do you think it would be successful and interesting? Give specific reasons to support your opinion.

2. Plimpton discusses the importance of identifying the audience for which your speech is intended. Why must you also consider your audience during the writing process?

3. In paragraph 11 the author mentions jokes of "the shaggy-dog variety." What does he mean by this? What other varieties of jokes can you name? Which are your favorite? Which are your least favorite? Should you tell jokes when making a speech? Why or why not?

4. Does Plimpton's discussion of how to design a speech make it seem any less terrifying to you? Why or why not? How would you feel if you were called on to make a speech in class?

IDEAS FOR WRITING

Guided Writing

Write a process analysis essay with the title "How to _____." Fill in the blank with something you know how to do very well, but which most people don't enjoy doing. Such topics as "how to prepare for final examinations," "how to succeed in a job interview," and "how to lose weight" might lend themselves to development.

1. Begin by attempting to put at ease your readers' fears about performing this process.
2. Tell some of the important results of doing this process well.
3. Divide the process into at least three major steps (but no more than six); explain each in detail.
4. Use classification to explain one of your process steps.
5. Include at least two anecdotes.
6. Keep the tone lighthearted and positive.
7. Include examples drawn from your own experience with this process.
8. Conclude by telling readers of the most pleasant aspect(s) of completing this process.

More Writing Projects

1. Tell about a time you had to make a speech— even if it was in the second grade. Explain the process of your speechmaking from the beginning to the end.
2. Explain how to tell a good joke.
3. Explain how you do a specific process which you don't enjoy.

Grace Lichtenstein

COORS BEER

Process analysis often deals with mechanical or technical procedures. In this short selection by Grace Lichtenstein, who is a correspondent for *The New York Times,* the author examines a mechanical process—the brewing of beer. As you read this piece, look for the methods that the author uses to make this technical process interesting and understandable to the general reader.

Words to Watch

palate (par. 1): taste or sense of taste
mystique (par. 2): special, almost mysterious attitudes and feelings
      surrounding a person, place, or thing
Spartan (par. 3): simple and severe
rancid (par. 4): not fresh; having a bad smell
permeate (par. 4): to spread through everything
nondescript (par. 4): lacking any recognizable character or quality
cellulose (par. 5): the main substance in woody parts of plants,
      used in many manufacturing processes

Coors is a light-bodied beer, meaning it is brewed 1
with less malt, fewer hops and more rice than beers with a
tangy taste. Compared with Heineken's or other more full-

bodied foreign beers, Coors does seem almost flavorless and it is this quality that could account for its popularity among young people just starting to get acquainted with the pleasures of beer drinking. A few locals scoff at Coors, calling it "Colorado Kool-Aid." But the fact is that, according to Ernest Pyler, "if you conducted a blindfold test of the four leading beers, the chances of picking our Coors would be minimal." Indeed, one national newspaper conducted an informal test among eight beer drinkers, finding that only three could correctly identify Coors. My own admittedly uneducated palate detects no difference between Coors and Schaefer. In short, the difference between Coors and any other decent beer could be 1,800 miles. Maybe, if Paul Newman suddenly switched to Schaefer, Denverites would pay $15 a case for it.

There is one aspect to the Coors mystique that does 2 have measurable validity. Company officials make much of the fact that Coors has good mountain water and the most expensive brewing process in the country. Several elements are unusual, though not unique.

Thousands of visitors have learned about the process 3 on guided tours through the antiseptic, Spartan plant. (For out-of-towners, the tour is often a pilgrimage—but for local students of the Colorado School of Mines, it's usually more in the line of a quick belt before classes. The tour lasts 30 minutes, at the end of which visitors are invited to quaff to their heart's content in the hospitality lounge. "I've come here 50 times," boasted one student as he polished off a glass at 11:30 one morning in the lounge.) Situated in the center of town, between two high, flat mesas in the foothills of the Rockies, the plant dominates the community just as the somewhat rancid smell of malt seems to permeate the air; one-fourth of the town's families are said to owe their jobs to the factory's operations. Anyone expecting to see in Golden the foaming white waterfall amid mountain pines that is pictured on every yellow can of Coors will be disappointed. The water used in the brewing comes from nondescript wells hidden in concrete blockhouses. The brewery now puts out about 12 million barrels of beer a year, but construction sites throughout the grounds bear witness to the company's hopes for doubling that capacity by 1984.

Like other beers, Coors is produced from barley. 4 Most of the big Midwestern brewers use barley grown in North Dakota and Minnesota. Coors is the single American brewer to use a Moravian strain, grown under company supervision, on farms in Colorado, Idaho, Wyoming and Montana. At the brewery, the barley is turned into malt by being soaked in water—which must be biologically pure and of a known mineral content—for several days, causing it to sprout and producing a chemical change—breaking down starch into sugar. The malt is toasted, a process that halts the sprouting and determines the color and sweetness (the more the roasting, the darker, more bitter the beer). It is ground into flour and brewed, with more pure water, in huge copper-domed kettles until it is the consistency of oatmeal. Rice and refined starch are added to make mash; solids are strained out, leaving an amber liquid malt extract, which is boiled with hops—the dried cones from the hop vine which add to the bitterness, or tang. The hops are strained, yeast is added, turning the sugar to alcohol, and the beer is aged in huge red vats at near-freezing temperatures for almost two months, during which the second fermentation takes place and the liquid becomes carbonated, or bubbly. (Many breweries chemically age their beer to speed up production; Coors people say only naturally aged brew can be called a true "lager.") Next, the beer is filtered through cellulose filters to remove bacteria, and finally is pumped into cans, bottles or kegs for shipping.

The most unusual aspect of the Coors process is that 5 the beer is not pasteurized, as all but a half-dozen of the 90 or so American beers are. In the pasteurization process, bottles or cans of beer are passed through a heating unit and then cooled. This destroys the yeast in the brew which could cause spoilage, if the cans or bottles or barrels are unrefrigerated for any long period. However, pasteurization also changes the flavor of beer. Coors stopped pasteurizing its product 18 years ago because it decided that "heat is an enemy of beer," according to a company spokesman.

Unpasteurized beer must be kept under constant 6 refrigeration. Thus, Coors does not warehouse any of its finished product, as many other brewers do, but ships everything out cold, immediately. In effect, my tour guide, a young management trainee wearing a beer-can tie clip, explained as we wandered through the packaging area, watching workers in surgical masks feed aluminum lids into machines that sealed cans whirling by on conveyor belts, the six-pack you buy in a store contains not only a very fresh beer but also a beer that could be considered draft, since it has been kept cold from vat to home refrigerator.

BUILDING VOCABULARY

1. For the italicized word in each example in Column A below select a definition from Column B.

Column A	Column B
a. locals *scoff* (par. 1)	1. drink heartily
b. *informal* test (par. 1)	2. locations
c. measurable *validity* (par. 2)	3. thickness
d. the *antiseptic* Spartan plant (par. 3)	4. not according to fixed rules
e. to *quaff* to their heart's content (par. 3)	5. a line of certain species
f. flat *mesas* (par. 3)	6. a concentrated form of something
g. construction *sites* (par. 3)	7. soundness
h. a Moravian *strain* (par. 4)	8. make fun of
i. the *consistency* of oatmeal (par. 4)	9. free from infection
j. liquid malt *extract* (par. 4)	10. hills

2. Use five of the italicized words in the first exercise in sentences of your own.

UNDERSTANDING THE WRITER'S IDEAS

1. What is a "light-bodied" beer?

2. What does the author mean when she states, "In short, the difference between Coors and any other decent beer could be 1,800 miles"?

3. What *is* special about Coors beer?

4. Why do college students like to visit the Coors plant?

5. Describe the setting of the Coors brewery. How does it contrast with the picture on the Coors can?

6. Explain in your own words the process by which Coors is produced.

7. Why is the pasteurization process important to the final flavor of any beer?

8. Why can Coors almost be considered a draft beer?

UNDERSTANDING THE WRITER'S TECHNIQUES

1. How do comparison and contrast operate in the first paragraph? Does the author also use definition in this paragraph? Where? For what purpose?

2. What is the function of paragraph 2? What is the purpose of paragraph 3? How does the author develop paragraph 3?

3. Analyze the author's use of transitional devices (see Glossary) between paragraphs 2 and 3.

4. Which paragraphs analyze the process of brewing Coors? Make a list of the steps on a sheet of paper. Is the process clear and complete? Does the author use process analysis simply to inform? Does she also provide commentary? Where?

5. Where does the author introduce personal or subjective elements into this essay? Why, at these points, does she provide personal rather than technical details?

EXPLORING THE WRITER'S IDEAS

1. Suppose that three unidentified brands of beer, cola, or cigarettes were placed before you. Would you be able to identify them by taste? What is the importance of "mystique" (or image) or "brand loyalty" to a product's success?

2. Can you think of other products that have a mystique associated with them? What are they, and what accounts for the mystique?

3. Would the fact that Paul Newman drinks Coors affect people's attitudes toward the brand? Why do manufacturers attempt to have certain celebrities associated with their products? Why should consumers be influenced by these associations?

4. Based on this essay, what are some ways to make a technical analysis of process interesting to the reader?

IDEAS FOR WRITING

Guided Writing

Explain how to make or to assemble a particular item or product. For example, you might want to explain how to prepare a certain dish; how to assemble a piece of equipment; how to produce something in a factory. You might want to follow Lichtenstein's example: Explain how a popular drink is made.

1. Start by introducing the reader to your "perfect product," indicating how it is possible to achieve high-quality results in its preparation.

2. Use as examples of the quality of the product, positive statements made by other individuals. These may be the ideas of friends, relatives, or experts.

3. Explain the "mystique," if there is one, surrounding the product.

4. After arousing reader interest sufficiently, de-

scribe the actual process involved, concentrating on all important details in the sequence.

5. In your last paragraph, try to capture the taste, look, or feel of the final product.

More Writing Projects

1. Consult an encyclopedia or other reference book to learn about the making of some product—steel, automobiles, plywood, and so forth. Then explain this process in your own words.

2. Set up an actual testing situation in your class. Have various members test three types of a particular item, such as chocolate, diet soda, a kitchen cleanser. Then write a report describing the process involved in the testing, as well as the process by which results were obtained.

Ernest Hemingway

CAMPING OUT

In this essay by Ernest Hemingway (1899–1961), the author uses the pattern of process analysis to order his materials on the art of camping. Hemingway wrote this piece for the *Toronto Star* in the early 1920s, before he gained worldwide recognition as a major American writer. In it, we see his lifelong interest in the outdoors and in his desire to do things well.

Words to Watch

relief map (par. 2): a map that shows by lines and colors the various heights and forms of the land
Caucasus (par. 2): a mountain range in southeastern Europe
proprietary (par. 7): held under patent or trademark
rhapsodize (par. 9): to speak enthusiastically
browse bed (par. 9): a portable cot
tyro (par. 11): an amateur; a beginner in learning something
dyspepsia (par. 13): indigestion
mulligan (par. 18): a stew made from odds and ends of meats and vegetables

Thousands of people will go into the bush this 1 summer to cut the high cost of living. A man who gets his two weeks' salary while he is on vacation should be able to put those two weeks in fishing and camping and be able to save one week's salary clear. He ought to be able to sleep comfortably every night, to eat well every day and to return to the city rested and in good condition.

But if he goes into the woods with a frying pan, an 2 ignorance of black flies and mosquitoes, and a great and abiding lack of knowledge about cookery the chances are that his return will be very different. He will come back with enough mosquito bites to make the back of his neck look like a relief map of the Caucasus. His digestion will be wrecked after a valiant battle to assimilate half-cooked or charred grub. And he won't have had a decent night's sleep while he has been gone.

He will solemnly raise his right hand and inform 3 you that he has joined the grand army of never-agains. The call of the wild may be all right, but it's a dog's life. He's heard the call of the tame with both ears. Waiter, bring him an order of milk toast.

In the first place he overlooked the insects. Black 4 flies, no-see-ums, deer flies, gnats and mosquitoes were instituted by the devil to force people to live in cities where he could get at them better. If it weren't for them everybody would live in the bush and he would be out of work. It was a rather successful invention.

But there are lots of dopes that will counteract the 5 pests. The simplest perhaps is oil of citronella. Two bits' worth of this purchased at any pharmacist's will be enough to last for two weeks in the worst fly and mosquito-ridden country.

Rub a little on the back of your neck, your forehead 6 and your wrists before you start fishing, and the blacks and skeeters will shun you. The odor of citronella is not offensive to people. It smells like gun oil. But the bugs do hate it.

Oil of pennyroyal and eucalyptol are also much 7 hated by mosquitoes, and with citronella they form the basis for many proprietary preparations. But it is cheaper and better to buy the straight citronella. Put a little on the mosquito netting that covers the front of your pup tent or canoe tent at night, and you won't be bothered.

To be really rested and get any benefit out of a 8
vacation a man must get a good night's sleep every night.
The first requisite for this is to have plenty of cover. It is
twice as cold as you expect it will be in the bush four nights
out of five, and a good plan is to take just double the bedding
that you think you will need. An old quilt that you can
wrap up in is as warm as two blankets.

Nearly all outdoor writers rhapsodize over the 9
browse bed. It is all right for the man who knows how to
make one and has plenty of time. But in a succession of one-
night camps on a canoe trip all you need is level ground for
your tent floor and you will sleep all right if you have plenty
of covers under you. Take twice as much cover as you think
that you will need, and then put two-thirds of it under you.
You will sleep warm and get your rest.

When it is clear weather you don't need to pitch your 10
tent if you are only stopping for the night. Drive four stakes
at the head of your made-up bed and drape your mosquito
bar over that, then you can sleep like a log and laugh at the
mosquitoes.

Outside of insects and bum sleeping the rock that 11
wrecks most camping trips is cooking. The average tyro's
idea of cooking is to fry everything and fry it good and
plenty. Now, a frying pan is a most necessary thing to any
trip, but you also need the old stew kettle and the folding
reflector baker.

A pan of fried trout can't be bettered and they don't 12
cost any more than ever. But there is a good and bad way
of frying them.

The beginner puts his trout and his bacon in and 13
over a brightly burning fire the bacon curls up and dries
into a dry tasteless cinder and the trout is burned outside
while it is still raw inside. He eats them and it is all right
if he is only out for the day and going home to a good meal
at night. But if he is going to face more trout and bacon the
next morning and other equally well-cooked dishes for the
remainder of two weeks he is on the pathway to nervous
dyspepsia.

The proper way is to cook over coals. Have several cans of Crisco or Cotosuet or one of the vegetable shortenings along that are as good as lard and excellent for all kinds of shortening. Put the bacon in and when it is about half cooked lay the trout in the hot grease, dipping them in corn meal first. Then put the bacon on top of the trout and it will baste them as it slowly cooks.

The coffee can be boiling at the same time and in a smaller skillet pancakes being made that are satisfying the other campers while they are waiting for the trout.

With the prepared pancake flours you take a cupful of pancake flour and add a cup of water. Mix the water and flour and as soon as the lumps are out it is ready for cooking. Have the skillet hot and keep it well greased. Drop the batter in and as soon as it is done on one side loosen it in the skillet and flip it over. Apple butter, syrup or cinnamon and sugar go well with the cakes.

While the crowd have taken the edge from their appetites with flapjacks the trout have been cooked and they and the bacon are ready to serve. The trout are crisp outside and firm and pink inside and the bacon is well done—but not too done. If there is anything better than that combination the writer has yet to taste it in a lifetime devoted largely and studiously to eating.

The stew kettle will cook you dried apricots when they have resumed their predried plumpness after a night of soaking, it will serve to concoct a mulligan in, and it will cook macaroni. When you are not using it, it should be boiling water for the dishes.

In the baker, mere man comes into his own, for he can make a pie that to his bush appetite will have it all over the product that mother used to make, like a tent. Men have always believed that there was something mysterious and difficult about making a pie. Here is a great secret. There is nothing to it. We've been kidded for years. Any man of average office intelligence can make at least as good a pie as his wife.

All there is to a pie is a cup and a half of flour, one-half teaspoonful of salt, one-half cup of lard and cold water. That will make pie crust that will bring tears of joy into your camping partner's eyes.

Mix the salt with the flour, work the lard into the 21 flour, make it up into a good workmanlike dough with cold water. Spread some flour on the back of a box or something flat, and pat the dough around a while. Then roll it out with whatever kind of round bottle you prefer. Put a little more lard on the surface of the sheet of dough and then slosh a little flour on and roll it up and then roll it out again with the bottle.

Cut out a piece of the rolled out dough big enough 22 to line a pie tin. I like the kind with holes in the bottom. Then put in your dried apples that have soaked all night and been sweetened, or your apricots, or your blueberries, and then take another sheet of the dough and drape it gracefully over the top, soldering it down at the edges with your fingers. Cut a couple of slits in the top dough sheet and prick it a few times with a fork in an artistic manner.

Put it in the baker with a good slow fire for forty- 23 five minutes and then take it out and if your pals are Frenchmen they will kiss you. The penalty for knowing how to cook is that the others will make you do all the cooking.

It is all right to talk about roughing it in the woods. 24 But the real woodsman is the man who can be really comfortable in the bush.

BUILDING VOCABULARY

1.   For each word below write your own definition, based on how the word is used in the selection. Check back to the appropriate paragraph in the essay.

    a. abiding (par. 2)
    b. assimilate (par. 2)
    c. valiant (par. 2)
    d. charred (par. 2)
    e. solemnly (par. 3)
    f. requisite (par. 8)

g. succession (par. 9)

h. studiously (par. 17)

i. concoct (par. 18)

j. soldering (par. 22)

UNDERSTANDING THE WRITER'S IDEAS

1. What is Hemingway's main purpose in this essay? Does he simply want to explain how to set up camp and how to cook outdoors?

2. What, according to the writer, are the two possible results of camping out on your vacation?

3. Why is oil of citronella the one insecticide that Hemingway recommends over all others?

4. Is it always necessary to pitch a tent when camping out? What are alternatives to it? How can you sleep warmly and comfortably?

5. Explain the author's process for cooking trout. Also explain his process for baking a pie.

6. Is it enough for Hemingway simply to enjoy "roughing it" while camping out?

UNDERSTANDING THE WRITER'S TECHNIQUES

1. Identify those paragraphs in the essay that involve process analysis, and explain how Hemingway develops his subject in each.

2. What is the main writing pattern in paragraphs 1 and 2? How does this method serve as an organizing principle throughout the essay?

3. How would you characterize the author's style of writing? Is it appropriate to a newspaper audience? Is it more apt for professional fishermen?

4. In what way does Hemingway employ classification in this essay?

5. Analyze the tone of Hemingway's essay.

6. The concluding paragraph is short. Is it effective, nevertheless, and why? How does it reinforce the opening paragraph?

EXPLORING THE WRITER'S IDEAS

1. Camping out was popular in the 1920s, as it is in the 1980s. What are some of the reasons that it remains so attractive today?

2. Hemingway's essay describes many basic strategies for successful camping. He does not rely on "gadgets," or modern inventions to make camping easier. Do such gadgets make camping more fun today than it might have been in the 1920s?

3. The author suggests that there is a right way and a wrong way to do things. Does it matter if you perform a recreational activity right as long as you enjoy doing it? Why?

IDEAS FOR WRITING

Guided Writing

Write a composition on how to do something wrong, and how to do it right—going on vacation, looking for a job, fishing, or whatever.

1. Reexamine the author's first three paragraphs and imitate his method of introducing the right and wrong ways about the subject, and the possible results.

2. Adopt a simple, informal, "chatty" style. Feel free to use a few well-placed cliches and other forms of spoken English. Use several similes.

3. Divide your subject into useful categories. Just as Hemingway treated insects, sleeping, and cooking, try to cover the main aspects of your subject.

4. Explain the process involved for each aspect of your subject. Make certain that you compare and contrast the right and wrong ways of your activity.

5. Write a short, crisp conclusion that reinforces your longer introduction.

More Writing Projects

1. Explain how people camp out today.
2. Describe how to get to your favorite vacation spot, and what to do when you get there.
3. If you have ever camped out, write a process paper explaining one important feature of setting up camp.

8

Cause-and-Effect Analysis

The analysis of cause and effect—often called *causal analysis*—seeks to explain why events occur, or what the outcome or *expected* results of a chain of happenings might be. Basically, cause-and-effect analysis looks for connections between things and reasons behind them. It involves a way of thinking that identifies conditions (the causes) and establishes results or consequences (the effects). In order to discuss an idea intelligently a writer needs to explore causes and effects. The strength of an explanation may lie simply in his or her ability to point out *why* something is so.

Like all the other writing patterns discussed in this text, cause-and-effect analysis reflects a kind of thinking we do every day. If someone were to ask you why you selected the college that you are now attending, you would offer reasons to explain your choice: the cost, the geographic location, the reputation of the institution, and so forth. These would be the *causes* that you have identified. On the other hand, someone might ask you if and why you like the college now that you are there. You could discuss your satisfaction (or lack of it) with the teachers, the course offerings, the opportunity to work part time, the availability of scholarship money and loans, the beauty of the campus, the variety in your social life. Those are the consequences or results—in other words, the *effects*—of your decision. Of course, basic reasoning and common sense are involved in the way that you identify causes and effects.

How do you determine causal relationships? First, you look at the *immediate* causes that gave rise to a situation—that is, you look at the causes most directly related to it, the ones you discover closest at hand. (Here you must be careful not to assume that because one event simply preceded another it also caused it.) But for most events a good analyst looks beyond immediate causes to more fundamental ones. These are the *ultimate* causes of a situation, the basic conditions that stimulated the more obvious ones.

For example, if you looked for causes to explain why your supervisor dismissed you from your job, your first response might be that you and she did not get along well. That could be an *immediate cause*. (Because one of your coworkers left your supervisor's office after a private conference with her just before you were fired, you could *not* assume safely that that coworker necessarily caused your dismissal.) But the immediate cause you uncovered could certainly be influenced by other underlying conditions. Perhaps your attendance record on the job was poor. Perhaps you did not get your work done quickly enough. Or, on the other hand, perhaps you worked so quickly and efficiently that your supervisor saw you as a threat to her own position. One or more of those and others like them might be the *ultimate* causes to explain why you lost the job.

Of course, as in the above example, causes you name for many situations may be thought of only as possibilities. It's often impossible to *prove* causes and effects absolutely. Yet in evaluating the causal relationships you present in an essay, readers expect you to offer evidence. Therefore, you do have to support the causes and effects you present with specific details drawn from personal experiences, from statistics, or from statements by experts, for example. The more details and evidence you offer, the better your paper will be.

When writers use causal analysis as a pattern, they can concentrate either on causes or effects, or they can attempt to balance the two. Moreover, in longer and more complicated papers, a writer can show how one cause produces an effect that, in turn, creates *another* set of causes leading to a second effect. Wherever the pattern takes you, remember to be thorough in presenting all links in your chain of analysis; to consider all possible factors; to avoid oversimplification; and to emphasize all important major and minor causes and effects.

Anne Roiphe

WHY MARRIAGES FAIL

Anne Roiphe is the author of the well-known novel about relationships, *Up The Sandbox!*, which was later made into a popular film. In this essay, notice how she presents a series of interconnected reasons for the currently high divorce rate.

Words to Watch

obsolete (par. 1): out-of-date; no longer in use
perils (par. 2): dangers
infertility (par. 2): the lack of ability to have children
turbulent (par. 2): very chaotic or uneasy
stupefying (par. 2): bewildering
obese (par. 3): very fat, overweight
entrapment (par. 4): the act of trapping, sometimes by devious
    methods
yearning (par. 4): a strong desire
euphoric (par. 7): characterized by a feeling of well-being
proverbial (par. 13): relating to a proverb or accepted truth
infidelity (par. 13): sexual unfaithfulness

These days so many marriages end in divorce that 1
our most sacred vows no longer ring with truth. "Happily
ever after" and "Till death do us part" are expressions that

seem on the way to becoming obsolete. Why has it become so hard for couples to stay together? What goes wrong? What has happened to us that close to one-half of all marriages are destined for the divorce courts? How could we have created a society in which 42 percent of our children will grow up in single-parent homes? If statistics could only measure loneliness, regret, pain, loss of self-confidence and fear of the future, the numbers would be beyond quantifying.

Even though each broken marriage is unique, we 2 can still find the common perils, the common causes for marital despair. Each marriage has crisis points and each marriage tests endurance, the capacity for both intimacy and change. Outside pressures such as job loss, illness, infertility, trouble with a child, care of aging parents and all the other plagues of life hit marriage the way hurricanes blast our shores. Some marriages survive these storms and others don't. Marriages fail, however, not simply because of the outside weather but because the inner climate becomes too hot or too cold, too turbulent or too stupefying.

When we look at how we choose our partners and 3 what expectations exist at the tender beginnings of romance, some of the reasons for disaster become quite clear. We all select with unconscious accuracy a mate who will recreate with us the emotional patterns of our first homes. Dr. Carl A. Whitaker, a marital therapist and emeritus professor of psychiatry at the University of Wisconsin explains, "From early childhood on, each of us carried models for marriage, femininity, masculinity, motherhood, fatherhood and all the other family roles." Each of us falls in love with a mate who has qualities of our parents, who will help us rediscover both the psychological happiness and miseries of our past lives. We may think we have found a man unlike Dad, but then he turns to drink or drugs, or loses his job over and over again or sits silently in front of the T.V. just the way Dad did. A man may choose a woman who doesn't like kids just like his mother or who gambles away the family savings just like his mother. Or he may choose a slender wife who seems unlike his obese mother but then turns out to have other addictions that destroy their mutual happiness.

A man and a woman bring to their marriage bed a 4
blended concoction of conscious and unconscious memories
of their parents' lives together. The human way is to
compulsively repeat and recreate the patterns of the past.
Sigmund Freud so well described the unhappy design that
many of us get trapped in: the unmet needs of childhood,
the angry feelings left over from frustrations of long ago,
the limits of trust and the reoccurrence of old fears. Once
an individual senses this entrapment, there may follow a
yearning to escape, and the result could be a broken,
splintered marriage.

Of course people can overcome the habits and atti- 5
tudes that developed in childhood. We all have hidden
strengths and amazing capacities for growth and creative
change. Change, however, requires work—observing your
part in a rotten pattern, bringing difficulties out into the
open—and work runs counter to the basic myth of marriage:
"When I wed this person all my problems will be over. I
will have achieved success and I will become the center of
life for this other person and this person will be my center,
and we will mean everything to each other forever." This
myth, which every marriage relies on, is soon exposed. The
coming of children, the pulls and tugs of their demands on
affection and time, place a considerable strain on that basic
myth of meaning everything to each other, of merging
together and solving all of life's problems.

Concern and tension about money take each partner 6
away from the other. Obligations to demanding parents or
still-depended-upon parents create further strain. Couples
today must also deal with all the cultural changes brought
on in recent years by the women's movement and the sexual
revolution. The altering of roles and the shifting of responsibilities have been extremely trying for many marriages.

These and other realities of life erode the visions of 7
marital bliss the way sandstorms eat at rock and the ocean
nibbles away at the dunes. Those euphoric, grand feelings
that accompany romantic love are really self-delusions, self-
hypnotic dreams that enable us to forge a relationship. Real
life, failure at work, disappointments, exhaustion, bad smells,

bad colds and hard times all puncture the dream and leave us stranded with our mate, with our childhood patterns pushing us this way and that, with our unfulfilled expectations.

The struggle to survive in marriage requires adaptability, flexibility, genuine love and kindness and an imagination strong enough to feel what the other is feeling. Many marriages fall apart because either partner cannot imagine what the other wants or cannot communicate what he or she needs or feels. Anger builds until it erupts into a volcanic burst that buries the marriage in ash.

It is not hard to see, therefore, how essential communication is for a good marriage. A man and a woman must be able to tell each other how they feel and why they feel the way they do; otherwise they will impose on each other roles and actions that lead to further unhappiness. In some cases, the communication patterns of childhood—of not talking, of talking too much, of not listening, of distrust and anger, of withdrawal—spill into the marriage and prevent a healthy exchange of thoughts and feelings. The answer is to set up new patterns of communication and intimacy.

At the same time, however, we must see each other as individuals. "To achieve a balance between separateness and closeness is one of the major psychological tasks of all human beings at every stage of life," says Dr. Stuart Bartle, a psychiatrist at the New York University Medical Center.

If we sense from our mate a need for too much intimacy, we tend to push him or her away, fearing that we may lose our identities in the merging of marriage. One partner may suffocate the other partner in a childlike dependency.

A good marriage means growing as a couple but also growing as individuals. This isn't easy. Richard gives up his interest in carpentry because his wife, Helen, is jealous of the time he spends away from her. Karen quits her choir group because her husband dislikes the friends she makes there. Each pair clings to each other and are angry with each other as life closes in on them. This kind of marital balance is easily thrown as one or the other pulls away and divorce follows.

Sometimes people pretend that a new partner will 13 solve the old problems. Most often extramarital sex destroys a marriage because it allows an artificial split between the good and the bad—the good is projected on the new partner and the bad is dumped on the head of the old. Dishonesty, hiding and cheating create walls between men and women. Infidelity is just a symptom of trouble. It is a symbolic complaint, a weapon of revenge, as well as an unraveler of closeness. Infidelity is often that proverbial last straw that sinks the camel to the ground.

All right—marriage has always been difficult. Why 14 then are we seeing so many divorces at this time? Yes, our modern social fabric is thin, and yes the permissiveness of society has created unrealistic expectations and thrown the family into chaos. But divorce is so common because people today are unwilling to exercise the self-discipline that marriage requires. They expect easy joy, like the entertainment on TV, the thrill of a good party.

Marriage takes some kind of sacrifice, not dreadful 15 self-sacrifice of the soul, but some level of compromise. Some of one's fantasies, some of one's legitimate desires have to be given up for the value of the marriage itself. "While all marital partners feel shackled at times, it is they who really choose to make the marital ties into confining chains or supporting bonds, says Dr. Whitaker. Marriage requires sexual, financial and emotional discipline. A man and a woman cannot follow every impulse, cannot allow themselves to stop growing or changing.

Divorce is not an evil act. Sometimes it provides 16 salvation for people who have grown hopelessly apart or were frozen in patterns of pain or mutual unhappiness. Divorce can be, despite its initial devastation, like the first cut of the surgeon's knife, a step toward new health and a good life. On the other hand, if the partners can stay past the breaking up of the romantic myths into the development of real love and intimacy, they have achieved a work as amazing as the greatest cathedrals of the world. Marriages that do not fail but improve, that persist despite imperfections, are not only rare these days but offer a wondrous shelter in which the face of our mutual humanity can safely show itself.

BUILDING VOCABULARY

1. Roiphe loads her essay with some very common expressions to make the discussion more easily understandable to the reader. Below is a list of ten such expressions. Use each in a sentence of your own.

   a. ring with truth (par. 1)
   b. crisis points (par. 2)
   c. tender beginnings (par. 3)
   d. mutual happiness (par. 3)
   e. marriage bed (par. 4)
   f. hidden strengths (par. 5)
   g. marital bliss (par. 7)
   h. healthy exchange (par. 9)
   i. childlike dependency (par. 11)
   j. social fabric (par. 14)

2. Locate and explain five terms that the author draws from psychology.

UNDERSTANDING THE WRITER'S IDEAS

1. What are the "sacred vows" the author mentions in paragraph 1? Identify the source of the expressions "happily ever after" and "till death do us part." What does she mean when she says that these expressions "seem on the way to becoming obsolete"?

2. What is a "single-parent home"?

3. How does Roiphe define "endurance" in a marriage? What does she mean by "outside pressures" in paragraph 2? What are some of these pressures? Does Roiphe feel they are the primary causes for marriages failing? Why?

4. According to the essay, how do we choose husbands and wives? What is the meaning of "our first home" in paragraph 3? According to Roiphe, for what reasons is the way we choose mates a possible cause for marriages failing?

5. What is the "basic myth" of marriage? How does it create a possibly bad marriage?

6. How have the women's movement and the sexual revolution created strains on modern marriages?

7. Explain what the writer means by "Real life, failure at work, disappointments, exhaustion, bad smells, bad colds, and hard times" in paragraph 7? How do they affect marriages?

8. What is the role of communications between husband and wife in a marriage? What are the results of poor communications? What solutions to this problem does Roiphe suggest?

9. What two types of "growth" does Roiphe suggest as necessary to a good marriage? Who are Richard, Helen, and Karen, named in paragraph 12?

10. According to Roiphe, what is the common cause for extramarital sexual affairs? What are her projected results of infidelity?

11. What does Roiphe identify as the primary cause of divorce? What does she propose as a solution to this problem?

12. According to the last paragraph, do you think Roiphe is in favor of each divorces? Why? In this paragraph, she presents both the positive and negative effects of divorce. What are the positive effects? the negative effects?

UNDERSTANDING THE WRITER'S TECHNIQUES

1. How does the title almost predict for the reader that the writer's main technique of development will be cause-and-effect analysis?

2. One strategy for developing an introductory paragraph is to ask a question. What is the purpose of the questions that the author asks in the opening paragraph?

What is the relationship among the questions? How do the questions themselves dictate a cause-effect pattern of development? How do they immediately involve the reader in the topic?

3. In which paragraph does Roiphe list the immediate or common causes of marital failure? Why is this placement effective?

4. The use of clear *topic sentences* for each paragraph can often be an important technique in writing a clear causal analysis because they usually identify main causes for the effect under discussion. Identify the topic sentences for paragraphs 3, 4, and 6. What causes for marriage failure does each identify?

5. What causal chain of behavior does Roiphe build in paragraphs 8 to 13?

6. Why does Roiphe begin paragraph 14 with the words "All right"? Whom is she addressing? How does this address compare with the technique used in her introduction?

7. What two authorities does Roiphe quote in this essay? How are their citations useful? How are they identified? In what ways do their identifications add to their credibility as sources of opinions or information on Roiphe's topic?

8. Where does Roiphe use statistics in this essay? Why is it especially important to the development of the article?

9. Roiphe makes use of *definition* (see page 141) in a number of places in this essay. What are her definitions of the following:

    a. "work" in a marriage (par. 5)
    b. "A good marriage" (par. 12)
    c. "divorce" (par. 16)
    d. "marriages that do not fail but improve" (par. 16)

Locate other places where she uses definition.

10. In some essays, the introduction and conclusion are each simply the first and last paragraphs. In this essay, the writer uses more than one paragraph for each. Which

paragraphs make up her introduction? Which make up the conclusion? Why might she have structured her introduction and conclusion in this way? How does the structure affect the essay?

11. You have learned that two of the most common types of comparisons used by writers to enliven their essays are *similes* and *metaphors*. Look up the definition of these terms in the Glossary to refresh your memory. In addition, writers may use *extended metaphors*. This technique relies upon a number of metaphoric comparisons which revolve around a main idea rather than a single comparison. In each of the following paragraphs identify and explain the comparisons indicated:

paragraph 2: extended metaphor

paragraph 7: metaphor

paragraph 8: metaphor

paragraph 13: metaphor

paragraph 14: simile

paragraph 15: metaphor

paragraph 16: similes, metaphors

How does Roiphe's frequent use of metaphors and similes affect the tone of the essay?

12. Why does Roiphe end her essay with references to successful marriages? Would you consider that as being off the topic? Why or why not?

EXPLORING THE WRITER'S IDEAS

1. Roiphe discusses quite a few causes for marriages failing. Discuss with the class some additional causes. Why are they also important?

2. Paragraph 6 states that "Couples today must also deal with all the cultural changes brought on in recent years by the women's movement and the sexual revolution." Identify these two social phenomena. Among the people you

know, have these cultural changes affected their marriages? How? If you are not married, and plan to marry, do you feel that the changes will present any foreseeable problems? If you are not married, and do not plan to marry, have they influenced your decision in any ways? What other effects have these two movements had in American society? Do you think these influences have been positive or negative? Why?

3. If you are married or in a close relationship, how did you choose your mate? If you are not married or in a relationship, what qualities would you look for in a mate? Why?

4. In paragraphs 6 and 7, Roiphe mentions "realities of life" that destroy romantic notions of "marital bliss." What other realities can you add to her list?

5. Paragraph 15 discusses the idea of self-sacrifice in marriage. Roiphe writes, "Some of one's fantasies, some of one's legitimate desires have to be given up for the value of the marriage itself." However, some people insist that for a marriage to survive, each partner must maintain complete integrity, that is, must not be forced into major sacrifices of values or life-styles. What is your opinion of these two opposing viewpoints?

6. Both Gregg Easterbrook in "Escape Valve" (pages 157–160) and the anonymous author of "I Wish They'd Do It Right" (pages 294–297) provide some insights into marriage that complement Roiphe's. How do their positions compare with hers? How, for example, could the principle of "automatic-out" explain to some degree why marriages fail?

IDEAS FOR WRITING

Guided Writing

Using cause-and-effect analysis, write an essay in which you explain *why marriages succeed.*

1. Limit your topic sufficiently so that you can concentrate your discussion on closely interrelated cause-and-effect patterns.

2. In the introduction, involve your reader with a series of pertinent questions.

3. Identify what many people think are common or immediate causes of successful marriages; then show how other causes are perhaps even more important.

4. In the course of your essay, cite at least one relevant statistic that will add extra importance to your topic.

5. Try to use at least one quotation from a reputable authority. Consult your library for books and articles that deal with marriage. Be sure to include full identification of your source.

6. Use clear topic sentences in each paragraph as you present analysis of the various causes for successful marriages.

7. Make use of metaphors, similes, and extended metaphors.

8. In your essay, offer necessary definitions of terms that are especially important to your topic. Try for at least one definition by negation.

9. Write a conclusion in which you make some commentary upon divorce. Make your comment as an outgrowth of your discussion of a successful marriage.

More Writing Projects

1. In an essay of approximately 750 to 1000 words, explain the reasons why you ever ended a relationship (a marriage, a close friendship, a relationship with a girlfriend or boyfriend). Also discuss how you knew when you had reached the "breaking point." Did you feel you had hung on too long or had given up too soon?

2. Write a long letter to a friend explaining why you think he or she should end or not end a marriage, relationship, or friendship. Be sure to include clear reasons.

3. Write an essay in which you explain the effects of divorce in the lives of the couple involved. Here, do not concern yourself with causes; look only at the results of the failed marriage.

Boyce Rensberger

WHY YOU LIKE SOME FOODS AND HATE OTHERS

In this essay, Boyce Rensberger explores the various reasons for our liking or disliking certain foods. He relates taste preferences to human evolution; and he discusses the ideas proposed about tastes by anthropologists. Pay special attention to the discussions of experiments designed to test people's taste preferences.

Words to Watch

aversion (par. 1): a strong feeling of dislike accompanied by a strong desire to avoid something

insights (par. 2): deep understandings

genetic (par. 3): dealing with hereditary changes in living things

evolution (par. 4): the process of changes through which living beings acquire distinguishing characteristics or traits

foraging (par. 4): wandering in search of food

induced (par. 6): influenced by reasons or persuasion

nausea (par. 12): a stomach illness accompanied by a hatred for food and by an urge to vomit

anesthetized (par. 12): under the influence of a substance which produces a loss of feeling without a loss of consciousness

ingrained (par. 13): deep-seated

assimilated (par. 18): absorbed traditions and values of a culture

viscosity (par. 20): the property of a fluid that prevents it from flowing

staple (par. 21): major or principal element

mainstay (par. 21): chief or main support

putrefaction (par. 22): rotting; decomposition of organic matter

$\mathbf{E}$verybody doesn't like something. Whether the aversion is to sautéed brains or McDonald's hamburgers, to Szechwan spiciness or Middle American blandness, everyone finds at least a few foods or flavors to be objectionable.

Yet, as common as taste aversions are, little is reliably known about how they are formed. They are just beginning to be studied by scientists, however, and some insights are developing.

There are, for example, genetic differences in people's abilities to taste some substances. Some people cannot taste certain bitter flavors, and hence enjoy foods that others find objectionably bitter.

Some authorities have suggested that the widely held strong preference for sweetness, craving for salt and aversion to sour or bitter flavors is innate, a product of evolution during the days when our foraging ancestors lived off the land. Things that taste sweet are usually nutritious and full of energy, while those that are bitter or sour tend more often to be poisonous. As tropical animals, our ancestors lost lots of salt in their sweat and needed to replace it to prevent sodium deficiency in the blood.

Our taste preferences and aversions, so this explanation goes, evolved to be generally reliable guides to eating in the wild. It is only after our relatively recent adoption of sedentary ways and synthetic foods that the preference for sweets and salt is getting us into nutritional trouble.

Although nutritionists often contend that a preference for very sweet foods is culturally induced or that people actually develop an addiction to sugar, Dr. Gary Beauchamp, a specialist in taste research, says there is no solid evidence to support this.

Dr. Beauchamp, of the University of Pennsylvania's Monell Chemical Senses Center, suggests that although people may consciously modify their food choices, the basic preference for sweetness remains. It has only become noticeable now that food technologists "have separated sweetness from the goodness of the natural food" and marketed a number of foods offering little else.

Rather than creating a preference for sweetness, 8
Dr. Beauchamp suggests, the food technologists are merely
exploiting an existing preference that, in the past, was no
problem.

Also there is solid evidence that, aside from the 9
aversion to sour and bitter flavors, the sense of taste plays
another role in preventing food poisoning. The evidence was
first seen in animal experiments. If a rat gets sick after
eating some unusual food, it will develop an immediate
aversion to the taste of that food.

In a form of learning quite unlike Pavlovian condi- 10
tioning, the taste aversion develops after a single episode
and the sickness may occur several hours after the food was
eaten. The aversion also persists for a long time. Conditioned
responses usually require many experiences to be learned
and the aversive response must occur immediately after the
stimulus. And they fade quickly.

The phenomenon occurs in many animals and is 11
called "bait shyness" among those who try to poison un-
wanted animals but find that if the animal survives, it
usually learns to avoid the bait.

Dr. John Garcia, a psychologist at the University of 12
California, Los Angeles, has found that laboratory rats can
be made to dislike sugar-flavored water, which they normally strongly prefer, by injecting them with a drug that
induces nausea several hours afterward. Experiments have
also shown that rats learn this taste aversion even if they
are totally anesthetized throughout the period of induced
nausea.

All of this evidence tells scientists that taste aver- 13
sions formed in this way are the effect of a powerful and
deeply ingrained biological capacity. Such powerful and obvious biological traits do not evolve into being and become
widespread unless they confer a distinct advantage to the
survival of the animal. There is now evidence that human
beings share this capacity.

In the only controlled experiment on learned taste 14
aversions in people, Dr. Ilene L. Bernstein, a University of
Washington psychiatrist, found that children could be made

to dislike a novel flavor of ice cream if they became sick after eating it. Children who did not get sick loved it.

Her experiment was aimed at learning why so many 15 cancer patients receiving drug therapy develop aversions to many kinds of food, even foods they once preferred. Cancer drugs often induce severe nausea, and, Dr. Bernstein reasoned, the patients might be victims of the bait-shy response.

She studied children with cancer who had to take 16 nausea-inducing drugs. One group received a new flavor of ice cream, called Mapletoff, before undergoing therapy. Later the children were given a choice of the ice cream and playing with a game. Less than a quarter chose the ice cream. Children who had tried Mapletoff but did not get sick from therapy, preferred Mapletoff to the game almost four to one.

While genetically controlled factors may account for 17 some taste aversions, cultural influences clearly play a more obvious role.

Anthropologists have found that food preferences are 18 among the most stable of cultural traditions. Long after immigrants and their descendants have assimilated most other aspects of their adopted country, including language, they will cling to their native cookery.

When the potato, native to Peru, was introduced in 19 Europe centuries ago, people resisted it as a bizarre-tasting oddity. It was 200 years before they generally adopted the potato into their diets.

While most people dislike foods that are strongly 20 sour and increase their dislikes in proportion to the sourness, at least one group in India says it prefers foods sour, and the sourer the better. This is an economically poor group whose basic foods are sour, and who, for example, eat tamarind fruits as if they were apples. Their culture is apparently their only difference with other Indians.

Cultural preferences apply not only to flavor but to 21 texture and viscosity. One finding has been that people tend to prefer their dietary staple to have a hearty, chewy consistency. To most Americans rice is just another side dish;

they prefer it light and fluffy. But in cultures where rice is the dietary mainstay, it is preferred heavier and more glutinous. When bread was a staple in the United States it was heavy and substantial. But now that it is no longer the staff of life, bread has been turned into fluff.

The role of smell in influencing food aversions and preferences is well known. People with colds often lose their appetites because they cannot smell food. However delicious a dish might appear to the eyes, if the nose perceives any odor like that of putrefaction, the tongue will probably never taste it. What is not so well appreciated is the role of the eyes in modifying food preferences. 22

Food technologists add orange coloring to their synthetic orange drinks not just to be consistent but because, without the color, the flavor does not taste as orangy. Thus grape-flavored drinks are colored purple, cherry drinks are red, and so on. When lemon drinks and lime drinks came out, however, food synthesizers were faced with a dilemma. Both juices are essentially colorless. How to inform consumers what flavor they were supposed to taste? The decision was to adopt the color of the rind. Thus lime drinks are green and lemon drinks are yellow. 23

In one experiment, researchers scrambled five flavors and colors and found that if, for example, the lemon-flavored drink was red, taste testers tended to call it strawberry. The test involved drinks flavored with lemon, orange, strawberry, grape and blueberry and colored yellow, orange, red, purple and blue. When the "right" color was combined with the flavor, 72 percent of the testers guessed the correct flavoring. But when the colors were scrambled only 22 percent could name the flavor. 24

The role of color is not limited to artificial flavors. Experienced wine tasters can also be fooled. In one experiment a white wine was colored to look like a rosé. Tasters concluded that it was sweeter. 25

Perhaps the ultimate example of the role of experience in influencing food preferences and aversions is that reported by Dr. Howard Schutz, a psychologist at the University of California at Davis. He notes that many people 26 have come to prefer the taste of canned tomato juice over that of fresh tomato juice.

"The taste of tin from the can," Dr. Schutz said, "has 27 been accepted as appropriate in tomato juice. That's what people expect. It's so important that aluminum-can makers have thought about adding the tin flavor to juice packed in their containers."

BUILDING VOCABULARY

1. For each italicized word in Column A, write the correct *antonym* (a word of opposite meaning) from Column B. Look up unfamiliar words in a dictionary.

Column A	Column B
a. to be *objectionable* (par. 1)	1. abundance
b. is *innate* (par. 4)	2. changeable
c. a sodium *deficiency* (par. 4)	3. unsettled
d. *reliable* guides (par. 5)	4. natural
e. *sedentary* ways (par. 5)	5. unoriginal
f. *synthetic* foods (par. 5)	6. acceptable
g. *novel* flavor (par. 14)	7. unsteady
h. most *stable* (par. 18)	8. undependable
i. *bizarre*-tasting (par. 19)	9. unnatural
j. to be *consistent* (par. 23)	10. typical

2. The following words are used in this essay to describe food. Look up their meanings and use each in a sentence of your own.

a. sautéed	f. nutritious
b. Szechwan	g. sodium
c. blandness	h. tamarind fruits
d. bitter	i. glutinous
e. sweetness	j. rind

UNDERSTANDING THE WRITER'S IDEAS

1. In your own words, what condition is the author setting out to analyze in this essay? Where does he state that condition?

2.   According to the evolutionary theory of taste preferences, why do we like some foods and hate others? What accounts for our liking of sweets? Our craving for salt? Our dislike of bitter-tasting foods? What two aspects of contemporary life may threaten this evolutionary process?

3.   What evidence does Rensberger offer to support the idea that our sense of taste acts as an inborn guard against food poisoning?

4.   What is Pavlovian conditioning? What is the phenomenon of "bait shyness"? How do the two processes differ?

5.   What is the main reason described to support the theory that taste aversions derive from ingrained biological necessities?

6.   Explain in your own words how cancer patients might be victims of the bait-shy response.

7.   Although some scientists attempt to explain taste aversions by genetic factors, anthropologists take another viewpoint. What is it? What three examples does Rensberger describe to illustrate this viewpoint?

8.   What is the role of the sense of smell in the process of determining tastes we dislike? How is the sense of sight involved in the process?

9.   Why do many people no longer like to drink fresh-pressed tomato juice, according to Rensberger's essay? Of what factor influencing food preferences is this taste phenomenon an example?

UNDERSTANDING THE WRITER'S TECHNIQUES

1.   Does Rensberger fulfill the purpose stated in the title? Does he give equal treatment to both aspects of the purpose? Explain.

2.   Explain the author's use of transitions. List all the transitional words and expressions in paragraphs 1 through 9.

3.   Explain Rensberger's use of classification in this selection. How does he classify types of tastes? What major

categories of causes for taste aversions and preferences does he discuss?

4.   Explain the use of cause and effect in paragraphs 13 to 16, paragraphs 17 to 21, and paragraphs 26 to 27. Does each cause have a single effect, or are there chains of inter-related causes?

5.   What specific authorities does Rensberger cite? Why does he quote those authors? What do they add to the essay? Where does he use statistics?

6.   Where is *process analysis* used in this selection? How can the experiments be understood as process analyses? Describe step by step Dr. Ilene Bernstein's process of testing her hypothesis (a *hypothesis* is a tentative assumption made in order to draw out and test its consequences) that cancer patients might be victims of bait-shy response.

7.   Compare your description of process in answer to question 6 with your explanation of the use of cause and effect in answer to question 4. How do process analysis and cause-and-effect analysis reinforce each other in this essay?

8.   What are the tone and purpose of the conclusion to this selection?

9.   What major audience would you say Rensberger is attempting to reach: scientists, administrators of food companies or restaurants, junior high school students, a general educated public? How can you tell?

EXPLORING THE WRITER'S IDEAS

1.   What foods can you think of that are considered tasty by one culture and inedible by another? Why do you think there is such a difference in food preferences among various cultures?

2.   Do you believe our tastes in food are more a result of our genetic makeup or of our cultural conditioning? Explain your opinion.

3.   In an introductory college psychology textbook or some other source, look up the terms *Pavlovian conditioning* and *operant conditioning*. What do they mean? How could conditioning be used to change people's tastes for

foods? In what ways are we conditioned by advertisements to prefer certain products over others? Analyze the process by which your tastes have been conditioned to like a certain product.

4. In paragraph 6, Rensberger says that some nutritionists believe people develop an addiction to sugar. Along with parents and consumer groups they point to the great amounts of sugar found in such foods as breakfast cereals, baby foods, soft drinks, and even in such unlikely items as cold cuts, frozen vegetables, and dairy products.

Check the ingredients of some of the foods you eat most often. Do you find sugar among the list of ingredients? (Ingredients are listed in order of the amounts found in the product, with the most prevalent ingredient listed first and the rest in descending order.) How often and at what point on the list of ingredients does sugar appear? What comment can you make about your own sugar consumption? Do you feel that Americans are a nation of "sugar junkies"? Explain.

5. Compare Rensberger's use of the term *addiction* with the ways Adam Smith (see pages 204–208) uses it in his essay on drugs.

IDEAS FOR WRITING

Guided Writing

Write an essay in which you explain why you hate or love a particular food. Select a specific food like spinach, olives, or mayonnaise. Or choose a group of foods like vegetables, cold cuts, or cereals.

1. Use classification to categorize the main reasons why you hate or love this food.

2. Develop each reason through examples of your positive or negative reactions to that food. Discuss the causes for each of these reactions and relate them to the larger category, which includes those reasons.

3. Devise a possible simple method of experimentation by which your readers could test their aversions or

preferences for this food. Describe the experiment carefully, step by step.

4. Explain how you first developed a like or dislike for this food.

5. Indicate through specific examples or incidents how each of the following factors influenced your taste or distaste for the type of food: cultural preferences, family tastes, color, smell, looks, texture, experience.

More Writing Projects

1. Devise an experiment in which you test people's food aversions or preferences. Begin with a specific hypothesis and try to make the experiment simple enough to try in class. Then write an essay in which you analyze the results for cause and effect.

2. Through cause-and-effect analysis, write an essay explaining why you prefer certain types of people as friends and why you avoid other types.

Linda Bird Francke

THE AMBIVALENCE OF ABORTION

In this autobiographical narrative, author Linda Bird
Francke tells about her mixed feelings toward the issue
of abortion. Although she has strong political convictions
on the subject, her ambivalence surfaces when she must
confront abortion personally. Notice how she blends descriptive details with personal insights to explain the
reasons for her uncertainty.

Words to Watch

dwell (par. 1): keep attention directed on something
heralded (par. 1): announced in a joyous manner
rationalize (par. 2): to justify one's behavior (especially to oneself)
freelance (par. 3): working without long-range contractual agreements
cycled (par. 5): moved through a complete series of operations or
   steps
common denominator (par. 10): similar traits or themes
rhetoric (par. 13): ways of speaking or writing effectively
fetus (par. 13): an unborn child still in the mother's womb
neurotic (par. 14): emotionally unstable
vaccinated (par. 14): injected with a harmless virus to produce
   immunity to a disease
inoculated (par. 14): treated with a serum or antibody to prevent
   disease
uterus (par. 16): the womb; the place within the mother where the
   fetus develops
sensation (par. 18): feeling
Novocain (par. 18): a drug used to numb the feeling of pain
quivered (par. 18): shook

We were sitting in a bar on Lexington Avenue when 1
I told my husband I was pregnant. It is not a memory I like
to dwell on. Instead of the champagne and hope which had
heralded the impending births of the first, second and third
child, the news of this one was greeted with shocked silence
and Scotch. "Jesus," my husband kept saying to himself,
stirring the ice cubes around and around. "Oh, Jesus."

Oh, how we tried to rationalize it that night as the 2
starting time for the movie came and went. My husband
talked about his plans for a career change in the next year,
to stem the staleness that fourteen years with the same investment-banking firm had brought him. A new baby would
preclude that option.

The timing wasn't right for me either. Having jug- 3
gled pregnancies and child care with what freelance jobs
I could fit in between feedings, I had just taken on a full-time
job. A new baby would put me right back in the nursery just
when our youngest child was finally school age. It was time
for *us,* we tried to rationalize. There just wasn't room in our
lives now for another baby. We both agreed. And agreed.
And agreed.

How very considerate they are at the Women's Ser- 4
vices, known formally as the Center for Reproductive and
Sexual Health. Yes, indeed, I could have an abortion that
very Saturday morning and be out in time to drive to the
country that afternoon. Bring a first morning urine speci-
men, a sanitary belt and napkins, a money order or $125
cash—and a friend.

My friend turned out to be my husband, standing 5
awkwardly and ill at ease as men always do in places that
are exclusively for women, as I checked in at nine A.M. Other
men hovered around just as anxiously, knowing they had to
be there, wishing they weren't. No one spoke to each other.
When I would be cycled out of there four hours later, the
same men would be slumped in their same seats, locked
downcast in their cells of embarrassment.

The Saturday morning women's group was more dis- 6
spirited than the men in the waiting room. There were
around fifteen of us, a mixture of races, ages and back-

grounds. Three didn't speak English at all and a fourth, a pregnant Puerto Rican girl around eighteen, translated for them.

There were six black women and a hodgepodge of 7 whites, among them a T-shirted teenager who kept leaving the room to throw up and a puzzled middle-aged woman from Queens with three grown children.

"What form of birth control were you using?" the volunteer asked each one of us. The answer was inevitably "none." She then went on to describe the various forms of birth control available at the clinic, and offered them to each of us.

The youngest Puerto Rican girl was asked through the interpreter which she'd like to use: the loop, diaphragm, or pill. She shook her head "no" three times. "You don't want to come back here again, do you?" the volunteer pressed. The girl's head was so low her chin rested on her breastbone. "Sí," she whispered.

We had been there two hours by that time, filling 10 out endless forms, giving blood and urine, receiving lectures. But unlike any other group of women I've been in, we didn't talk. Our common denominator, the one which usually floods across language and economic barriers into familiarity, today was one of shame. We were losing life that day, not giving it.

The group kept getting cut back to smaller, more 11 workable units, and finally I was put in a small waiting room with just two other women. We changed into paper bathrobes and paper slippers, and we rustled whenever we moved. One of the women in my room was shivering and an aide brought her a blanket.

"What's the matter?" the aide asked her. "I'm 12 scared," the woman said. "How much will it hurt?" The aide smiled. "Oh, nothing worse than a couple of bad cramps," she said. "This afternoon you'll be dancing a jig."

I began to panic. Suddenly the rhetoric, the abortion 13 marches I'd walked in, the telegrams sent to Albany to counteract the Friends of the Fetus, the Zero Population Growth buttons I'd worn, peeled away, and I was all alone with my microscopic baby. There were just the two of us there, and soon, because it was more convenient for me and my husband, there would be one again.

How could it be that I, who am so neurotic about life 14 that I step over bugs rather than on them, who spend hours planting flowers and vegetables in the spring even though we rent out the house and never see them, who make sure the children are vaccinated and inoculated and filled with vitamin C, could so arbitrarily decide that this life shouldn't be?

"It's not a life," my husband had argued, more to 15 convince himself than me. "It's a bunch of cells smaller than my fingernail."

But any woman who has had children knows that 16 certain feeling in her taut, swollen breasts, and the slight but constant ache in her uterus that signals the arrival of a life. Though I would march myself into blisters for a woman's right to exercise the option of motherhood, I discovered there in the waiting room that I was not the modern woman I thought I was.

When my name was called, my body felt so heavy the 17 nurse had to help me into the examining room. I waited for my husband to burst through the door and yell "stop," but of course he didn't. I concentrated on three black spots in the acoustic ceiling until they grew in size to the shape of saucers, while the doctor swabbed my insides with antiseptic. 18

"You're going to feel a burning sensation now," he said, injecting Novocain into the neck of the womb. The pain was swift and severe, and I twisted to get away from him. He was hurting my baby, I reasoned, and the black saucers quivered in the air. "Stop," I cried. "Please stop." He shook his head, busy with his equipment. "It's too late to stop now," he said. "It'll just take a few more seconds."

What good sports we women are. And how obedient. 19 Physically the pain passed even before the hum of the machine signaled that the vacuuming of my uterus was completed, my baby sucked up like ashes after a cocktail party. Ten minutes start to finish. And I was back on the arm of the nurse.

There were twelve beds in the recovery room. Each 20
one had a gaily flowered draw sheet and a soft green or blue
thermal blanket. It was all very feminine. Lying on these
beds for an hour or more were the shocked victims of their
sex, their full wombs now stripped clean, their futures less
encumbered.

It was very quiet in that room. The only voice was 21
that of the nurse, locating the new women who had just
come in so she could monitor their blood pressure, and checking out the recovered women who were free to leave.

Juice was being passed about, and I found myself 22
sipping a Dixie cup of Hawaiian Punch. An older woman
with tightly curled bleached hair was just getting up from
the next bed. "That was no goddamn snap," she said, resting
before putting on her miniskirt and high white boots. Other
women came and went, some walking out as dazed as they
had entered, others with a bounce that signaled they were
going right back to Bloomingdale's.

Finally then, it was time for me to leave. I checked 23
out, making an appointment to return in two weeks for an
IUD insertion. My husband was slumped in the waiting
room, clutching a single yellow rose wrapped in a wet paper
towel and stuffed into a Baggie.

We didn't talk the whole way home, but just held 24
hands very tightly. At home there were more yellow roses
and a tray in bed for me and the children's curiosity to
divert.

It had certainly been a successful operation. I didn't 25
bleed at all for two days just as they had predicted, and then
I bled only moderately for another four days. Within a week
my breasts had subsided and the tenderness vanished, and
my body felt mine again instead of the eggshell it becomes
when it's protecting someone else.

My husband and I are back to planning our summer 26
vacation and his career switch.

And it certainly does make more sense not to be 27
having a baby right now—we say that to each other all the
time. But I have this ghost now. A very little ghost that only
appears when I'm seeing something beautiful, like the full

moon on the ocean last weekend. And the baby waves at me. And I wave at the baby. "Of course, we have room," I cry to the ghost. "Of course, we do."

BUILDING VOCABULARY

1. Develop definitions of your own for the italicized words by relying on context clues, that is, clues from surrounding words and sentences. Then check your definition against a dictionary definition.

a. "My husband talked about his plans for a career change in the next year, *to stem* the staleness that fourteen years with the same investment-banking firm had brought him. A new baby would *preclude* that *option*." (par. 2)

b. "Though I would march myself into blisters for a woman's right to *exercise* the *option* of motherhood, I discovered there in the waiting room that I was not the modern woman I thought I was." (par. 16)

c. "The pain was *swift* and *severe,* and I twisted to get away from him." (par. 18)

d. "Lying on these beds for an hour or more were the shocked victims of their sex, their full wombs now stripped clean, their futures less *encumbered.*" (par. 20)

e. "It had certainly been a successful operation. I didn't bleed at all for two days just as they had predicted, and then I bled only *moderately* for another four days." (par. 25)

2. For each italicized word in Column A, write the correct *synonym* (a word of similar meaning) from Column B. Look up unfamiliar words in a dictionary.

Column A	Column B
a. *impending* birth (par. 1)	1. decreased
b. *hovered* around (par. 5)	2. complying
c. looked *downcast* (par. 5)	3. confused
d. more *dispirited* (par. 6)	4. lingered
e. *puzzled* middle-aged woman (par. 7)	5. about to happen
f. *inevitably* "none" (par. 8)	6. tight
g. *taut* swollen breasts (par. 16)	7. distract

h. how *obedient* (par. 19)
i. curiosity to *divert* (par. 24)
j. had *subsided* (par. 25)

8. dejected
9. unavoidable
10. discouraged

UNDERSTANDING THE WRITER'S IDEAS

1. What is the setting in which Francke breaks the news to her husband that she is pregnant? How does he receive the news?

2. What reasons does the husband give for not wanting another child? Why does Francke feel it is a bad time for herself as well?

3. What is the attitude of the men waiting at the abortion clinic? Explain.

4. Why is there a women's group meeting before Francke actually gets her abortion? Are all the women pretty much alike at this meeting? How so? What is Francke's attitude toward these other women? Give specific examples to support your answer.

5. What common reason do all the women in the group share for being pregnant?

6. In the past, what was the author's viewpoint concerning women's rights to have abortions? What specific examples does she give to illustrate this point of view? Do you assume that she still holds this opinion? Why?

7. What examples does Francke give to illustrate that she supports life? Are they convincing?

8. Explain what the author means by the statement "Though I would march myself into blisters for a woman's right to exercise the option of motherhood, I discovered there in the waiting room that I was not the modern woman I thought I was." (par. 16)

9. When she is in the examining room, what does the author do to deal with her anxieties about the abortion?

10. Explain what the woman means when she says to Francke, " 'That was no goddamn snap.' "

11. How does Francke know the operation has been successful?

UNDERSTANDING THE WRITER'S TECHNIQUES

1. What rhetorical strategy does the word "ambivalence" in the title suggest? How does Francke use that strategy in the very first paragraph? Where does she use it elsewhere in the essay?

2. Does Francke successfully explain the ambivalence named in the title? Why or why not?

3. Which does this analysis concentrate on more—causes, effects, or a combination of the two? What evidence can you offer to support your answer? What specifically is the relationship between cause and effect in paragraphs 6 to 10? Analyze the pattern of cause and effect in paragraphs 19 to 22.

4. What is the use of narration in this essay? What is the narrative *point of view* (see Glossary) in this selection? How is it used to enhance the essay?

5. What would you say is the overall tone of the selection? The author uses repetition in this essay to help set that tone. How does the repetition in "We both agreed. And agreed. And agreed." (par. 3) contribute to it?

6. *Paradox* is a special variety of irony (see Glossary) in which there is a clear contradiction in a situation. A paradox is a statement or attitude which, on the surface, seems unlikely, and yet, on analysis, can indeed be true. For example, it is paradoxical that the author should have such ambivalent feelings about abortion while she is sitting in an abortion clinic. Why is that situation considered paradoxical? What other paradoxes do you find in this essay?

7. What is the function of description in this essay? Select passages in which you feel the descriptions are especially vivid. How is description used by the author to characterize the women mentioned in paragraph 22? Are the women stereotyped in this description? Explain.

8. Only toward the last part of the essay does Francke use any metaphors or similes—some of them quite startling. Identify the metaphors or similes in paragraph 19, paragraph 25, and paragraph 27. Why do you think she saved this figurative language for the end?

9.   Analyze the last paragraph. What causes and effects discussed throughout the essay are echoed here? What new ones are suggested? Compare the effect of the statement " 'Of course, we have room' " to the statement in paragraph 3, "There just wasn't room. . . ." How does this repetition affect the conclusion?

10.   Writers who write about highly charged emotional issues must take special care to avoid *sentimentality*— the excessive display of emotion (see Glossary). Has Francke been successful in avoiding it everywhere in the essay? How has she used concrete descriptions to avoid being sentimental? Does the conclusion strike you as being excessively emotional or does it strike you simply as a dramatic but effective closing? Explain your responses.

EXPLORING THE WRITER'S IDEAS

1.   When this article was originally published in 1976, it appeared under the *pseudonym* (a fictitious name) "Jane Doe." What reason might Linda Francke have had for not using her real name? Why do you think that a few years later she admitted to the authorship of the article? In general, what do you think about a writer publishing his or her work under an assumed name? Explain. What historical examples can you offer for the use of pseudonyms?

2.   Francke describes some very intimate personal emotions and experiences in her attempt to explain what causes her ambivalence toward abortion. On the basis of the material presented, do you think she is justified in feeling ambivalent? Do you feel she should have been more definite one way or the other? Why?

3.   In her description of the Saturday morning women's group (pars. 6 to 10), Francke shows that the women present were of all types—"a mixture of races, ages, and backgrounds." This suggests, of course, that abortion is a subject affecting all women. Does it, in fact, affect all women equally? Explain your answer.

4.   In paragraph 5, the author describes her husband as "standing awkwardly and ill at ease as men always do in

places that are exclusively for women." What sorts of places are exclusively for persons of one sex? Discuss how you felt and acted if you were ever in a place which was really more for persons of the opposite sex.

5. Much controversy about abortion revolves around modern definitions of life and death. Some people argue that life begins at conception; others argue that life begins at birth. With which group do you agree? Why? How has modern science complicated our concepts of life and death?

IDEAS FOR WRITING

Guided Writing

Select an important issue facing society, an issue with which you have had personal experience and about which you have mixed feelings. After you fill in the blank, write an essay titled "Two Sides of _____." In your essay explore the reasons for your ambivalence. You can select from a wide range of social, moral, health, or education topics. For example, you might want to consider ambivalence toward interracial dating or marriages, a compulsory draft, legalization of drugs, cigarette smoking, a liberal arts education—but feel free to select any issue which is especially important to you.

1. Write the essay as a first-person narrative. Begin with an incident when you first clearly realized the ambivalent nature of the issue, and explain why or how this particular incident focused your attention on the subject.

2. Tell about how and for what reasons you came to a decision to take a certain action despite your mixed feelings. What rationalizations did you or others use to help you feel you were doing the right thing?

3. Narrate in detail the sequence of events that followed your decision. Make the narrative come to life with concrete sensory detail. As you tell your story, analyze the various causes and effects of your decision and actions.

4. Discuss how the same event you experienced affects others. Explain how the causes and effects of the action are different or similar for you and for others.

5. Explain how you felt immediately before, during, and after the crucial experience.

6. In your conclusion, express your deepest feelings about the consequences of your decision and experiences. Use similes, metaphors, and an echo of your original attempts to rationalize your ambivalence.

More Writing Projects

1. Write an essay in which you analyze the reasons for your own attitudes toward abortion.

2. Write an essay in which you explain the causes and/or effects of a political standpoint you feel very strongly about.

3. In an essay of analysis, propose the effects on children if elementary schools throughout the country offered compulsory sex education programs.

4. In 1968, Black Panther party leader Eldridge Cleaver ended a speech with the statement, "If you're not part of the solution, you're part of the problem." Analyze what you think Cleaver meant by that statement.

Susan Jacoby

WHEN BRIGHT GIRLS DECIDE THAT MATH IS "A WASTE OF TIME"

In this article, Susan Jacoby explains how cultural expectations and societal stereotyping are overshadowed by women's own decisions to keep themselves away from scientific and technological studies. Notice how she uses narrative and process analysis to reinforce the causes and effects she is exploring here.

Words to Watch

sanguine (par. 3): cheerful, hopeful
vulnerable (par. 6): open to attack or suggestion
syndrome (par. 7): a group of symptoms that characterize a condition
akin to (par. 7): similar to
phobia (par. 7): a group of symptoms that characterize a condition
akin to (par. 7): similar to
phobia (par. 7): an excessive fear of something
constitute (par. 7): to make up; compose
epitomize (par. 8): to be a prime example of
prone (par. 15): disposed to; susceptible
accede to (par. 16): give in to

Susannah, a 16-year-old who has always been an 1
A student in every subject from algebra to English, recently

informed her parents that she intended to drop physics and calculus in her senior year of high school and replace them with a drama seminar and a work-study program. She expects a major in art or history in college, she explained, and "any more science or math will just be a waste of my time."

Her parents were neither concerned by nor opposed 2 to her decision. "Fine, dear," they said. Their daughter is, after all, an outstanding student. What does it matter if, at age 16, she has taken a step that may limit her understanding of both machines and the natural world for the rest of her life?

This kind of decision, in which girls turn away from 3 studies that would given them a sure footing in the world of science and technology, is a self-inflicted female disability that is, regrettably, almost as common today as it was when I was in high school. If Susannah had announced that she had decided to stop taking English in her senior year, her mother and father would have been horrified. I also think they would have been a good deal less sanguine about her decision if she were a boy.

In saying that scientific and mathematical ignorance 4 is a self-inflicted female wound, I do not, obviously, mean that cultural expectations play no role in the process. But the world does not conspire to deprive modern women of access to science as it did in the 1930's, when Rosalyn S. Yalow, the Nobel Prize-winning physicist, graduated from Hunter College and was advised to go to work as a secretary because no graduate school would admit her to its physics department. The current generation of adolescent girls—and their parents, bred on old expectations about women's interests—are active conspirators in limiting their own intellectual development.

It is true that the proportion of young women in 5 science-related graduate and professional schools, most notably medical schools, has increased significantly in the past decade. It is also true that so few women were studying advanced science and mathematics before the early 1970's that the percentage increase in female enrollment does not yet translate into large numbers of women actually working in science.

6 The real problem is that so many girls eliminate themselves from any serious possibility of studying science as a result of decisions made during the vulnerable period of midadolescence, when they are most likely to be influenced—on both conscious and subconscious levels—by the traditional belief that math and science are "masculine" subjects.

7 During the teen-age years the well-documented phenomenon of "math anxiety" strikes girls who never had any problem handling numbers during earlier schooling. Some men, too, experience this syndrome—a form of panic, akin to a phobia, at any task involving numbers—but women constitute the overwhelming majority of sufferers. The onset of acute math anxiety during the teen-age years is, as Stalin was fond of saying, "not by accident."

8 In adolescence girls begin to fear that they will be unattractive to boys if they are typed as "brains." Science and math epitomize unfeminine braininess in a way that, say, foreign languages do not. High-school girls who pursue an advanced interest in science and math (unless they are students at special institutions like the Bronx High School of Science where everyone is a brain) usually find that they are greatly outnumbered by boys in their classes. They are, therefore, introduing on male turf at a time when their sexual confidence, as well as that of the boys, is most fragile.

9 A 1981 assessment of female achievement in mathematics, based on research conducted under a National Institute for Education grant, found significant differences in the mathematical achievements of 9th and 12th graders. At age 13 girls were equal to or slightly better than boys in tests involving algebra, problem solving and spatial ability; four years later the boys had outstripped the girls.

10 It is not mysterious that some very bright high-school girls suddenly decide that math is "too hard" and "a waste of time." In my experience, self-sabotage of mathematical and scientific ability is often a conscious process. I remember deliberately pretending to be puzzled by geometry

problems in my sophomore year in high school. A male teacher called me in after class and said, in a baffled tone, "I don't see how you can be having so much trouble when you got straight A's last year in my algebra class."

The decision to avoid advanced biology, chemistry, 11 physics and calculus in high school automatically restricts academic and professional choices that ought to be wide open to anyone beginning college. At all coeducational universities women are overwhelmingly concentrated in the fine arts, social sciences and traditionally female departments like education. Courses leading to degrees in science- and technology-related fields are filled mainly by men.

In my generation, the practical consequences of 12 mathematical and scientific illiteracy are visible in the large number of special programs to help professional women overcome the anxiety they feel when they are promoted into jobs that require them to handle statistics.

The consequences of this syndrome should not, how- 13 ever, be viewed in narrowly professional terms. Competence in science and math does not mean one is going to become a scientist or mathematician any more than competence in writing English means one is going to become a professional writer. Scientific and mathematical illiteracy—which has been cited in several recent critiques by panels studying American education from kindergarten through college— produces an incalculably impoverished vision of human experience.

Scientific illiteracy is not, of course, the exclusive 14 province of women. In certain intellectual circles it has become fashionable to proclaim a willed, aggressive ignorance about science and technology. Some female writers specialize in ominous, uninformed diatribes against genetic research as a plot to remove control of childbearing from women, while some well-known men of letters proudly announce that they understand absolutely nothing about computers, or, for that matter, about electricity. This lack of understanding is nothing in which women or men ought to take pride.

Failure to comprehend either computers or chro- 15

mosomes leads to a terrible sense of helplessness, because the profound impact of science on everyday life is evident even to those who insist they don't, won't, can't understand why the changes are taking place. At this stage of history women are more prone to such feelings of helplessness than men because the culture judges their ignorance less harshly and because women themselves acquiesce in that indulgence.

Since there is ample evidence of such feelings in 16 adolescence, it is up to parents to see that their daughters do not accede to the old stereotypes about "masculine" and "feminine" knowledge. Unless we want our daughters to share our intellectual handicaps, we had better tell them no, they can't stop taking mathematics and science at the ripe old age of 16.

BUILDING VOCABULARY

1. Like Anne Roiphe (pages 249–254), Susan Jacoby uses a number of common expressions, but these are at a higher level of *diction* (the writer's choice of words depending on audience and purpose). Below are some of these expressions, which may contain words that are unfamiliar to you. First, look up any unfamiliar words in your dictionary. Then, write a short explanation of each expression as Jacoby uses it.

    a. sure footing (par. 3)
    b. cultural expectations (par. 4)
    c. overwhelming majority (par. 7)
    d. male turf (par. 8)
    e. spatial ability (par. 9).
    f. the exclusive province (par. 14)
    g. ominous, uninformed diatribes (par. 14)
    h. acquiesce in that indulgence (par. 15)
    i. ample evidence (par. 16)
    j. our intellectual handicaps (par. 16)

2. Explain the connotations (see Glossary) that the following words have for you: "disability" (par. 3), "conspire" (par. 4), adolescent (par. 4), "vulnerable" (par. 6), "acute"

(par. 8). Use each of these words correctly in sentences of your own.

UNDERSTANDING THE WRITER'S IDEAS

1. What condition is Jacoby trying to analyze? Is the main *effect* analyzed in this cause-and-effect analysis? On what primary cause does she blame women's "scientific and mathematical ignorance"? What exactly does she mean by that term? How is society to blame? What is the "process" mentioned in paragraph 4? What point does the example of Rosalyn S. Yalow illustrate?

2. Why does Jacoby think that the greater proportion of women students now in science and medical graduate and professional schools does not really mean that there are many women working in these areas?

3. According to Jacoby, when do most girls decide not to study the sciences? Why does this happen?

4. What is "math anxiety"? Who suffers more from it—boys or girls? Why? What does the author mean by "brains" (par. 8)?

5. Who was Joseph Stalin (par. 7)?

6. What subjects does Jacoby identify as "feminine"? Which are "unfeminine"?

7. According to the research evidence discussed in paragraph 9, how do the math abilities of girls and boys change between ninth and tenth grades? What does Jacoby say is the *cause* for this change? What are the *results*?

8. Explain what Jacoby means by the expression "self-inflicted female wound" (par. 4) and "self-sabotage" (par. 10). How are these expressions similar? How are they different?

9. What is the difference between what men and women study at coeducational universities?

10. What does Jacoby mean by "mathematical and scientific illiteracy" (par. 12)? Do only women suffer from this syndrome? According to Jacoby, why does it lead to "an incalculably impoverished vision of human experience"? What does she mean by this phrase? What examples of scientific illiteracy does Jacoby offer?

11. Why does the author think women feel more helpless than men do about scientific changes?

12. What suggestion does Jacoby offer in her conclusion?

UNDERSTANDING THE WRITER'S TECHNIQUES

1. Which paragraphs make up the introductory section of this essay? What cause-and-effect relationship does Jacoby establish and how does she present it? How does Jacoby use narration in her introduction? How does she use illustration?

2. What is the thesis statement of this essay? Why is it placed where it is? Find another statement before it that expresses a similar cause-and-effect relationship. How are the two different?

3. Both sentences of paragraph 5 begin with the phrase "It is true," yet the sentences contradict each other. How and why does the author set up this contradiction? What is the effect on Jacoby's analysis of beginning paragraph 6 with the words "the real problem is . . ."?

4. How does she use *process analysis* (see pages 214–215) from paragraph 6 to paragraph 8?

5. Where does the author use definition in this essay?

6. Trace the cause-and-effect developments in paragraphs 7 and 8.

7. In paragraph 9, Jacoby mentions a study conducted under "a National Institute for Education grant." How does the evidence she presents support her position in the essay?

8. What is the effect of the phrase "in my experience" in paragraph 10? What expository technique does she use there?

9. Trace the cause-and-effect patterns in paragraphs 11 through 13. Be sure to show the interrelationship between the causes and the effects (that is, how can the effect of something also be the cause of something else?).

10. How is the first sentence of paragraph 15 ("Failure to comprehend . . .") a good example in itself of cause-and-effect development?

11. Why does Jacoby use quotation marks around the words "masculine" and "feminine" in the phrase " 'masculine' and 'feminine' knowledge" (par. 16)?

12. What is the overall tone of this essay? At three points, Jacoby switches tone and uses irony (see Glossary). Explain the irony in the following sentences:

  a. "What does it matter if, at age 16, she had taken a step that may limit her understanding of both machines and the natural world for the rest of her life?" (par. 2)

  b. "The onset of acute math anxiety during the teen-age years is, as Stalin was fond of saying, 'not by accident'." (par. 7)

  c. "Unless we want our daughters to share our intellectual handicaps, we had better tell them no, they can't stop taking mathematics and science at the ripe old age of 16." (par. 16)

Compare the irony in paragraph 16 with that in paragraph 2. How is the impact the same or different?

13. Who do you think is the intended *audience* for this essay? Cite evidence for your answer.

14. Jacoby uses a variety of transitional devices to connect smoothly the ideas expressed in the various paragraphs of this essay. Look especially at paragraphs 1 to 4. How does the writer achieve coherence between paragraphs? What transitional elements do you find in the opening sentences of each of those paragraphs? What other transitions do you find throughout the essay?

EXPLORING THE WRITER'S IDEAS

1. One of the underlying suggestions in this essay is that the society has long considered there to be "masculine" and "feminine" subjects to study. What is your opinion on this issue? Do you feel that any subjects are particularly more suited to men or women? Which? Why? Are there any other school activities that you feel are exclusively masculine or feminine? Why? Are there any jobs that are more suited to men or women?

2. In paragraph 4, Jacoby mentions the "old expectations about women's interests." What do you think these expectations are? What do you consider *new* expectations for women?

3. A *stereotype* is an opinion of a category of people that is unoriginal and often based in strong prejudices. For example, some prejudicial stereotypes include "All immigrants are lazy"; "All Republicans are rich"; "All women are terrible drivers." What other stereotypes do you know? Where do you think they originate? (Reread Berlitz's essay on pages 165–170.)

4. Reread the essay by Richard Restak on pages 122–127. How do Restak's ideas compare with Jacoby's? Do you agree more with either one? Why?

5. The general implication of paragraph 8 is that people minimize their skills in order to be socially acceptable. In your experience, where have you seen this principle operating? Do people sometimes pretend to be unable to achieve something? What motivates them, do you think?

6. A recent study shows that among major nations in the world America's students—boys and girls—are the worst mathematics students. How do you account for the poor showing of Americans as mathematicians? How would you remedy this situation?

IDEAS FOR WRITING

Guided Writing

Select a job or profession that is usually male-dominated. Write a cause-and-effect analysis explaining how and why women both have been excluded from this profession *and* (or) have self-selected themselves from the job. (Some examples may include firefighters, physicians, marines, bank executives, carpenters, and so on.)

1. Begin with an anecdote to illustrate the condition that you are analyzing.

2. Present and analyze the partial causes of this condition that arise from society's expectations and norms.

3. State your main point clearly in a thesis statement.

4. Clearly identify what you consider "the real problem."

5. If you believe that women have deliberately excluded themselves, explain when and how the process of self-selection begins for women.

6. Analyze the consequences of this process of self-selection and give examples of the results of it.

7. Provide evidence that supports your analysis.

8. Link paragraphs with appropriate transitions.

9. In your conclusion offer a suggestion to change or improve this situation.

More Writing Projects

1. Margaret Mead, the famous anthropologist, once wrote, "Women in our society complain of the lack of stimulation, of the loneliness, of the dullness of staying at home." Write a causal analysis of this situation.

2. Write an analysis of why boys and men exclude themselves from a certain field of profession—nursing, cooking, grammar-school teaching, and so on.

9

Argumentation
and Persuasion

Argumentation in prose is an attempt to convince the reader to have the opinion *you* have on a subject; frequently, it also involves an effort to persuade the reader to act in a particular manner. In many ways, argumentation is a good end point for a course in writing. In a formal argument, you can use, according to your purpose, all the prose strategies and principles of sound composition practiced until now.

You can see how important it is to state your thesis very clearly in argumentation, and to support your main point with convincing minor points. You have to make these points according to reason, and you need to arrange them so they have the greatest effect on your reader. Moreover, as in any prose, writers of argument must offer the reader particulars of details, whether sensory, quoted, statistical, or based upon historical evidence. Finally, techniques of comparison, process analysis, description, narration, cause and effect, definition, all can help strengthen an argument.

Although argumentation reflects all these earlier prose techniques, it is important for you to understand the special characteristics of this method. To begin with, although argumentation as a written form is often emotional, it differs sharply from those little battles and those major disagreements with friends over coffee or in hallways outside class. Perhaps that last shouting match between you and your friend about who would win the World Series is, no doubt, one that you would call an argument: There is a disagreement there for which each of you tries to make your own point of view stick. Yet often these argumentative conversations deteriorate into loss of temper, angry personal comments about your friend's judgment or character, departures from the argument itself, and inability to reason.

In written arguments, writers always should keep clearly in mind the point they wish to make, and should not lose sight of it. They may try to convince readers that some issue requires action ("Colleges and businesses should follow special admissions procedures for minority applicants"). Or, they may try to convince readers that something is true ("wives are taken for granted"). Whatever the point, writers always offer their reasons for their beliefs in a logical way, without losing command of their subject and without attacking anyone personally; they may, though, attack someone's ideas or attitudes.

The main point in an argument—often termed the *major proposition*—is an idea which is debatable or can be disputed. As such it differs from theses in ordinary essays, which state main ideas without necessarily taking sides. The major proposition gives an essay its "argumentative edge." Frequently this argumentative edge appears in the very title of the essay, and it should form the basis of a crisp introductory paragraph laying out the terms of the position that you plan to take.

Once you state clearly and carefully your major proposition at the outset of the essay, you must then proceed to *convince* readers about the position that you have taken. There are basic strategies to succeed in this goal, beginning with the ordered presentation of reasons to defend the major proposition. We term these reasons *minor propositions*—in other words, assertions designed to support your main argument. To support each minor proposition, the writer must offer *evidence* in the form of facts, statistics, testimony from authorities, and personal experience. Here, a variety of writing methods, ranging from comparison and contrast to definition to causal analysis, can serve to develop minor propositions effectively.

In addition to presenting your own argument logically and convincingly, you must also recognize and deal with opposing arguments, a technique called *refutation*. Obviously, there has to be more than one side to any debatable issue, and you have to take this fact into account. For one thing, acknowledgment of the opposition indicates fairness on your part—a willingness to recognize that there *are* two sides to the argument. More significantly, your refutation of rival propositions, both major and minor, makes your own case more convincing. Whether at the outset of your argumentative essay or in the body as you are developing your own minor propositions, you should take care to indicate opposing views and to refute them effectively.

An argumentative essay ultimately is only as strong as the logic that a writer brings to it. Such logical errors as hasty generalizations (main ideas unsupported by sufficient evidence), attacks on the opposition's character, faulty conclusions that do not follow from the facts, faulty analogies, and excessive appeals to emotion damage your argument. In short, any convincing argument requires clear, orderly thinking. By learning how to present ideas logically through the preparation of convincing argumentative essays, you will strengthen your overall reasoning ability. You will also learn how to deal with those arguments, many of which are important, that occur in your daily life.

Jane Doe

I WISH THEY'D DO IT RIGHT

In this essay from the *New York Times,* a mother who wishes not to be identified (hence, the name Jane Doe, a pseudonym) argues against a feature of her son's life-style. As you read this selection, notice how the author attempts to understand her son's position, while maintaining and supporting her own.

Words to Watch

appraised (par. 2): told the value
Leboyer (par. 2): a physician whose ideas on birth without violence have drawn many followers to his method
legitimacy (par. 2): fact of being legal
surfeited (par. 7): filled with excess amount
executing (par. 7): carrying out
wedlock (par. 8): state of marriage
facetious (par. 8): amusing; humorous
bypassing (par. 9): avoiding
sanctuary (par. 12): holy place
assiduously (par. 12): constantly
foibles (par. 13): weaknesses of character
mandated (par. 13): commanded
adamancy (par. 14): stubbornness
harassment (par. 15): attacks; disturbances

My son and his wife are not married. They have lived together for seven years without benefit of license. Though occasionally marriage has been a subject of conjecture, it did not seem important until the day they announced, jubilantly, that they were going to have a child. It was happy news. I was ready and eager to become a grandmother. Now, I thought, they will take the final step and make their relationship legal.

I was appraised of the Lamaze method of natural childbirth. I was prepared by Leboyer for birth without violence. I admired the expectant mother's discipline. She ate only organic foods, abstained from alcohol, avoided insecticides, smog and trauma. Every precaution was taken to insure the arrival of a healthy, happy infant. No royal birth had been prepared for more auspiciously. All that was lacking was legitimacy.

Finally, when my grandson was two weeks old, I dared to question their intentions.

"We don't believe in marriage," was all that was volunteered.

"Not even for your son's sake?" I asked. "Maybe he will."

Their eyes were impenetrable, their faces stiffened to masks. "You wouldn't understand," I was told.

And I don't. Surely they cannot believe they are pioneering, making revolutionary changes in society. That frontier has long been tamed. Today marriage offers all the options. Books and talk shows have surfeited us with the freedom offered in open marriage. Lawyers, psychologists and marriage counselors are growing rich executing marriage contracts. And divorce, should it come to that, is in most states easy and inexpensive.

On the other hand, living together out of wedlock can be economically impractical as well as socially awkward. How do I present her—as my son's roommate? his spouse? his spice, as one facetious friend suggested? Even my son flounders in these waters. Recently, I heard him refer to her as his girl friend. I cannot believe that that description will be endearing to their son when he is able to understand.

I have resolved that problem for myself, bypassing 9
their omission, introducing her as she is, as my daughter-
in-law. But my son, in militant support of his ideology,
refutes any assumption, however casual, that they have
taken vows.

There are economic benefits which they are denying 10
themselves. When they applied for housing in the married-
students dormitory of the university where he is seeking his
doctorate, they were asked for their marriage certificate.
Not having one, they were forced to find other, more
expensive quarters off campus. Her medical insurance,
provided by the company where she was employed, was
denied him. He is not her husband. There have been and
will be other inconveniences they have elected to endure.

Their son will not enjoy the luxury of choice about 11
the inconveniences and scurrility to which he will be subject
from those of his peers and elders who dislike and fear
society's nonconformists.

And if in the future, his parents should decide to 12
separate, will he not suffer greater damage than the child
of divorce, who may find comfort in the knowledge that his
parents once believed they could live happily ever after, and
committed themselves to that idea? The child of unwed
parents has no sanctuary. His mother and father have
assiduously avoided a pledge of permanency, leaving him
drifting and insecure.

I know my son is motivated by idealism and honesty 13
in his reluctance to concede to what he considers mere
ceremony. But is he wise enough to know that no one
individual can fight all of society's foibles and frauds. Why
does he persist in this, a battle already lost? Because though
he rejects marriage, California, his residence, has declared
that while couples living together in imitation of marriage
are no longer under the jurisdiction of the family court, their
relationship is viewed by the state as an implicit contract
somewhat like a business agreement. This position was
mandated when equal property rights were granted a woman
who had been abandoned by the man she had lived with for
a number of years.

Finally, the couple's adamancy has been depriving 14
to all the rest of the family. There has been no celebration
of wedding or anniversaries. There has been concealment
from certain family elders who could not cope with the
situation. Its irregularity has put constraint on the grandparents, who are stifled by one another's possible embarrassment or hurt.

I hope that one day very soon my son and his wife 15
will acknowledge their cohabitation with a license. The rest
of us will not love them any more for it. We love and support
them as much as possible now. But it will be easier and
happier for us knowing that our grandson will be spared the
continued explanation and harassment, the doubts and
anxieties of being a child of unmarried parents.

BUILDING VOCABULARY

1. Check the definitions of each of these words.
Then explain how its prefix and/or suffix, named alongside,
contributes to its meaning.

Prefix or Suffix

a. conjecture (par. 1)	con	
b. impenetrable (par. 3)	im	able
c. concede (par. 13)	con	
d. concealment (par. 14)	con	ment
e. constraint (par. 14)	con	
f. cohabitation (par. 15)	co	tion

2. You know that by changing the form of a word
(and, as a result, usually its grammatical function) you can
change its meaning. Determine the definition of each word
in Column A below. Then, write a definition of the word
related to it in Column B.

Column A	Column B
jubilantly (par. 1)	jubilation

abstained (par. 2)	abstention
trauma (par. 2)	traumatic
auspiciously (par. 2)	inauspicious
endearing (par. 8)	endearment
militant (par. 10)	militancy
endure (par. 10)	endurable
scurrility (par. 11)	scurrilous
implicit (par. 13)	implied
stifled (par. 14)	stifling

3. Write original sentences for any five words defined in the Words to Watch section.

UNDERSTANDING THE WRITER'S IDEAS

1. Why did the writer think her son should get married?

2. Why does she compare the coming birth of her son's child to a "royal birth"?

3. Why does she not understand when her son and his woman say that they do not believe in marriage?

4. Why does the writer believe that marriage offers all the options? What is "open marriage"?

5. Why does the writer have problems in introducing her son's girlfriend? Why does she think that living together without being married is impractical?

6. What problems does she forsee for her grandchild if his parents do not marry?

7. What law did the state of California pass in regard to couples who live together? How, according to the writer, has this affected her son's decision.

8. How has the rest of the family been deprived, according to the writer?

UNDERSTANDING THE WRITER'S TECHNIQUES

1. What is Doe's major premise in this essay? One sentence about a third of the way through could be called the *thesis sentence*. Which do you think it is?

2. It is not until paragraph 7 that the writer actually begins arguing her point. What is the purpose of paragraphs 1 and 2? Are they necessary to the essay? Why?

3. What minor premise does she make and develop in paragraph 7?

4. In paragraph 8 she takes up the problems that she sees for people who do not agree with her point; in the rest of the essay she offers several minor premises to explain what those problems would be. What minor premise do paragraphs 8 and 9 develop? paragraph 10? 11 and 12? 14?

5. Paragraph 13 attempts to set up a *causal* relationship. What is it? Does the writer convince you of the reason for her son's behavior?

6. What is the *tone* of this essay (see Glossary)? Would you say the writing shows *anger, indifference, control, distance, coolness, passion,* or *resignation*? Support your response.

7. In this essay the writer uses the *passive voice* in a number of places. (A sentence like "I was told" is passive: The subject of the sentence is acted upon; it does not itself carry out some action.) A passive construction helps a writer stress an action that is performed, and helps avoid a stress on the person or thing performing that action. Usually too many passives weaken a writer's style. What examples of passive voice do you find here? Has the writer used passive effectively, or has she overused it? Does the passive voice contribute anything to the tone?

8. Comment on the writer's use of transitions in the first sentence of each of these paragraphs: 3, 7, 8, 9, 12, 14.

9. How do the closing paragraphs serve as a summary of the writer's position? Why does she focus on the unborn child at the end? Is this reference sentimental (see Glossary)? Does Doe rely on other emotional appeals throughout her essay? List examples.

10. Where in the essay does the writer deal with the opposition—the reasons why her son and his woman might *not* want to marry? Should she have offered any other opposing arguments to strengthen her own position? Or, do

you think she was wise in avoiding too much discussion of the opposition's point of view?

EXPLORING THE WRITER'S IDEAS

1. Why do you think many young people in our current times often decide not to marry, despite the fact that they live together and have children? What benefits do you see in such arrangements? What problems, other than those Doe spells out, do you see?

2. The writer says she cannot understand the life-style her son and his woman have chosen. Is this simply a reflection of the "generation gap"? Or, do you think there are more basic, philosophical differences here that transcend age?

3. Do you agree with the writer's view of the problems for the child if it is born illegitimate? Why? Are people today more willing than in the past to accept socially a child born to unwed parents? Why?

4. Several of the writer's points focus on the problems unmarried couples cause their families. Should young people consider the effects of their decisions on their parents? Why or why not?

5. The writer suggests that her son's idealism is an important factor in his behavior. What is "idealism"? Do you agree that "no one individual can fight all of society's foibles and frauds"? Why? Is it possible to be an idealist and to live happily in today's world?

6. By the title the author suggests that there is a "right" and a "wrong" way. Is it possible that these are merely *alternative* ways, the traditional view of marriage and the more contemporary concept of "living together"? Should there be room in this society (politically, legally, economically, socially) for alternative life-styles? Why?

7. Many people say that in a "living together" relationship, the woman suffers most because the man, if he leaves, avoids all responsibilities for woman, child, and home. Do you agree? Why?

8. What is a "common law marriage"? Does your state recognize such marriages as legal?

WRITING PROJECTS

Guided Writing

Write an essay in which you explain the advantages of a young man and woman living together unmarried. (You might even write this from the point of view of Jane Doe's son or daughter-in-law.)

1. Decide on the main thrust of your essay and write a thesis statement which makes clear your major premise.

2. In two or three paragraphs describe briefly the most convincing reasons for life together without marriage. Give specific illustrations to support your point.

3. In the rest of the essay discuss the problems for a young man and woman who *do* get married, problems which living together without marriage does not bring up. (These are your *minor premises*.) Again, be specific in offering reasons to explain why marriage is *not* an attractive alternative for two people who love each other.

4. Connect your ideas with carefully chosen transitions.

5. Save your most convincing minor premise for last.

6. Write a conclusion summarizing your main argument.

More Writing Projects

1. Write an essay in which you defend or oppose some other "alternative life-style" available in today's culture. You might wish to argue for or against communal living, open marriage, or homosexuality, for example.

2. Write an essay in which you argue about the responsibilities an adult should (or should not) have to his parents.

Joseph Wood Krutch

THE VANDAL AND
THE SPORTSMAN

Joseph Wood Krutch is a renowned author, scholar, and
social commentator. Here he argues forcefully—sometimes
even righteously—against sports hunting. He uses language for its fullest impact, telling us of "pure evil," "a
fathomless abyss," and "wicked ideas." This essay, from
The Best Nature Writing of Joseph Wood Krutch, is a
model of both logical and emotional appeal in argumentative writing.

Words to Watch

impediment (par. 8): obstacle
vitality (par. 3): the quality distinguishing the living from the
    dead
wantonly (par. 3): without moral restraint
unassailable (par. 5): unquestionable
compassion (par. 6): deep understanding of others' feelings
quail (par. 7): a stout-bodied game bird
delinquency (par. 7): living immorally
cultivate (par. 7): develop

It would not be quite true to say that "some of my 1
best friends are hunters." Nevertheless, I do number among
my respected acquaintances some who not only kill for the

sake of killing but count it among their keenest pleasures. I can think of no better illustration of the fact that men may be separated at some point by a fathomless abyss yet share elsewhere much common ground.

To me it is inconceivable how anyone should think 2 an animal more interesting dead than alive. I can also easily prove to my own satisfaction that killing "for sport" is the perfect type of that pure evil for which metaphysicians have sometimes sought.

Most wicked deeds are done because the doer pro- 3 poses some good to himself. The liar lies to gain some end; the swindler and thief want things which, if honestly got, might be good in themselves. Even the murderer may be removing an impediment to normal desires or gaining possession of something which his victim keeps from him. None of these usually does evil for evil's sake. They are selfish or unscrupulous, but their deeds are not gratuitously evil. The killer for sport has no such comprehensible motive. He prefers death to life, darkness to light. He gets nothing except the satisfaction of saying, "Something which wanted to live is dead. There is that much less vitality, consciousness, and, perhaps, joy in the universe. I am the Spirit that Denies." When a man wantonly destroys one of the works of man we call him Vandal. When he wantonly destroys one of the works of God we call him Sportsman.

The hunter-for-food may be as wicked and as mis- 4 guided as vegetarians sometimes say; but he does not kill for the sake of killing. The rancher and the farmer who exterminate all living things not immediately profitable to them may sometimes be working against their own best interests; but whether they are or are not, the hope to achieve some supposed good by their exterminations. If to do evil not in the hope of gain but for evil's sake involves the deepest guilt by which man can be stained, then killing for killing's sake is a terrifying phenomenon and as strong a proof as we could have of that "reality of evil" with which present-day theologians are again concerned.

Despite all this I know that sportsmen are not 5 necessarily monsters. Even if the logic of my position is unassailable, the fact still remains that men are not logical creatures; that most if not all are blind to much they might be expected to see and are habitually inconsistent; that both the blind spots and the inconsistencies vary from person to person.

To say as we all do: "Any man who would do A 6 would do B," is to state a proposition mercifully proved false almost as often as it is stated. The murderer is not necessarily a liar any more than the liar is necessarily a murderer, and few men feel that if they break one commandment there is little use in keeping the others. Many have been known to say that they considered adultery worse than homicide but not all adulterers are potential murderers and there are even murderers to whom incontinence would be unthinkable. So the sportsman may exhibit any of the virtues—including compassion and respect for life—everywhere except in connection with his "sporting" activities. It may even be often enough true that, as "antisentimentalists" are fond of pointing out, those tenderest toward animals are not necessarily most philanthropic. They no more than sportsmen are always consistent.

When the Winchester gun company makes a prop- 7 aganda movie concluding with a scene in which a "typical American boy" shoots a number of quail and when it then ends with the slogan "Go hunting with your boy and you'll never have to go hunting for him," I may suspect that the gun company is moved by a desire to sell more guns at least as much as by a determination to do what it can toward reducing the incidence of delinquency. I will certainly add also my belief that there are even better ways of diminishing the likelihood that a boy will grow up to do even worse things. Though it seems to me that he is being taught a pure evil I know that he will not necessarily cultivate a taste for all or, for that matter, any one of the innumerable other forms under which evil may be loved.

BUILDING VOCABULARY

1. Match the words or phrases in Column A with a word or phrase in Column B which most closely matches its meaning.

Column A	Column B
a. keenest (par. 1)	1. immeasurable depths
b. fathomless abyss (par. 1)	2. ideas used to damage an opposing cause
c. pure evil (par. 2)	3. understandable reason
d. gratuitously evil (par. 3)	4. dishonest
e. unscrupulous (par. 3)	5. absolute immorality
f. comprehensible motive (par. 3)	6. lack of self-restraint
g. habitually inconsistent (par. 5)	7. most special
h. incontinence (par. 6)	8. with great generosity
i. philanthropic (par. 6)	9. usually changeable
j. propaganda (par. 7)	10. vicious without cause

2. Both "metaphysicians" (par. 2) and "theologians" (par. 4) deal with questions of virtues (par. 6). Look up each word and write a definition.

3. What are the crimes of "adultery" and "homicide" (par. 6)?

UNDERSTANDING THE WRITER'S IDEAS

1. Does Krutch have many close friends who are hunters? How do you know? What does he think of his acquaintances that do enjoy hunting? Explain the sentence that tells you this information.

2. What is Krutch's opinion of hunting as a sport?

3. According to Krutch, what is the major motivation for which people do bad things? What examples does he offer to support his opinion? What does Krutch say is the primary motivation for sports hunters? How does this motivation differ from that of other "evil doers"?

4. For what does the author substitute the phrase "killer for sport" (par. 3)? Why?

5. Explain the difference between a Vandal and a Sportsman in your own words.

6. How are the hunters-for-food different from sports hunters? How are the ranchers and farmers different?

7. Try to explain the meaning of the sentence at the end of paragraph 4 which begins, "If to do evil. . . ."

8. Explain the statement "men are not logical creatures" (par. 5) as it is used by Krutch in this essay.

9. What excuses does the author offer for sports hunters? Do you feel he believes these excuses? Why? In paragraph 6 what does he say about the ethics of sports hunting?

10. What does the phrase "if they break one commandment" refer to?

11. What is the Winchester gun company? What is Krutch's opinion of the film made by that company?

UNDERSTANDING THE WRITER'S TECHNIQUES

1. In your own words, what is Krutch's *major proposition* in this essay? Does he ever state it as a single thesis statement? Why?

2. How does Krutch use logical explanation and appeals to intelligence in this essay? What is he trying to "prove"?

3. A special type of argumentative strategy is *ethical* appeal, in which the writer addresses the moral standards of his or her audience. What is the nature of Krutch's ethical appeal? How is it presented?

4. Throughout this essay Krutch uses very emotionally charged language to describe or explain things. One of the techniques of argumentation is to use such language subtly to influence your readers' opinions. For example, in paragraph 3, Krutch helps the reader to make unconscious connections between a sports hunter and "wicked deeds," a "liar," a "swindler," a "thief," and a "murderer." How and why does he do this?

Read through the essay once again and find as many other examples of emotionally charged language as you can. How do these emotional or nonlogical appeals affect Krutch's intended audience?

5. One of the techniques the author uses is to put quotation marks (" ") around words or groups of words other than for the purpose of quotation or citation. What does the quotation mark indicate about the enclosed words? Find all

the places Krutch uses this technique and explain the meaning of each word or phrase.

6. Krutch also uses exaggeration to influence his readers. *Hyperbole* is a type of very extravagant exaggeration—heightened exaggeration, so to speak. Explain the hyperbole of the last part of paragraph 3, from "the Killer for sport had . . ." to the end. How does this section influence your opinion? Why?

7. A good argumentative essay will in some way deal with the opposition's argument to show that the writer has at least recognized that differing opinions exist. Usually, however, a writer will rebut (disprove) the opposition argument to enhance the correctness of his or her own opinions. Where in this essay does Krutch present the opposition argument? How does he deal with it? How does he feel about the correctness of his own opinions? What one sentence tells us so?

8. What is the tone of this essay? Give at least three examples to support your answer, at lease one of which should come from the introductory paragraph.

9. What is the purpose of the discussion of the film made by the Winchester gun company? How does it connect to the rest of the essay? How does Krutch use *extended example* (see page 66) in this discussion?

10. Explain the significance of the title.

EXPLORING THE WRITER'S IDEAS

1. In paragraph 3, Krutch compares sports hunters to liars, thieves, even murderers. Do you think they are comparable? Why?

Krutch also says sports hunters enjoy killing and death. Do you agree or disagree? Why?

2. Krutch makes a distinction between hunters-for-food and sports hunters. What do you think are the differences between the two? Do you feel either is more or less justified in his or her activity? Why?

3. The expression in quotations in the first paragraph ("some of my best friends are hunters") is a parody

of an expression often used by people attempting to hide or defend their prejudices. For example, a person might say, "But some of my best friends are Jewish (or black, or Irish, or Chinese, or . . .)" after making an ethnic slur or offensive remark. What is the purpose of Krutch's parody here? What does it tell us about the author?

4. Are there degrees of humaneness in sports hunting? For example, is it more humane to use a rifle, a shotgun, or a bow and arrow? Why?

If you have ever gone sports hunting, describe how you felt when you pulled the trigger or let the arrow fly. Explain what made you feel this way.

5. Research the sports hunting laws in your state. What are they? Do you think they are fair? If possible, find out on what basis some of the laws, quotas, and restrictions were made.

6. Krutch is very forceful and dogmatic in this essay, perhaps even a bit self-righteous at times. For instance, in paragraph 5 he says, ". . . the logic of my position is unassailable." How did the tone of this essay affect you? Were you ever put off by it or did it draw you nearer to the writer's position?

IDEAS FOR WRITING

Guided Writing

Write an argumentative essay in which you support or oppose hunting.

1. Acknowledge your opposition in the first paragraph of the essay. Explain your possible closeness to such individuals, but take a critical attitude toward their position regarding hunting.

2. Tell why it is "inconceivable" to you that anyone would support or oppose hunting.

3. Logically refute the propositions of those who oppose your position. After explaining your opposition's viewpoint, you can *deny* that their point is right or true; or

you can *admit* that what they say seems reasonable, but that they have left out important ideas; or you can try to find a *shortcoming* in the way they reason about the topic.

4. Make your essay strong in *emotional* appeals. Lace your essay generously with emotionally charged terms and comparisons.

5. Introduce *ethical* appeals in support of your argument.

6. Carefully draw distinctions between different types of opponents.

7. End your essay with an extended example from an outside source that substantiates your proposition, that is, that puts your opponents in an unfavorable position.

More Writing Projects

1. Write a letter to the editor in which you argue for or against handgun controls.

2. Write an argumentative essay that responds to the following quotation from the American novelist and screenplay writer Nathaniel West: "In America violence is daily."

Judy Syfers

I WANT A WIFE

Judy Syfers, a wife, and mother of two children, argues in this essay for a wife of her own. Although her argument might seem strange, her position will become apparent once you move into the essay. She presents many points to support her position, so you want to keep in mind those you think are the strongest.

Words to Watch

nurturant (par. 3): someone who feeds and takes care of children as they grow up
hors d'oeuvres (par. 6): food served before the regular courses of the meal
monogamy (par. 8): the habit of having only one mate; the practice of marrying only once during life

I belong to that classification of people known as 1 wives. I am A Wife. And, not altogether incidentally, I am a mother.

Not too long ago a male friend of mine appeared on 2 the scene fresh from a recent divorce. He had one child, who is, of course, with his ex-wife. He is obviously looking for another wife. As I thought about him while I was ironing one evening, it suddenly occurred to me that I, too, would like to have a wife. Why do I want a wife?

I would like to go back to school so that I can become 3 economically independent, support myself, and, if need be, support those dependent upon me. I want a wife who will work and send me to school. And while I am going to school I want a wife to keep track of the children's doctor and dentist appointments. And to keep track of mine, too. I want a wife to make sure my children eat properly and are kept clean. I want a wife who will wash the children's clothes and keep them mended. I want a wife who is a good nurturant attendant to my children, who arranges for their schooling, makes sure that they have an adequate social life with their peers, takes them to the park, the zoo, etc. I want a wife who takes care of the children when they are sick, a wife who arranges to be around when the children need special care, because, of course, I cannot miss classes at school. My wife must arrange to lose time at work and not lose the job. It may mean a small cut in my wife's income from time to time, but I guess I can tolerate that. Needless to say, my wife will arrange and pay for the care of the children while my wife is working.

I want a wife who will take care of *my* physical 4 needs. I want a wife who will keep my house clean. A wife who will pick up after me. I want a wife who will keep my clothes clean, ironed, mended, replaced when need be, and who will see to it that my personal things are kept in their proper place so that I can find what I need the minute I need it. I want a wife who cooks the meals, a wife who is a *good* cook. I want a wife who will plan the menus, do the necessary grocery shopping, prepare the meals, serve them pleasantly, and then do the cleaning up while I do my studying. I want a wife who will care for me when I am sick and sympathize with my pain and loss of time from school. I want a wife to go along when our family takes a vacation so that someone can continue to care for me and my children when I need a rest and change of scene.

I want a wife who will not bother me with rambling 5 complaints about a wife's duties. But I want a wife who will listen to me when I feel the need to explain a rather difficult point I have come across in my course of studies. And I want a wife who will type my papers for me when I have written them.

I want a wife who will take care of the details of my 6 social life. When my wife and I are invited out by my friends, I want a wife who will take care of the babysitting arrangements. When I meet people at school that I like and want to entertain, I want a wife who will have the house clean, will prepare a special meal, serve it to me and my friends, and not interrupt when I talk about the things that interest me and my friends. I want a wife who will have arranged that the children are fed and ready for bed before my guests arrive so that the children do not bother us. I want a wife who takes care of the needs of my guests so that they feel comfortable, who makes sure that they have an ashtray, that they are passed the hors d'oeuvres, that they are offered a second helping of the food, that their wine glasses are replenished when necessary, that their coffee is served to them as they like it.

And I want a wife who knows that sometimes I need 7 a night out by myself.

I want a wife who is sensitive to my sexual needs, 8 a wife who makes love passionately and eagerly when I feel like it, a wife who makes sure that I am satisfied. And, of course, I want a wife who will not demand sexual attention when I am not in the mood for it. I want a wife who assumes the complete responsibility for birth control, because I do not want more children. I want a wife who will remain sexually faithful to me so that I do not have to clutter up my intellectual life with jealousies. And I want a wife who understands that *my* sexual needs may entail more than strict adherence to monogamy. I must, after all, be able to relate to people as fully as possible.

If, by chance, I find another person more suitable as 9 a wife than the wife I already have, I want the liberty to replace my present wife with another one. Naturally, I will expect a fresh, new life; my wife will take the children and be solely-responsible for them so that I am left free.

When I am through with school and have a job, I 10
want my wife to quit working and remain at home so that
my wife can more fully and completely take care of a wife's
duties.

My God, who *wouldn't* want a wife? 11

BUILDING VOCABULARY

1. After checking a dictionary write definitions of
each of these words:

     a. attendant (par. 3)
     b. adequate (par. 3)
     c. peers (par. 3)
     d. tolerate (par. 3)
     e. rambling (par. 5)
     f. replenished (par. 6)
     g. adherence (par. 8)

2. Write an original sentence for each word above.

UNDERSTANDING THE WRITER'S IDEAS

1. What incident made Syfers think about wanting
a wife?

2. How would a wife help the writer achieve economic independence?

3. In what ways would a wife take care of the
writer's children? Why would the writer like someone to
assume those responsibilities?

4. What physical needs would Syfers's "wife" take
care of?

5. How would a wife deal with the writer's social
life? Her sex life?

UNDERSTANDING THE WRITER'S TECHNIQUES

1. In formal argumentation, we often call the
writer's main point the *major* or *main proposition*. What is
Syfers's major proposition? Is it simply what she says in

paragraph 2, or is the proposition more complex than that? State it in your own words.

2. What is the value of the question Syfers asks in paragraph 2? Where else does she ask a question? What value does this other question have in its place in the essay? What impact does it have on the reader?

3. The points a writer offers to support the major proposition are called *minor propositions*. What minor propositions does Syfers present to show why she wants a wife? In which instance do they serve as topic sentences within paragraphs? What details does she offer to illustrate those minor propositions?

4. What order has the writer chosen to arrange the minor propositions? Why has she chosen such an order? Do you think she builds from the least to the most important reasons for having a wife? What changes would you urge in the order of the minor propositions?

5. Most of the paragraphs here develop through illustration. Where has Syfers used a *simple listing* of details? Why has she chosen that format?

6. Syfers's style is obviously straightforward, her sentences for the most part simple and often brief. Why has she chosen such a style? What is the effect of the repetition of "I want" at the start of so many sentences? Why has Syfers used several short paragraphs (5, 7, 9, 10,11) in addition to longer ones?

7. What is the author's *tone* (see Glossary)? Point out the uses of *irony* (see Glossary) in the essay. How does irony contribute to Syfers's main intent in this essay? How does the fact that Syfers is a woman contribute to this sense of irony?

EXPLORING THE WRITER'S IDEAS

1. By claiming she wants a wife, Syfers is showing us all the duties and responsibilities of the woman in a contemporary household. Has Syfers represented these duties fairly? Do husbands generally expect their wives to do all these things?

2. To what degree do wives today fit Syfers' description? How could a wife avoid many of the responsibilities spelled out in the essay? How does the "modern husband" figure in the way many couples meet household responsibilities now?

3. Syfers has characterized all the traditional and stereotyped roles usually assigned to wives. What "wifely responsibilities" has she left out?

4. Has Syfers presented a balanced picture of the issues or is her argument one-sided? Support your opinion with specific references to the essay. Could the author have dealt effectively with opposing arguments? Why or why not? What might these opposing arguments be?

5. Answer the question in the last line of the essay.

IDEAS FOR WRITING

Guided Writing

Write an essay of 750 to 1,000 words, which you call, "I Want a Husband."

1. Write the essay from the point of view of a *man*. As Syfers wrote as a woman who wanted a wife, you write this essay as a man who wants a *husband*.

2. Start your essay with a brief personal story as in paragraph 2 in "I Want a Wife."

3. Support your main point with a number of minor points. Expand each minor point with details that explain your premises.

4. Arrange your minor premises carefully so that you build to the most convincing point at the end.

5. Use a simple and straightforward style. Connect your points with transitions; use repetition as one transitional device.

6. Balance your longer paragraphs with occasional shorter ones.

7. End your essay with a crisp, one-sentence question of your own.

More Writing Projects

1.   Write an essay in which you argue *for* or *against* this issue: "A married woman belongs at home."

2.   Write an essay in which you argue about whose role you think harder to play effectively in today's society: the role of the mother or the role of the father.

Rachel L. Jones

WHAT'S WRONG WITH BLACK ENGLISH

When she wrote this article, which appeared as a guest editorial in *Newsweek,* Rachel Jones was a sophomore at Southern Illinois University. She takes what had often been an unpopular opinion among her fellow students and defends it skillfully through a mixture of personal narration, interesting language, and pointed references.

Words to Watch

linguist (par. 1): an expert in languages
peers (par. 2): equals, contemporaries
doggedly (par. 4): with great determination
rabid (par. 5): violent, furious; suffering from rabies
deduced (par. 5): concluded by reasoning
implications (par. 5): underlying meanings or results
articulate (par. 6): able to express oneself readily and effectively
assimilating (par. 9): absorbing into a cultural tradition
ideology (par. 9): system of beliefs

William Labov, a noted linguist, once said about 1 the use of black English, "It is the goal of most black Americans to acquire full control of the standard language without giving up their own culture." He also suggested that there are certain advantages to having two ways to express one's feelings. I wonder if the good doctor might also consider the goals of those black Americans who have full control of standard English but who are every now and then troubled by that colorful, grammar-to-the-winds patois that is black English. Case in point—me.

I'm a 21-year-old black born to a family that would 2 probably be considered lower-middle class—which in my mind is a polite way of describing a condition only slightly better than poverty. Let's just say we rarely if ever did the winter-vacation thing in the Caribbean. I've often had to defend my humble beginnings to a most unlikely group of people for an even less likely reason. Because of the way I talk, some of my black peers look at me sideways and ask, "Why do you talk like you're white?"

The first time it happened to me I was nine years 3 old. Cornered in the school bathroom by the class bully and her sidekick, I was offered the opportunity to swallow a few of my teeth unless I satisfactorily explained why I always got good grades, why I talked "proper" or "white." I had no ready answer for her, save the fact that my mother had from the time I was old enough to talk stressed the importance of reading and learning, or that L. Frank Baum and Ray Bradbury were my closest companions. I read all my older brothers' and sisters' literature textbooks more faithfully than they did, and even lightweights like the Bobbsey Twins and Trixie Belden were allowed into my bookish inner circle. I don't remember exactly what I told those girls, but I somehow talked my way out of a beating.

'White pipes'. I was reminded once again of my 4 "white pipes" problem while apartment hunting in Evanston, Ill., last winter. I doggedly made out lists of available places and called all around. I would immediately be invited over—and immediately turned down. The thinly concealed looks of shock when the front door opened clued me in, along with the flustered instances of "just getting off the phone with the girl who was ahead of you and she wants the rooms." When I finally found a place to live, my roommate stirred up old memories when she remarked a few months later, "You know, I was surprised when I first saw you. You sounded white over the phone." Tell me another one, sister.

I should've asked her a question I've wanted an answer to for years: how does one "talk white"? The silly side of me pictures a rabid white foam spewing forth when I speak. I don't use Valley Girl jargon, so that's not what's meant in my case. Actually, I've pretty much deduced what people mean when they say that to me, and the implications are really frightening.

It means that I'm articulate and well-versed. It means that I can talk as freely about John Steinbeck as I can about Rick James. It means that "ain't" and "he be" are not staples of my vocabulary and are only used around family and friends. (It is almost Jekyll and Hyde-ish the way I can slip out of academic abstractions into a long, lean, double-negative-filled dialogue, but I've come to terms with that aspect of my personality.) As a child, I found it hard to believe that's what people meant by "talking proper"; that would've meant that good grades and standard English were equated with white skin, and that went against everything I'd ever been taught. Running into the same type of mentality as an adult has confirmed the depressing reality that for many blacks, standard English is not only unfamiliar, it is socially unacceptable.

James Baldwin once defended black English by saying it had added "vitality to the language," and even went so far as to label it a language in its own right, saying, "Language [i.e., black English] is a political instrument" and a "vivid and crucial key to identity." But did Malcolm X urge blacks to take power in this country "any way y'all can"? Did Martin Luther King Jr. say to blacks, "I has been to the mountaintop, and I done seed the Promised Land"? Toni Morrison, Alice Walker and James Baldwin did not achieve their eloquence, grace and stature by using only black English in their writing. Andrew Young, Tom Bradley and Barbara Jordan did not acquire political power by saying, "Y'all crazy if you ain't gon vote for me." They all have full command of standard English, and I don't think that knowledge takes away from their blackness or commitment to black people.

Soulful. I know from experience that it's important 8 for black people, stripped of culture and heritage, to have something they can point to and say, "This is ours, *we* can comprehend it, *we* alone can speak it with a soulful flourish." I'd be lying if I said that the rhythms of my people caught up in "some serious rap" don't sound natural and right to me sometimes. But how heartwarming is it for those same brothers when they hit the pavement searching for employment? Studies have proven that the use of ethnic dialects decreases power in the marketplace. "I be" is acceptable on the corner, but not with the boss.

Am I letting capitalistic, European-oriented think- 9 ing fog the issue? Am I selling out blacks to an ideal of assimilating, being as much like white as possible? I have not formed a personal political ideology, but I do know this: it hurts me to hear black children use black English, knowing that they will be at yet another disadvantage in an educational system already full of stumbling blocks. It hurts me to sit in lecture halls and hear fellow black students complain that the professor "be tripping dem out using big words dey can't understand." And what hurts most is to be stripped of my own blackness simply because I know my way around the English language.

I would have to disagree with Labov in one respect. 10 My goal is not so much to acquire full control of both standard and black English, but to one day see more black people less dependent on a dialect that excludes them from full participation in the world we live in. I don't think I talk white, I think I talk right.

BUILDING VOCABULARY

1. The author uses several examples of black English in the essay. On a sheet of paper write out all the terminology from black English that you can identify. Then write definitions and/or standard spellings for each word or phrase.

2. Use these colloquial expressions from the essay in sentences of your own. Then rewrite the sentences, using "standard" English.

a. "look at me sideways" (par. 2)
b. "to swallow a few of my front teeth" (par. 3)
c. "clued me in" (par. 4)
d. "tell me another one. . . ." (par. 4)
e. "hit the pavement" (par. 8)

3. The author refers to "Valley Girl jargon" (par. 5), otherwise known as Valspeak," a type of language common originally to certain segments of teenage culture in southern California, but now easily recognized across the country. List examples of "Valspeak" and be prepared to explain their meanings.

UNDERSTANDING THE WRITER'S IDEAS

1. What is William Labov's theory of black English? What is Jones's opinion of Labov's theory?

2. What is Jones's background?

3. What is the "unlikely group" Jones mentions in paragraph 2? Why does she call it that?

4. Who are L. Frank Baum and Ray Bradbury? What are the Bobbsey twins, Jekyll and Hyde, and Trixie Belden? What is the author's relation to these characters?

5. What are "white pipes"? How did Jones realize she had "white pipes" when she was apartment hunting in Evanston, Illinois?

6. What, according to Jordan, does it mean to "talk white"? How does it compare with "talking proper"? What is "standard English"?

7. What does the author like about black English? What does she think is not good about it?

8. Explain in your own words the "depressing reality" mentioned in paragraph 6.

9. What is James Baldwin's opinion of black English? How does Jones feel about his opinion? What is her point about the correlation between successful black writers and politicians and the use of black English?

10. What does Jones mean by "capitalistic, European-oriented thinking" (par. 9)? How is it opposed to the use of black English?

11. What is the main point of Jones's conclusion?

UNDERSTANDING THE WRITER'S TECHNIQUES

1. Is the main proposition or thesis in this essay directly stated or implied? Explain your answer.

2. How does the title indicate the author's position in this argument?

3. Why does the author introduce William Labov in her first paragraph? How does she *refute* him in the course of the essay? What other instances of refutation do you find in this written argument?

4. Writers can employ argumentation for a variety of purposes, ranging from persuading people to support a cause to trying to refute a theory. What are Jordan's purposes in this argumentative essay? Cite evidence to support your response.

5. Who is Jordan's audience? Might any part of the audience disagree with her? Who? How does she take such opposition into account in terms of the *tone* of her essay?

6. Why does the author use personal narration in this essay?

7. Explain Jones's use of cause-and-effect analysis in her discussion of black English and job hunting and of black English and education. How does she use causal analysis to logically support her argument?

8. Why does Jones begin paragraph 9 with a series of rhetorical questions? What is the effect? Where else does she use questions, and toward what end?

9. What types of emotional appeals does Jones make to her audience? How effective are these appeals in convincing readers?

10. How does the concluding paragraph logically reinforce or repeat Jones's main proposition?

EXPLORING THE WRITER'S IDEAS

1. In paragraph 8, Jones states, "Studies have proven that the use of ethnic dialects decreases power in the marketplace." What does she mean by "ethnic dialects"? In this

essay she deals with the black English ethnic dialect. What other variations on the English language—either ethnic or regional dialects—can you name? How well can you understand other variations? If you were an employer, would a job applicant's use of an ethnic dialect influence your hiring decision? Why or why not?

2. What are your experiences with black English? Do you feel, as James Baldwin does, that it is "a language in its own right"? Why?

3. Compare Jones's attitudes about black cultural identity to those of Andrea Lee in her essay "Black and Well-To-Do." (pages 47–49)

4. In recent years there has been an ongoing debate—mostly in the cities—over bilingual education. Those in favor of it say that in neighborhoods or regions where a language other than standard English is commonly spoken (such as Spanish or Chinese), schools should teach courses in both languages. Those opposed say that all American students, regardless of their cultural ties, must be taught standard English. Where do you stand on this issue? Cite reasons to support your position.

IDEAS FOR WRITING

Guided Writing

Write an essay using the title "What's Wrong with _____" and fill in the blank with a cultural, political, sociological, or educational issue with which you have had direct involvement.

1. Begin with a reference to an outside authority on the issue. In your first paragraph, question that authority's analysis. Make the entire essay strong in refutation.

2. At the end of the first paragraph or the beginning of the second, establish your own claim as an authority on the issue.

3. Do not state your thesis or proposition directly, but instead use an implied thesis.

4. Narrate an incident or two that establishes your personal involvement and provides evidence for your main proposition.

5. If appropriate, use colloquial, slang, idiomatic, and figurative expressions throughout your essay.

6. Make allusions to well-known people to help illustrate the relative "rightness" or "wrongness" of the issue.

7. Use cause-and-effect analysis and/or comparison and contrast as support for your main proposition.

8. In your conclusion, indicate why the issue is wrong, especially for you. Indicate its effects on you personally and your methods of combating it.

More Writing Projects

1. Write an argument in favor of the use of black English (or any ethnic dialect) as a second language.

2. Write an argument entitled "What's Right with _____" in which you defend a commonly *un*popular issue.

3. Write an essay of persuasion on any topic of great concern to you for which you can use one of the essays in this book as a reference authority.

10

Prose for Further Reading

Lillian Hellman

MEMOIR OF A NEW ORLEANS BOARDING HOUSE

Much has come into American life since my childhood that makes things easier and nicer for almost everybody, but much has also been lost, and the shabby substitutes have deprived us of good and modest pleasures. It seems to me, to name a simple few, that we are less for the loss of the climbing sweet pea, the elm tree, and jogging in place could be a violation of the pleasure of walking through woods or just walking downtown.

A major loss in American life to me—perhaps because I knew one of them so well and stayed so often in so many others—is the boarding house, completely replaced now by the ugly, cold motel. The boarding houses ran, depending on the city and its size, all the way from handsome, redeemed mansions with fine food and pleasant service through the not-very-nice houses where people with small incomes, or those passing through, could live, not well but in a less cold atmosphere, and eat better than the junk food of motel coffee shops.

My Aunt Jenny's boarding house in New Orleans was considered upper middle class. There were no lunches served but there were enormous breakfasts, and dinners that very few good French restaurants could now duplicate.

Breakfast always included a variety of dishes: whatever fresh fish was in season, creamed finnan haddie if no fish was running well, ham hash or corned beef hash, hot biscuits, scrambled eggs with brains, and always for Sunday breakfast a large dish of tripe.

Two or three times a week my aunt and I, and the upstairs maid, a sad girl named Collie, of no age, no color, who was given shelter and food by my aunt and was, I think, a long way from being all there in the head, would take a streetcar ride down to the French market to buy food for the elaborate dinners. We would return home with snapping turtle meat, chickens that weighed no more than one pound, and in season a basket of crawfish to be made into a most difficult soup called crawfish bisque.

We would also carry back very often, Collie on one handle and I on the other, a large basket of unopened oysters, which always caused my aunt to give a lecture on the contempt she felt for oysters Rockefeller, and to explain her own fine recipe of simply frizzling the oysters in butter, cream and chives.

In season—and that phrase was a piece of nonsense-politesse because Cajuns shot in all seasons—a very old Cajun, who was always accompanied by one of many 6- or 7-year-old boys, would appear at my aunt's kitchen door to sell wild duck, quail, or pheasants. Three for a dollar no matter what birds you bought. The young boy was there for the purpose of plucking and cleaning the birds. He was given 50 cents for his work and as much cake and milk as he wanted. My favorite little boy—I think I was about the same age at the time—took snuff.

My aunt's house had a good reputation, although there were many more fancy boarding houses along St. Charles Avenue. Jenny's house had an almost permanent population. But, of course, sometimes somebody moved away and sometimes people even died although most of them lived to rather a fine age. A few of them had to move after my aunt's retirement, but most of them came back to call on her from time to time, or would write notes complaining that their new places were too stiff, too expensive and not homey.

The word homey understandably amused Jenny, who certainly had not ever meant to make a home for them.

I didn't then and I don't now understand what went on in my Aunt Jenny's head because she was like nobody else I've ever known. She was a very tall, heavy woman, with a pretty, soft face that did not suit her body. She had a high temper that she had learned to control, except sometimes in the early morning. Her sister, Hannah, was not pretty, the face too strong, but she was a soft darling. Hannah had a good job in the city, but she rose at 6 in order to watch over Jenny's possible early morning tempers and to sweep the steps and porch of the house.

The people most likely to bring out Jenny's temper were a Mr. Steffens, a handsome man who was a stockbroker, and his wife, Lucia, who was nothing at all except Mr. Steffens's wife. Mr. Steffens was a flirt, and knew about his own good looks. I never saw very much harm in him but Jenny did and had a tendency not to speak to him at all, and too much tendency to speak in a very sharp voice to Mrs. Steffens for whose indolence she had the greatest contempt. Mrs. Steffens slept a great deal, resting immediately after breakfast, then riding downtown for lunch and shopping, always returning about 3 o'clock for another long nap that took her up to the 6:30 Dubonnet before dinner.

She was a patsy for my aunt's unpleasant questions at breakfast: what bargains had she found in the stores the day before, had she managed to walk by her own feet across Canal Street or had she been escorted or wheeled in some unknown vehicle, or had her doctor given her a new draught for afternoon sleeping that was different from the after-breakfast draught?

Jenny was in a different kind of morning bad humor with Edward, who was a small, thin man, in love, I think, with my mother, who was too innocent to think of his open affection as possibly sexual (and it probably wasn't) but my mother always came to Edward's help when Jenny and others made fun of him because she like him and felt sorry for him.

Edward's last name was Roncourt and somehow it

had been found out that it had once been De Roncourt and that his grandfather had been a count in Northern France. My aunt had questions to ask about what the French aristocracy had been like, knowing full well that Edward had never been to France, and my mother's defense of Edward's stumbling embarrassment both tickled and irritated Jenny. She teased my poor mother about what she called "l'affaire de Roncourt" until my mother once burst into tears and locked her door for the rest of the day. That night, for the first and last time, I saw Hannah lose her temper with Jenny. After that the teasing stopped.

There were also two elderly lady boarders whose names I no longer remember and one elderly gentleman who was their cousin. I think I don't remember them because I don't remember their ever speaking, or maybe I don't remember them because Jenny completely ignored them.

But in looking back, I would not be too certain of my own opinions of any of the guests because I loved and admired Jenny and saw things too much through her eyes and one of the reasons I think I did was that I spent so much time in the kitchen with her where she was in her best humor.

Akira Kurosawa

BABYHOOD

I was in the washtub naked. The place was dimly lit, and I was soaking in hot water and rocking myself by holding on to the rims of the tub. At the lowest point the tub teetered between two sloping boards, the water making little splashing noises as it rocked. This must have been very interesting for me. I rocked the tub with all my strength. Suddenly it overturned. I have a very vivid memory of the strange feeling of shock and uncertainty at that moment, of the sensation of that wet and slippery space between the boards against my bare skin, and of looking up at something painfully bright overhead.

After reaching an age of awareness, I would occasionally recall this incident. But it seemed a trivial thing, so I said nothing about it until I became an adult. It must have been after I had passed twenty years of age that for some reason I mentioned to my mother that I remembered these sensations. For a moment she just stared at me in surprise; then she informed me that this could only have been something that occurred when we went to my father's birthplace up north in Akita Prefecture to attend a memorial service for my grandfather. I had been one year old at the time.

The dimly lit place where I sat in a tub lodged between two boards was the room that served as both kitchen and bath in the house where my father was born. My mother had been about to give me a bath, but first she put me in the tub of hot water and went into the next room to take off her kimono. Suddenly she heard me start wailing at the top of my lungs. She rushed back and found me spilled out of the tub on the floor crying. The painfully bright, shiny thing over head, my mother explained, was probably a hanging oil lamp of the type still used when I was a baby.

This incident with the washtub is my very first memory of myself. Naturally, I do not recall being born. However, my oldest sister, now deceased, used to say, "You were a strange baby." Apparently I emerged from my mother's womb without uttering a sound, but with my hands firmly clasped together. When at last they were able to pry my hands apart, I had bruises on both palms.

I think this story may be a lie. It was probably made up to tease me because I was the youngest child. After all, if I really had been born such a grasping person, by now I would be a millionaire and surely would be riding around in nothing less than a Rolls-Royce.

After the washtub incident of my first year, I can now recall only a few other events from my babyhood, in a form resembling out-of-focus bits of film footage. All of them are things seen from my infant's vantage point on my nurse's shoulders.

One of them is something seen through a wire net. People dressed in white flail at a ball with a stick, run after it as it dances and flies through the air, and pick it up and throw it around. Later I understood that this was the view from behind the net of the baseball field at the gymnastics school where my father was a teacher. So I must say that my liking for baseball today is deep-rooted; apparently I've been watching it since babyhood.

Another memory from babyhood, also a sight viewed from my nurse's back, comes to mind: a fire seen from a great distance. Between us and the fire stretches an expanse of dark water. My home was in the Ōmori district of Tokyo, so this was probably the Ōmori shore of Tokyo Bay, and since the fire appeared very far away, it must have taken place somewhere near Haneda (now the site of one of Tokyo's international airports). I was frightened by this distant fire and cried. Even now I have a strong dislike of fires, and especially when I see the night sky reddened with flames I am overcome by fear.

One last memory of babyhood remains. In this case, too, I am on my nurse's back, and from time to time we enter a small dark room. Years later I would occasionally recall this frequent occurrence and wonder what it was. Then one day all at once, like Sherlock Holmes solving a mystery, I understood: my nurse, with me still on her back, was going to the toilet. What an insult!

Many years later my nurse came to see me. She looked up at this person who had reached nearly six feet and more than 150 pounds and just said, "My dear, how you've grown," as she clasped me around the knees and broke into tears. I had been ready to reproach her for the indignities she had caused me to suffer in the past, but suddenly I was moved by this figure of an old woman I no longer recognized, and all I could do was stare vacantly down at her.

Maya Angelou
"THE FIGHT"

The last inch of space was filled, yet people continued to wedge themselves along the walls of the Store. Uncle Willie had turned the radio up to its last notch so that youngsters on the porch wouldn't miss a word. Women sat on kitchen chairs, dining-room chairs, stools and upturned wooden boxes. Small children and babies perched on every lap available and men leaned on the shelves or on each other.

The apprehensive mood was shot through with shafts of gaiety, as a black sky is streaked with lightning.

"I ain't worried 'bout this fight. Joe's gonna whip that cracker like it's open season."

"He gone whip him till that white boy call him Momma."

At last the talking was finished and the string-along songs about razor blades were over and the fight began.

"A quick jab to the head." In the Store the crowd grunted. "A left to the head and a right and another left." One of the listeners cackled like a hen and was quieted.

"They're in a clench, Louis is trying to fight his way out."

Some bitter comedian on the porch said, "That white man don't mind hugging that niggah now, I betcha."

"The referee is moving in to break them up, but Louis finally pushed the contender away and it's an uppercut to the chin. The contender is hanging on, now he's backing away. Louis catches him with a short left to the jaw."

A tide of murmuring assent poured out the doors and into the yard.

"Another left and another left. Louis is saving that mighty right . . ." The mutter in the Store had grown into a baby roar and it was pierced by the clang of a bell and the announcer's "That's the bell for round three, ladies and gentlemen."

As I pushed my way into the Store I wondered if the announcer gave any thought to the fact that he was addressing as "ladies and gentlemen" all the Negroes around the world who sat sweating and praying, glued to their "master's voice."

There were only a few calls for R. C. Colas, Dr. Peppers, and Hire's root beer. The real festivities would begin after the fight. Then even the old Christian ladies who taught their children and tried themselves to practice turning the other cheek would buy soft drinks, and if the Brown Bomber's victory was a particularly bloody one they would order peanut patties and Baby Ruths also.

Bailey and I lay the coins on top of the cash register. Uncle Willie didn't allow us to ring up sales during a fight. It was too noisy and might shake up the atmosphere. When the gong rang for the next round we pushed through the near-sacred quiet to the herd of children outside.

"He's got Louis against the ropes and now it's a left to the body and a right to the ribs. Another right to the body, it looks like it was low . . . Yes, ladies and gentlemen, the referee is signaling but the contender keeps raining the blows on Louis. It's another to the body, and it looks like Louis is going down."

My race groaned. It was our people falling. It was another lynching, yet another Black man hanging on a tree. One more woman ambushed and raped. A Black boy whipped and maimed. It was hounds on the trail of a man running through slimy swamps. It was a white woman slapping her maid for being forgetful.

The men in the Store stood away from the walls and

at attention. Women greedily clutched the babes on their laps while on the porch the shufflings and smiles, flirtings and pinching of a few minutes before were gone. This might be the end of the world. If Joe lost we were back in slavery and beyond help. It would all be true, the accusations that we were lower types of human beings. Only a little higher than the apes. True that we were stupid and ugly and lazy and dirty and, unlucky and worst of all, that God Himself hated us and ordained us to be hewers of wood and drawers of water, forever and ever, world without end.

We didn't breathe. We didn't hope. We waited.

"He's off the ropes, ladies and gentlemen. He's moving towards the center of the ring." There was no time to be relieved. The worst might still happen.

"And now it looks like Joe is mad. He's caught Carnera with a left hook to the head and a right to the head. It's a left jab to the body and another left to the head. There's a left cross and a right to the head. The contender's right eye is bleeding and he can't seem to keep his block up. Louis is penetrating every block. The referee is moving in, but Louis sends a left to the body and it's the uppercut to the chin and the contender is dropping. He's on the canvas, ladies and gentlemen."

Babies slid to the floor as women stood up and men leaned toward the radio.

"Here's the referee. He's counting. One, two, three, four, five, six, seven . . . Is the contender trying to get up again?"

All the men in the store shouted, "NO."

"—eight, nine, ten." There were a few sounds from the audience, but they seemed to be holding themselves in against tremendous pressure.

"The fight is all over, ladies and gentlemen. Let's get the microphone over to the referee . . . Here he is. He's got the Brown Bomber's hand, he's holding it up . . . Here he is . . ."

Then the voice, husky and familiar, came to wash over us—"The winnah, and still heavyweight champeen of the world . . . Joe Louis."

Champion of the world. A Black boy. Some Black mother's son. He was the strongest man in the world. People drank Coca-Colas like ambrosia and ate candy bars like Christmas. Some of the men went behind the Store and poured white lightning in their soft-drink bottles, and a few of the bigger boys followed them. Those who were not chased away came back blowing their breath in front of themselves like proud smokers.

It would take an hour or more before the people would leave the Store and head for home. Those who lived too far had made arrangements to stay in town. It wouldn't do for a Black man and his family to be caught on a lonely country road on a night when Joe Louis had proved that we were the strongest people in the world.

John Slote

THE SOCIAL SPORT

A few summers ago, I played for two softball teams. One, called Radio Sports, was made up of athletic, serious guys. We wore uniforms and prepared scouting reports on other teams. But though we won most games by fifteen runs, we were unhappy. I always felt our team competed not only against its opponents but against the game itself. We tried to take ourselves more seriously than the sport would let us.

The members of the other team I played on that summer were staffers on a magazine for which I worked part-time. At four-thirty in the afternoon we would start changing into T-shirts and jeans, and then we would all take the elevator downstairs and make our way to the field. Our team, one of hundreds that played in the parks those afternoons (so promiscuously entwined that someone else's right fielder rubbed shoulders with your shortstop), was a motley bunch. Our beer tasted cold and metallic. The art director, in right field, kept dropping fly balls and getting angry. The catcher's fiancé was good at third, and the pitcher wasn't bad; but, still, we rarely won a game. I didn't know it then, but that mattered to me. I used to leave the park with a nagging feeling in my stomach, a feeling I did not like or understand.

Softball is the game of baseball made less challenging. It is a social sport, since everyone can play it. But when we play the game, we also admit that we can't be everything we want to be—baseball is too good (and difficult) for us. And yet, though easier, softball can be good, too. If the players know how to play their positions, the game can be *played* hard; at the same time, it needn't sacrifice the social appeal that is perhaps its greatest virtue. Somewhere between my magazine team (it didn't even have a name) and Radio Sports, there exists the ideal softball team—a team mature enough to be sociable and innocent enough to play to win.

No position suffers more from the changes that turn baseball into softball than do those of pitcher and catcher. The pitcher's big, difficult hardball delivery becomes an underhand lob with a swollen ball. The catcher no longer has to guard the bases against theft, since in softball there is no base stealing. Thus a team of mixed abilities will stick its less accomplished players at these positions, where—their pride wounded—they wither. No good can come of this. The battery is essential to the team.

At the core of the best softball game is a pitcher who pitches well enough that the other team hits its way to base rather than walks there. It is difficult to strike too many batters out, but a pitcher can at least make batters earn their hits and spare his outfielders the indignity of having to run into the neighboring game's infield to retrieve home runs. And, depending on the amount of arch the rules allow, the pitcher *can* get clever; he can deliver a steeply dropping ball that falls to earth at the back of the strike zone, armpit-level—a pitch that forces the batter to go back on his heels. Or the pitcher can throw to a point just above the batter's front kneecap on the outside corner of the plate, forcing him to lunge forward for the pitch. While in softball a pitcher cannot hope to dominate the game as he can in hardball, he can—by throwing accurately, by fielding his own position aggressively, by racing to cover first, for example, every time the first baseman has to make a play on a hit ball—give his team and the game an edge.

No one wants to be the catcher. It's dirty, dangerous, and uncomfortable back there. But there is much to be made of the catcher's unique relationship with the game. Only he looks out at the whole theater of action. Only he can speed up or slow down the tempo of the game by holding the ball between pitches. Only he can—and must—be responsible for making sure the outfielders are in their correct positions and that everyone knows how many outs there are and where the play is going. He must also watch to see that the pitcher is properly pampered, or harangued, and that he does not fly off the handle if he does not like a call. In short, the catcher takes charge of things. He must also take charge of himself, taking care to protect himself with a cup and to keep his throwing hand in a fist while the pitch is coming to avoid jammed fingers from foul tips. No one else will look out for him.

In my experience, the defensive player who handles the most chances (and handles them most spectacularly) is the shortstop. Thus it is a good thing that there are shortstops in this world, wearing their wristbands and looking sharp, tossing away loose pebbles, and readying themselves to come swooping gracefully in on a ground ball before they fire it to first in a cloud of dust. Elsewhere in the infield, one need not be so fancy; a little brute courage, hustle, and aggressiveness will do.

But for any infielder, the trick is to get in front of the ball, to keep your eyes on it, and to take *control* in whatever way you can. At third you've got time to field the ball off your chest before you make the long, hard, fast throw to first. At second base, since your throw is relatively easy, you can play deep and increase your range; you also have time to drop to your knees to field a ground ball. But at first base the most important thing is to not drop good throws and to not stay glued to the bag: better to let the batter make it to first than to let him take second on an errant throw that might have been stopped had you gotten your body out in front of it.

If for some reason your team does not have a shortstop and *you* end up there, you should try your best to summon all your nerve; you're not only going to have to play like a shortstop, you'll have to look like one, too. While success or failure in the field depends on your ability to move off the balls of your feet, to go far to your left and right, to field the ball cleanly and throw in one artful motion—on a typically weedy, unkempt softball field, it's that dash of vanity your team will count on most.

Things tend to get a bit more complex in the outfield. To play out there, you have to learn to judge the flight of sailing softballs, learn to get a jump on the ball (that is, commit yourself one way or another before you're really ready to) by the sound it makes off the batter's stick, learn to come in hard on ground balls and go back on long flies without getting all twisted up and confused. You have to learn to run evenly on the front of your feet to soften the impact of your steps: trouncing tensely over the outfield ground with your eyes following the ball, you'll suddenly feel the earth quaking beneath you and see your vision go bouncing off to somewhere the ball isn't. In the outfield it is almost always a good idea to take ground balls down on one knee, for there is no one else behind you if the ball hits a cigarette butt and skips your glove. Good outfielders know the earth: they know that a line drive landing on hard, dry ground bounces high overheard. A good outfielder can haul in a fly ball at the same time he is building momentum for his throw. A good outfielder can even fake base runners into thinking he is going to catch a ball that he's really going to take on a bounce.

You can learn to do these things, to glide like a gazelle and coolly snap a ball shut in your mitt while reaching far over your shoulder. But to be an outfielder in a game, you must be a conqueror not only of balls and space but of mind. For having waited inning after inning for some action in the outfield, having reacted time and time again to the swing of the bat only to see an infielder get the play, having been stranded far from anyone for far too long with nothing at all to do, it will inevitably be your first reaction, when at last the ball seems headed out your way, to think: "How ironic, how *awfully* ironic it would be if after all this waiting around doing nothing I missed this ball." Then you are in trouble.

To play the outfield, you must use the waiting time to your advantage. You must think. You must make the play in your mind before it comes up in real life. You must know at every moment exactly what is going on: how many outs there are, where the runners are, where they'll be headed by the time, say, a ground ball through the infield starts toward you. You must fantasize every possibility. If you do, and the moment comes to make a play, *then* it will be time to sit back and let it happen: the ball will come bouncing merrily out to you as little figures dash around the bases like gophers: you will kneel, catch the ball, and come up throwing without a moment's hesitation; and then you will watch as the ball sails through the air to third, where your baseman colleague will casually nail the runner on his way from first.

The ideal softball team plays like a team. It knows how to whip the ball around the horn after an out, knows how to relay the ball in from the outfield, knows who takes whose throw, who covers what bag when. That's what you must work toward: the unity that happens when you hear the sound of one another's voices in the field: when you feel together, solid.

In softball it is the offensive team's task to crack the fielding team's defense. For the team that's up to bat, that means putting the ball in play, forcing the action, and running the bases like a bunch of madpeople. Punch the ball out over the shortstop, make the left fielder throw you out at second. The more the other guys have to throw and catch the ball, the more often your team will cross home plate. (And don't forget to touch the bases; push your inside foot against the inside corner of the bag for turning power.)

Like the pitcher and the catcher on defense, the softball hitter must live with the knowledge that this whole game has been concocted to make his task easy. It is this knowledge, I think, that causes one to lunge and overswing at the plate, that causes one's concentration to collapse just as that big, fat, ridiculous target comes drifting up before one's eyes. Patience, poise, concentration, a continuous view of the ball, a loose and level swing—all this is imperative; as a hitter you must be humble, respect the game, and maintain all the fundamentals. Swing for ground balls before pop-ups, and line drives before long high flies. Let the other team make the difficult play.

The point in softball is to keep steep pressure on the other guys. That's the way to score runs. But the more pressure you put on your opponents, the more pressure you put on the game itself. In some cases this may cause the game to crack. There are some precautions you can take.

When there are no umpires, it is important to approach the contest warily, to fortify it with plenty of rules and regulations and formal agreements. Everyone may be feeling chummy at the game's beginning but how will they be feeling when the score is 2–2 in the last inning and someone tries a squeeze play? Likewise, sooner or later someone is bound to put the foul lines to the test or suddenly claim that sliding is not allowed. Even the most informal game must have their fierce formalities. Standards for what constitutes a ball and strike must be rigidly maintained. There has to be an accepted way of making "out" and "safe" calls at the bases, and there have to be bases. The anchored, canvas type of bag is still the base worth getting. Second best is a rubber slab. After that your choices dwindle. A T-shirt gets tangled up in one's feet. A piece of cardboard blows away, and a mark in the dirt is kind of hard to see.

Softball is a social sport, but what one remembers from a softball game is not only the society but the score, and one's own performance. Thinking back to playing on the magazine team, I can still see myself popping up to third one time in Central Park. Remembering the Radio Sports team, I think of the time I hit a pitch right between the seams for a home run an inning just before the rain came, and then everyone ran for cover.

I think of the night games we played down by the East River, a red boat drifting by left field, and how we once played a team of women professional basketball players: stretching out a single, I slid into the blonde at second and was safe. I remember her legs. I think of the time we played a team sponsored by Meatloaf, the singer, who arrived in his own limousine and pitched. Afterward he stayed out in the field by himself, berating the umpire because he could not bear the score. I had doubled off him twice.

Marsha Rabe

PASSAGES

There is land in central Illinois that is as flat as the floor. It does not roll and ripple into hills, nor does it fill, lift, and erupt like sails into mountains the way some land does. The most it grants, and this begrudgingly, is to warp and buckle where rare and subtle sorts of lumps appear; but these lumps are not hills and this land is very flat.

It happens more frequently of late that when I imagine my father, I see him not as the large, soft, hazy man I have always known, but as a boy of nine, standing on a dark spot in this flat Illinois land, standing near a railroad crossing. It is night and it is hot. Summer here is dreadful, windless. The air clots and settles close to the ground, while the sky, smeared thick with stars, floats farther away than at other times of the year. It is cricket season, baseball season.

My father's father was a passenger conductor on the Chicago and Alton Railroad. He had the best and fastest run from Chicago to St. Louis. It was 1915 when on Friday afternoon my grandfather, who had gone to Chicago on a morning train, phoned Walt Hempfing, the dispatcher in my father's hometown, and asked him to call my grandmother and tell her to pack an overnight bag and have Louis, my father, at the crossing that night at 11 o'clock so he could pick him up as his train swept through town. "The Cubs are in St. Louis tomorrow, Walt. Jim Lavender is pitching. It's time Louis sees a big league game. It's time he sees the Cubs."

The signal switch near where my father stands lights and begins to swing back and forth. In the clockwork flashing back and forth, back and forth like a pendulum, I see that my father is a little boy. He is wearing baggy knickers that bellow around his thick, straight legs like a cloud. Long, thin socks pucker at his knees and tuck into high-button shoes cut just above his ankles. He also wears a loose, wrinkled white shirt, a long, thin tie, and a cloth-banded straw hat. From his left hand hangs a small suitcase, and in his right he holds a pocket watch. His head is bent—I cannot see his face for the flashing shadows and the brim of his hat—but I *can* see that he is looking into the palm of his right hand to check the time.

As I watch, the signal switch begins to clang and my father looks to his left. A train is coming. First to arrive is its whistle, a metallic honk like an elephant's call. Then its threading lights appear, bright across the cow pastures and corn fields, blinking on and off behind the trees and barns, scintillating, seeming to shatter and then, miraculously, to heal and reappear, whole. My father watches, then notes the time. 10:58. It's on time.

So there he is and I see him, a little boy on a hot night, waiting on flat, adamant land, while a huge, punctual monster uncoils toward him, rushing and rising up out of the dark, hurtling across the still fields, frightening small animals and birds, shocking the earth itself. The train is the only thing with lights for miles around, and his father is bringing it to him. For a long time he watches, because the land is so flat and he can see so far, and all the time I watch him watching I try to imagine how grand he must feel, the object of all this roaring commotion, of this hissing power.

Here it comes, closer, larger, louder. Brakes grind, out pours steam like a wet sigh. The engine chokes, jolts, and gently stops in front of him. Directly, deliberately in front of him. His father lowers a large hand and whisks him aboard. Sweaty smiles and grave excitement all around, and they are off, off to St. Louis, off to Jim Lavender, and off to the Cubs, who lost that game, my father tells me, 3 to 2.

Richard Rodriguez
COMPLEXION

Complexion. My first conscious experience of sexual excitement concerns my complexion. One summer weekend, when I was around seven years old, I was at a public swimming pool with the whole family. I remember sitting on the damp pavement next to the pool and seeing my mother, in the spectators' bleachers, holding my younger sister on her lap. My mother, I noticed, was watching my father as he stood on a diving board, waving to her. I watched her wave back. Then saw her radiant, bashful, astonishing smile. In that second I sensed that my mother and father had a relationship I knew nothing about. A nervous excitement encircled my stomach as I saw my mother's eyes follow my father's figure curving into the water. A second or two later, he emerged. I heard him call out. Smiling, his voice sounded, buoyant, calling me to swim to him. But turning to see him, I caught my mother's eye. I heard her shout over to me. In Spanish she called through the crowd: 'Put a towel on over your shoulders.' In public, she didn't want to say why. I knew.

That incident anticipates the shame and sexual inferiority I was to feel in later years because of my dark complexion. I was to grow up an ugly child. Or one who thought himself ugly. (*Feo.*) One night when I was eleven or twelve years old, I locked myself in the bathroom and carefully regarded my reflection in the mirror over the sink. Without any pleasure I studied my skin. I turned on the faucet. (In my mind I heard the swirling voices of aunts, and even my mother's voice, whispering, whispering incessantly about lemon juice solutions and dark, *feo* children.) With a bar of soap, I fashioned a thick ball of lather. I began soaping my arms. I took my father's straight razor out of the medicine cabinet. Slowly, with steady deliberateness, I put the blade against my flesh, pressed it as close as I could without cutting, and moved it up and down across my skin to see if I could get out, somehow lessen, the dark. All I succeeded in doing, however, was in shaving my arms bare of their hair. For as I noted with disappointment, the dark would not come out. It remained. Trapped. Deep in the cells of my skin.

Throughout adolescence, I felt myself mysteriously marked. Nothing else about my appearance would concern me so much as the fact that my complexion was dark. My mother would say how sorry she was that there was not money enough to get braces to straighten my teeth. But I never bothered about my teeth. In three-way mirrors at department stores, I'd see my profile dramatically defined by a long nose, but it was really only the color of my skin that caught my attention.

I wasn't afraid that I would become a menial laborer because of my skin. Nor did my complexion make me feel especially vulnerable to racial abuse. (I didn't really consider my dark skin to be a racial characteristic. I would have been only too happy to look as Mexican as my light-skinned older brother.) Simply, I judged myself ugly. And, since the women in my family had been the ones who discussed it in such worried tones, I felt my dark skin made me unattractive to women.

Thirteen years old. Fourteen. In a grammar school art class, when the assignment was to draw a self-portrait, I tried and I tried but could not bring myself to shade in the face on the paper to anything like my actual tone. With disgust then I would come face to face with myself in mirrors. With disappointment I located myself in class photographs—

my dark face undefined by the camera which had clearly described the white faces of classmates. Or I'd see my dark wrist against my long-sleeved white shirt.

I grew divorced from my body. Insecure, overweight, listless. On hot summer days when my rubber-soled shoes soaked up the heat from the sidewalk, I kept my head down. Or walked in the shade. My mother didn't need anymore to tell me to watch out for the sun. I denied myself a sensational life. The normal, extraordinary, animal excitement of feeling my body alive—riding shirtless on a bicycle in the warm wind created by furious self-propelled motion—the sensations that first had excited in me a sense of my maleness, I denied. I was too ashamed of my body. I wanted to forget that I had a body because I had a brown body. I was grateful that none of my classmates ever mentioned the fact.

I continued to see the *braceros,* those men I resembled in one way and, in another way, didn't resemble at all. On the watery horizon of a Valley afternoon, I'd see them. And though I feared looking like them, it was with silent envy that I regarded them still. I envied them their physical lives, their freedom to violate the taboo of the sun. Closer to home I would notice the shirtless construction workers, the roofers, the sweating men tarring the street in front of the house. And I'd see the Mexican gardeners. I was unwilling to admit the attraction of their lives. I tried to deny it by looking away. But what was denied became strongly desired.

In high school physical education classes, I withdrew, in the regular company of five or six classmates, to a distant corner of a football field where we smoked and talked. Our company was composed of bodies too short or too tall, all graceless and all—except mine—pale. Our conversation was usually witty. (In fact we were intelligent.) If we referred to the athletic contests around us, it was with sarcasm. With savage scorn I'd refer to the 'animals' playing football or baseball. It would have been important for me to have joined them. Or for me to have taken off my shirt, to have let the sun burn dark on my skin, and to have run barefoot on the warm wet grass. It would have been very important.

Too important. It would have been too telling a gesture—to admit the desire for sensation, the body, my body.

Fifteen, sixteen. I was a teenager shy in the presence of girls. Never dated. Barely could talk to a girl without stammering. In high school I went to several dances, but I never managed to ask a girl to dance. So I stopped going. I cannot remember high school years now with the parade of typical images: bright drive-ins or gliding blue shadows of a Junior Prom. At home most weekend nights, I would pass evenings reading. Like those hidden, precocious adolescents who have no real-life sexual experiences, I read a great deal of romantic fiction. 'You won't find it in your books,' my brother would playfully taunt me as he prepared to go to a party by freezing the crest of the wave in his hair with sticky pomade. Through my reading, however, I developed a fabulous and sophisticated sexual imagination. At seventeen, I may not have known how to engage a girl in small talk, but I had read *Lady Chatterley's Lover*.

It annoyed me to hear my father's teasing: that I would never know what 'real work' is; that my hands were so soft. I think I knew it was his way of admitting pleasure and pride in my academic success. But I didn't smile. My mother said she was glad her children were getting their educations and would not be pushed around like *los pobres*. I heard the remark ironically as a reminder of my separation from *los braceros*. At such times I suspected that education was making me effeminate. The odd thing, however, was that I did not judge my classmates so harshly. Nor did I consider my male teachers in high school effeminate. It was only myself I judged against some shadowy, mythical Mexican laborer—dark like me, yet very different.

Ben Yagoda

WHAT EVERY MAN SHOULD KNOW: HOW TO KEEP YOUR PLACE NICE

Like so many middle-class American boys, I gained from my education a wonderful mastery of the conjugation of irregular French verbs and none of home economics. So I found when I first started to live alone that I had no idea how to keep my place nice. Everything was so baffling. Should wood floors be vacuumed or swept? Not being the kind of person who, when confronted with an unfamiliar task, experiments with different methods until he finds a workable one, I didn't do either. And dusting—the notion bemused me no end. Where, I wondered, does the dust go? Is the idea that when you wipe dust off a table it goes on the floor, where you're supposed to vacuum it, or what? Of course, while I occupied myself with these metaphysical queries nothing got done—except the gathering of grime. Eventually I'd call my mother, get some idea of the accepted procedure, and tackle the problem.

Through innumerable such telephone calls, and through my own investigations, I came to discover that cleaning house is not nearly as daunting as I imagined it to be. It follows not some arcane set of rules and procedures but common sense.

Let's begin at the beginning. Dirt comes in three principal forms, the first of which (because it's the easiest to deal with) is clutter. Sometimes getting rid of clutter is actually fun—the key is having a place to store it, even if you're only throwing things in the closet. And with a minimum of effort, some simple straightening up makes a big difference in the appearance of your abode. A friend of mine says that if he's pressed for time, he can make his place go from dump-ness to presentability merely by stashing the several pairs of shoes he generally has strewn across the floor.

The second kind of dirt is dust, defined as stuff that's not stuck to a surface but is too small to pick up and throw away. In time (days in New York City, weeks in Arizona, but eventually everywhere), everything gets dusty. It's an act of nature, like the forming of dew. How do you get rid of dust? In almost every case, with a vacuum cleaner. Wiping with a cloth cannot help but spread it around; a vacuum swallows it. As one expert memorably put it, you should "vacuum everything big enough or rigid enough not to get sucked up the nozzle."

Unless you have a preponderance of wall-to-wall carpets, your best bet is probably a canister vacuum, rather than an upright model. Canisters (which can be had for under one hundred dollars) come with attachments for cleaning rugs and carpets, as well as ones that can tackle bare floors, radiators, drapes, plants, books, lamps, paintings, air conditioners, walls, floorboards, upholstered furniture, wicker furniture, and practically anything else you can think of. Actually, you probably *wouldn't* think of vacuuming a lot of this stuff, but you should. Dust is bad. Too much of it in a sofa, for instance, does at least two unwelcome things: it weakens the fabric of the upholstery, which makes it wear out sooner, and it transmits dust to the air, which makes a lot of people sneeze.

Cleaning consultant and author Don Aslett claims that you can reduce your dust by half by putting a three-by-five mat—rubber bottomed, carpet topped—inside and outside your entrance. If you can live with that decorwise, it's probably a good idea.

The third kind of dirt, grime, can't be vacuumed up; it has to be rubbed out. What's important here is having the right tools and the right cleanser. As for the former, you can handle most any surface if you have sponges, a bucket and mop (the string kind is preferable to the sponge), and dry things to wipe with. For these, the conventional wisdom says to use soft rags; old diapers is the classic example. I don't know about you, but I don't have too many old diapers around the apartment—or a washing machine in my spare room to clean them every time they get dirty. So I use soft paper towels. They're less economical, but they get the job done and they're convenient as hell. (They're also fine for dusting the surfaces a vacuum cleaner can't get at—the tops of picture frames, for example.)

Choosing what kind of cleaning substance to use appears to be a more confusing decision, but it really isn't. Though cleaning experts and household-hints columnists like to provide elaborate recipes for mixing your own concoctions (with such ingredients as ammonia, vinegar, baking soda, and laundry detergent), it's much more convenient, and only a little more expensive, to choose from the products arrayed in the unfamiliar cleaning-goods aisle of the supermarket. This stuff all works reasonably well, and you can't go wrong if you just read the labels on the products. If you're looking to consolidate your purchases, an all-purpose cleanser like Mr. Clean or Top Job—augmented with a wood cleaner-polish—can take care of just about all your needs.

I have, however, one caveat to this anything-goes cleanser philosophy. It has to do with what is for some reason probably the most popular cleanser among men: white scouring powder, like Comet or Ajax. Porcelain sinks and bathtubs are designed for easy cleaning by even mild cleansers. I hate to say it, fellows, but when you rub and rub with an abrasive, you're ruining the surface, so that eventually an abrasive is the *only* thing that will get it clean. Even if your sinks are already on their way out, it's better to use a milder cleanser on your sponge; Clorox's Soft Scrub is a good bet.

I now come to windows, the cleaning chore that has probably struck more anomie into more hearts than any other household task save over cleaning. Still, clean windows can make a dramatic difference in how a room looks. And there's a trick to them. Forget all you've read and been told about waiting for a cloudy day, wiping with newspapers, and all that. Buy a squeegee. Just mix up a bucketfull of warm water with a little ammonia (in this case homemade brew *is* called for), wash the window with the sponge end of the squeegee, and wipe it dry with the rubber end. Done.

This, however, leaves open the question of how to deal with the *outside* of the window, which brings me to my next topic: Where to draw the line. Unless you live on the first floor, have one of those detachable insulated windows, or are Philippe Petit, you probably won't *want* to wash the outside of your windows and should have them done professionally. I would also put cleaning the oven in the draw-the-line category. I myself get around the need to perform this task by being incredibly careful about not getting my oven dirty. (I haven't broiled a steak there for seven years.) Similarly, refinishing your floors and shampooing your rugs are outside jobs that most people dread doing and probably wouldn't do well. Hiring someone to do them is much better than sitting around feeling guilty.

As this suggests, psychology has a great deal to do with keeping house. It doesn't sound like much, but turning on all the lights and opening the windows before I start cleaning helps me a lot. If you don't go about them sensibly, your household tasks will begin to seem Sisyphean, a legacy that is never completed. So take a little bit at a time. Before you start to clean, always know exactly what you plan to do and how much time you plan to spend doing it. That way, when you're finished you'll have a satisfying sense of completeness instead of a sense that there's so much more to do.

Even if you follow all these guidelines, though, there's bound to be a time when the dirt gets you so frustrated that you're paralyzed. Then there's only one thing to do.

Call Mom.

Jane E. Brody

THE EVIDENCE BUILDS AGAINST MARIJUANA

Millions of marijuana-smoking young Americans, jaded by alarmists and politically motivated but poorly documented reports of marijuana's alleged risks, are convinced that it is a safe drug, especially when compared to alcohol.

However, as a growing number of persons smoke a more potent marijuana at ever-younger ages, scientists are gathering an impressive—though still inconclusive—body of evidence indicating that the nation's second leading recreational drug (alcohol is No. 1) is indeed hazardous to health.

In fact, some leading drug experts who once dismissed marijuana as a drug of minor consequence now express serious concern about the possible risks and patterns of use, particularly among teen-agers.

Among those who now take a dim view of marijuana are Dr. Sidney Cohen, a drug expert at the University of California at Los Angeles, who once described marijuana as "a trivial weed," and Dr. Robert L. DuPont, former director of the National Institute on Drug Abuse, who had lobbied for marijuana's legalization.

According to these and other experts, it is no longer possible to say that marijuana is an innocuous drug with few if any health effects aside from intoxication. Although the evidence for immediate effects on the brain is most convincing, a number of recent studies show damaging effects that suggest long-term health hazards involving many different body functions. These include the heart, lungs and reproductive organs.

The problem with accurately defining the hazards of marijuana is that the way in which it is used by Americans has not yet been subjected to long-term study. Decades of experience with marijuana in other countries is not necessarily relevant here, where a stronger form of the drug is used, primarily by people in their formative years, and where patterns of inhalation are likely to differ.

It may be 20 years or more before the necessary studies can be conducted among Americans. Therefore, it is especially important to heed the "early warning signs" of the long-term hazards of smoking marijuana. One need only recall that it took half a century of heavy cigarette smoking by millions of Americans before the health risks of tobacco were widely recognized. By then, so many had become so hooked on the "innocuous weed" that today, 25 years after the first major report on the health hazards of cigarettes, more than 50 million Americans still smoke cigarettes, and smoking remains the nation's leading preventable cause of illness and premature death.

The following are among the reasons for the mounting concern about marijuana:

Patterns of use. Some 43 million Americans have tried marijuana and the latest national survey in 1977 showed that 16 million were current users. Current users included 4 percent of 12-year-olds, 15 percent of 14-year-olds, and 31 percent of 18- to 21-year-olds. More than four million youngsters aged 12 to 17 were using marijuana in 1977, and one in nine high school seniors used marijuana daily. The survey showed that the proportion of youngsters who had begun using marijuana before the ninth grade had nearly doubled since 1972.

Marijuana is far less popular among adults, and most who use it tend to smoke it only occasionally. There is relatively little concern about occasional use by adults, except for pregnant women and persons with heart disease, lung disease or emotional disorders.

Potency. Drug experts are disturbed about the rapidly increasing potency of the marijuana generally available to Americans. In 1975, the average sample of confiscated marijuana contained 0.4 percent of the mind-altering chemical THC (tetrahydrocannabinol). By last year,* because of improved cultivation practices, the average was 4 percent of the active drug—a tenfold increase in potency. And one cultivated form increasingly available in this country contains 7 percent THC.

This is especially worrisome because, unlike alcohol, which is soluble in water and rapidly washed out of the body, THC and related cannabinoids in marijuana are fat-soluble and can remain and accumulate in the body for a week or longer after marijuana is smoked.

Brain effects. Immediate effects on the brain are the least controversial and best defined of marijuana's hazards. Like alcohol, marijuana is intoxicating and a marijuana high impairs memory, learning, speech, reading comprehension, arithmetic problem-solving and the ability to think. Long-term intellectual effects are not known.

Some researchers have described what they called "a motivational syndrome" among young marijuana smokers, who, with frequent use of the drug, tend to lose interest in school, friends and sexual intercourse. However, it is not known whether marijuana use is a direct cause or merely one symptom of a general underlying problem. Persistent brain abnormalities and changes in emotion and behavior have been demonstrated in monkeys given large doses of marijuana.

Also like alcohol, marijuana interferes with psychomotor functions such as reaction time, coordination, visual perception and other skills important for driving and operating machinery safely. Actual tests of marijuana-intoxicated drivers have clearly shown that their driving is impaired, yet they tend to think they are driving better than usual. In several surveys 60 to 80 percent of marijuana users said they sometimes drive while high.

Although not physically addicting, people can be-

* 1979.

come psychologically hooked on the drug. Marijuana may aggravate existing emotional problems. The most common adverse emotional effect is an "acute panic reaction," in which the user may become terrified and paranoid and require hospital treatment. In 1978, some 10,000 persons were treated in hospital emergency rooms for adverse marijuana reactions.

Lung damage. Marijuana cigarettes are unfiltered and smokers tend to inhale deeply, exposing sensitive lung tissue to potent, irritating chemicals. One study among marijuana smokers showed that five marijuana cigarettes a week were more damaging to the lungs than six packs of cigarettes smoked over the same period. Marijuana smoking irritates the air passages and diminishes the amount of air the lungs can hold and exhale, the studies show.

Like tobacco, marijuana smoke impairs lung defenses against infections and foreign inhaled matter. In animal studies, it has caused extensive lung inflammation. Bronchitis may occur in people who smoke marijuana regularly.

Marijuana smoke contains 150 chemicals in addition to THC, and the effects of most of these are not known. One ingredient is benzopyrene, a known cancer-causing agent that is 70 percent more abundant in marijuana smoke than in tobacco smoke. There is also more "tar" in marijuana than in high-tar cigarettes. When painted on the skin of mice, marijuana tar can produce tumors. However, there is as yet no good evidence of any cancer-causing effects in people. If there is such an effect, it is not likely to become apparent for another two decades.

Heart effects. Marijuana has an even greater effect on heart function than tobacco. It can raise the heart rate by as much as 50 percent. This is of no known consequence to young healthy persons. But in those with poor heart function, this effect can be dangerous and may also produce chest pains (angina). Most doctors would caution heart patients to steer clear of marijuana.

Hormone and reproductive effects. Several, but not all, studies have shown that marijuana smoking can lower the level of the male sex hormone, testosterone, in the blood, though it usually remains within the range of normal. Sperm abnormalities, including reduced numbers of sperm and abnormal sperm movement and shapes, have also been found in relation to marijuana use.

In females, preliminary studies suggest an adverse effect on the menstrual cycle in 40 percent of the women who smoke marijuana at least four times a week. The result may be infertility. In animal studies, the levels of growth hormone and the female sex hormones, estrogen and progesterone, have been reduced by marijuana.

Marijuana can cross the placenta and reach the developing fetus; pregnant monkeys given THC were far more likely to suffer abortions or deliver dead babies.

Studies by Dr. Gabriel G. Nahas of Columbia University showed an effect of marijuana on the hypothalamus, the body's master gland that directs the functions of other hormone-producing glands.

Immune impairment. Evidence from both animal and human studies have suggested damage to basic body defenses against disease. However, it is not known whether marijuana smokers are any more likely to get sick than other persons of similar life circumstances. As the National Institute on Drug Abuse concludes in its latest report to Congress on marijuana: "It is very difficult to anticipate the problems which will arise in a given society in advance. Thus, any attempt to compare the health impact of marijuana with that of alcohol and tobacco at *current* levels of use is certain to minimize the hazards of marijuana."

James T. Baker

HOW DO WE FIND THE STUDENT IN A WORLD OF ACADEMIC GYMNASTS AND WORKER ANTS?

Anatole France once wrote that "the whole art of teaching is only the art of awakening the natural curiosity of young minds." I fully agree, except I have to wonder if, by using the word "only," he thought that the art of awakening such natural curiosity was an easy job. For me, it never has been—sometimes exciting, always challenging, but definitely not easy.

Robert M. Hutchins used to say that a good education prepares students to go on educating themselves throughout their lives. A fine definition, to be sure, but it has at times made me doubt that my own students, who seem only too eager to graduate so they can lay down their books forever, are receiving a good education.

But then maybe these are merely the pessimistic musings of someone suffering from battle fatigue. I have almost qualified for my second sabbatical leave, and I am scratching a severe case of the seven-year itch. About the only power my malaise has not impaired is my eye for spotting certain "types" of student. In fact, as the rest of me declines, my eye seems to grow more acute.

Has anyone else noticed that the very same students

people college classrooms year after year? Has anyone else found the same bodies, faces, personalities returning semester after semester? Forgive me for violating my students' individual "personhoods," but reality makes it so tempting to see them as types. Doubtless you will recognize at least some of them. They have twins, or perhaps clones, on your campus, too.

There is the eternal Good Time Charlie (or Charlene), who makes every party on and off the campus, who by November of his freshman year has worked his face into a case of terminal acne, who misses every set of examinations because of "mono," who finally burns himself out physically and mentally by the age of 19 and drops out to go home and recuperate, and who returns at 20 after a long talk with Dad to major in accounting.

There is the Young General Patton, the one who comes to college on an R.O.T.C. scholarship and for a year twirls his rifle at basketball games while loudly sniffing out pinko professors, who at midpoint takes a sudden but predictable, radical swing from far right to far left, who grows a beard and moves in with a girl who refuses to shave her legs, who then makes the just as predictable, radical swing back to the right and ends up preaching fundamentalist sermons on the steps of the student union while the Good Time Charlies and Charlenes jeer.

There is the Egghead, the campus intellectual who shakes up his fellow students—and even a professor or two— with references to esoteric formulas and obscure Bulgarian poets, who is recognized by friend and foe alike as a promising young academic, someday to be a professional scholar, who disappears every summer for six weeks ostensibly to search for primeval human remains in Colorado caves, and who at 37 is shot dead by Arab terrorists while on a mission for the C.I.A.

There is the Performer—the music or theater major, the rock or folk singer—who spends all of his or her time working up an act, who gives barely a nod to mundane subjects like history, sociology, or physics, who dreams only of the day he or she will be on stage full time, praised by critics, cheered by audiences, who ends up either pregnant or responsible for a pregnancy and at 30 is either an insurance salesman or a housewife with a very lush garden.

There is the Jock, of course—the every-afternoon intramural champ, smelling of liniment and Brut, with bulging calves and a blue-eyed twinkle, the subject of untold numbers of female fantasies, the walking personification of he-man-ism—who upon graduation is granted managerial rank by a California bank because of his golden tan and low golf score, who is seen five years later buying the drinks at a San Francisco gay bar.

There is the Academic Gymnast—the guy or gal who sees college as an obstacle course, as so many stumbling blocks in the way of a great career or a perfect marriage— who strains every moment to finish and be done with "this place" forever, who toward the end of the junior year begins to slow down, to grow quieter and less eager to leave, who attends summer school, but never quite finishes those last six hours, who never leaves "this place," and who at 40 is still working at the campus laundry, still here, still a student.

There is the Medal Hound, the student who comes to college not to learn or expand any intellectual horizons but simply to win honors—medals, cups, plates, ribbons, scrolls—who is here because this is the best place to win the most the fastest, who plasticizes and mounts on his wall every certificate of excellence he wins, who at 39 will be a colonel in the U.S. Army and at 55 Secretary of something or other in a conservative Administration in Washington.

There is the Worker Ant, the student (loosely rendered) who takes 21 hours a semester and works 49 hours a week at the local car wash, who sleeps only on Sundays and during classes, who will somehow graduate on time and be the owner of his own vending-machine company at 30 and be dead of a heart attack at 40, and who will be remembered for the words chiseled on his tombstone:

All This Was Accomplished Without Ever Having So Much As Darkened The Door Of A Library.

There is the Lost Soul, the sad kid who is in college only because teachers, parents, and society at large said so, who hasn't a career in mind or a dream to follow, who hasn't a clue, who heads home every Friday afternoon to spend the weekend cruising the local Dairee-Freeze, who at 50 will have done all his teachers, parents, and society said to do, still without a career in mind or a dream to follow or a clue.

There is also the Saved Soul—the young woman who has received, through the ministry of one Gospel freak or another, a Holy Calling to save the world, or at least some special part of it—who majors in Russian studies so that she can be caught smuggling Bibles into the Soviet Union and be sent to Siberia where she can preach to souls imprisoned by the Agents of Satan in the Gulag Archipelago.

Then, finally, there is the Happy Child, who comes to college to find a husband or wife—and finds one—and there is the Determined Child, who comes to get a degree—and gets one.

Enough said.

All of which, I suppose, should make me throw up my hands in despair and say that education, like youth and love, is wasted on the young. Not quite.

For there does come along, on occasion, that one of a hundred or so who is maybe at first a bit lost, certainly puzzled; who may well start out a Good Timer, an Egghead, a Performer, a Jock, a Medal Hound, a Gymnast, a Worker Ant; who may indeed have trouble settling on a major, who will be distressed by what sometimes passes for education, who might even be a temporary dropout; but who has a vital capacity for growth and is able to fall in love with learning, who acquires a taste for intellectual pleasure, who becomes in the finest sense of the word a Student.

This is the one who keeps the most jaded of us going back to class after class, and he or she must be oh-so-carefully cultivated. He or she must be artfully awakened, given the tools needed to continue learning for a lifetime, and let grow at whatever pace and in whatever direction nature dictates.

For I try always to remember that this student is me, my continuing self, my immortality. This person is my only hope that my own search for Truth will continue after me, on and on, forever.

Norman Cousins

BACK TO HIPPOCRATES

People speak about holistic medicine today as though it were a new concept. Essentially, it is 2,000 years old. Hippocrates said it first when he spoke of the healing resources of the individual human being. Hippocrates viewed the treatment of disease as a dual process. One part was represented by systematic medicine; the other part was the full activation of the patient's own healing system. Since those early beginnings, however, there has been a consistent gravitational shift away from the patient as the center of the healing process. Increasingly, the physician came to the fore as the dominant force.

Once again, however, after 2,000 years, there is a shift in emphasis. Today the role of the patient in overcoming disease and maintaining good health is coming to the forefront. The perceptions of Hippocrates are given scientific substance by new knowledge about the ability of the human brain to exercise a measure of control over the autonomic nervous system. The end result, inevitably, is increased respect for the concept of the physician-patient partnership. Research about the functioning of the immunological system is bringing us back to the original Hippocratic concept of the patient not as a passive vessel into which the physician pours his therapeutic skills and his medicaments, but as a sovereign human being capable of generating powerful responses to disease.

To be sure, there is nothing new about knowledge concerning the effects of fear, panic, dread, despair, depression, hate, and rage on the total human organism. What is new is the growing knowledge concerning the biochemical effects of the will to live, hope, faith, confidence, cheerfulness, and laughter. The ancient idea that the healing system is connected to a belief system—that attitudes play a vital part in the recovery process—is finding systematic verification in current medical research. At the Menninger Foundation in Topeka, Kansas, and at dozens of other medical centers throughout the world, people are being treated for illnesses by mind-training that demolishes the notion that the brain is barred from any supervisory function over the autonomic nervous system.

These developments are not juxtaposed against modern medicine and surgery but are an integral part of it. A good place to observe these ideas at work is at St. Joseph Hospital in Houston, Texas, where Dr. John Stehlin, oncologist and surgeon, works with patients whose prospects for recovery had been considered to be slight. Dr. Stehlin doesn't minimize the seriousness of their illness in talking to patients, but he puts most of his emphasis on the patient's will to live and on a confident approach to treatment. The cancer floor at St. Joseph Hospital features what is called "The Living Room." It is a place where people take leave of their apprehensions and where they can generate good spirits. Dr. Stehlin has a blue-ribbon collection of video cassettes of comedies.

Even the nuns are expected by Dr. Stehlin to contribute to the upbeat mood. I heard one of the nuns tell a patient about an episode in a nightclub. As she told it, the headwaiter was astonished to see a man slip off his chair and fall under the table. "Madam," he said, "your husband has just slipped under the table." "Sir," she said, "my husband has just come through the door."

Does laughter have any beneficial effects? The evidence is mounting that it does. Dr. William Fry of Stanford University School of Medicine, who is one of the leading researchers in this field, points to the fact that laughter enhances respiration and stimulates the endocrine system.

Drs. Jonathan Levine and Howard Fields of the University of California, San Francisco, have done research showing that laughter stimulates endorphin and encephalin activity, thus accounting for the phenomenon frequently observed that hearty belly laughter sometimes sets the stage for pain-free sleep. Meanwhile, there seems to be little doubt that the physical activity induced by laughter is a form of internal jogging that confers benefits of its own.

Few things are more characteristic of severely ill patients than their emotional needs. Serious disease almost always produces fear and even panic. The reason so many cancer patients have difficulty in sleeping is not just because of their pain but because of their fears. Similarly, the reason so many heart-attack patients never reach the hospital is not just because of the condition itself but because the panic-produced constriction of the blood vessels imposes an additional and intolerable burden on the heart.

It is clear, therefore, that treatment of physical illness without corresponding attention to the emotional needs of the patient can only have a partial effect. Conversely, the physician who gives appropriate attention to the emotional needs of his patients not infrequently finds that he has helped clear the way for the effective use of his ministrations. Here in Los Angeles, working with cancer patients, I have observed that patients who "program" themselves emotionally to make good use of chemotherapy are generally the ones who are best able to tolerate powerful medication.

There is little doubt about the fact that fear is the great accelerator of disease. Conversely, hope, faith, confidence, and the will to live set an auspicious stage for efforts toward recovery. The physician, therefore, must be an expert not just in chasing disease germs but in pursuing the connection between the human belief system and the healing system.

GLOSSARY

Abstract and concrete are ways of describing important qualities of language. Abstract words are not associated with real, material objects that are related directly to the five senses. Such words as "love," "wisdom," "patriotism," and "power" are abstract because they refer to ideas rather than to things. Concrete language, on the other hand, names things that can be perceived by the five senses. Words like "table," "smoke," "lemon," and "halfback" are concrete. Generally you should not be too abstract in writing. It is best to employ concrete words naming things that can be seen, touched, smelled, heard, or tasted in order to support your more abstract ideas.

Allusion is a reference to some literary, biographical, or historical event. It is a "figure of speech" (a fresh, useful comparison) used to illuminate an idea. For instance, if you want to state that a certain national ruler is insane, you might refer to him as a "Nero"—an allusion to the Emperor who burned Rome.

Alternating method in comparison and contrast involves a point-by-point treatment of the two subjects that you have selected to discuss. Assume that you have chosen five points to examine in a comparison of the Volkswagen "Rabbit" (subject A) and the Honda "Accord" (subject) B): cost, comfort, gas mileage, road handling, and frequency of repair. In applying the alternating method, you would begin by discussing cost in relation to A + B; then comfort in relation to A + B, and so on. The alternating method permits you to isolate points for a balanced discussion.

Ambiguity means uncertainty. A writer is ambiguous when using a word, phrase, or sentence that is not clear. Ambiguity usually results in misunderstanding, and should be avoided in essay writing. Always strive for clarity in your compositions.

Analogy is a form of figurative comparison that uses a clear illustration to explain a difficult idea or function. It is unlike a formal comparison in that its subjects of comparison are from different categories or areas. For example, an analogy likening "division of labor" to the activity of bees in a hive makes the first concept more concrete by showing it to the reader through the figurative comparison with the bees.

Antonym is a word that is opposite in meaning to that of another word: "hot" is an antonym of "cold"; "fat" is an antonym of "thin"; "large" is an antonym of "small."

Argumentation is a form of writing in which you offer reasons in favor of or against something. (See Chapter 9, pp. 291–293).

Block method in comparison and contrast involves the presentation of all information about your first subject (A), followed by all information about the second subject (B). Thus, using the objects of comparison explained in the discussion of the "alternating method" (see entry, p. 365), you would for the block method first present all five points about the Volkswagen. Then you would present all five points about the Honda. When using the block method, remember to present the same points for each subject, and to provide an effective transition in moving from subject A to subject B.

Causal analysis is a form of writing that examines causes and effects of events or conditions as they relate to a specific subject (see Chapter 8, pp. 246–248).

Characterization is the description of people. As a particular type of description in an essay, characterization attempts to capture as vividly as possible the features, qualities, traits, speech, and actions of individuals.

Chronological order is the arrangement of events in the order that they happened. You might use chronological order to trace the history of the Vietnam War, to explain a scientific process, or to present the biography of a close relative or friend. When you order an essay by chronology, you are moving from one step to the next in time.

Classification is a pattern of writing where the author divides a subject into categories and then groups elements in each of those categories according to their relationships to each other (see Chapter 6, pp. 174–175).

Clichés are expressions that were once fresh and vivid, but have become tired and worn from overuse. "I'm so hungry that

I could eat a horse" is a typical cliché. People use clichés in conversation, but writers should generally avoid them.

Closings or "conclusions" are endings for your essay. Without a closing, your essay is incomplete, leaving the reader with the feeling that something important has been left out. There are numerous closing possibilities available to writers: summarizing main points in the essay; restating the main idea; using an effective quotation to bring the essay to an end; offering the reader the climax to a series of events; returning to the conclusion and echoing it; offering a solution to a problem; emphasizing the topic's significance; or setting a new frame of reference by generalizing from the main thesis. Whatever type of closing you use, make certain that it ends the essay in a firm and emphatic way.

Coherence is a quality in effective writing that results from the careful ordering of each sentence in a paragraph, and each paragraph in the essay. If an essay is coherent, each part will grow naturally and logically from those parts that come before it. Coherence depends on the writer's ability to organize materials in a logical way, and to order segments so that the reader is carried along easily from start to finish. The main devices used in achieving coherence are *transitions,* which help to connect one thought with another.

Colloquial language is language used in conversation and in certain types of informal writing, but rarely in essays, business writing, or research papers. There is nothing wrong with colloquialisms like "cool," "What's happening?" or "pal" when used in conversational settings. However, they are often unacceptable in essay writing—except when used sparingly for special effects.

Comparison/contrast is a pattern of essay writing treating similarities and differences between two subjects. (See Chapter 4, pp. 105–106).

Composition is a term used for an essay or for any piece of writing that reveals a careful plan.

Concrete (See Abstract/Concrete)

Connotation/denotation are terms specifying the way a word has meaning. Connotation refers to the "shades of meaning" that a word might have because of various emotional associations it calls up for writers and readers alike. Words like "American," "physician," "mother," "pig," and "San Francisco" have strong connotative overtones to them. With denotation, however, we are concerned not with the suggestive meaning of a word but with its exact, literal meaning. Denotation refers to the "dictionary definition" of a word—its exact meaning. Writers must understand the connotative and denotative value of words, and must control the shades of meaning that many words possess.

Context clues are hints provided about the meaning of a word by another word or words, or by the sentence or sentences coming before or after it. Thus in the sentence, "Mr. Rome, a true *raconteur*, told a story that thrilled the guests," we should be able to guess at the meaning of the italicized word by the context clues coming both before and after it. (A "raconteur" is a person who tells good stories.)

Definition is a method of explaining a word so that the reader knows what you mean by it. (See Chapter 5, pp. 141–142.)

Derivation is how a word originated and where it came from. Knowing the origin of a word can make you more aware of its meaning, and more able to use it effectively in writing. Your dictionary normally lists abbreviations (for example, O.E. for Old English, G. for Greek) for word origins and sometimes explains fully how they came about.

Description is a type of writing that uses details of sight, color, sound, smell, and touch to create a word picture and to explain or illustrate an idea. (See Chapter 1, pp. 1–2.)

Dialogue is the exact duplication in writing of something people say to each other. Dialogue is the reproduction of speech or conversation; it can add concreteness and vividness to an essay, and can also help to reveal character. When using dialogue, writers must be careful to use correct punctuation. Moreover, to use dialogue effectively in essay writing, you must develop an ear for the way other people talk, and an ability to create it accurately.

Diction refers to the writer's choice or use of words. Good diction reflects the topic of the writing. Orwell's diction, for example, is formal, despite colloquial language in the spoken dialogue he quotes. Least Heat Moon's diction (Chapter 1) is more varied, including subtle descriptions in standard diction and conversational sarcasms. Levels of diction refer both to the purpose of the essay and to the writer's audience. Skillful choice of the level of diction keeps the reader intimately involved with the topic.

Division is that aspect of classification (see Chapter 6, pp. 174–275) where the writer divides some large subject into categories. For example, you might divide "fish" into salt water and fresh water fish; or "sports" into team and individual sports. Division helps writers to split large and potentially complicated subjects into parts for orderly presentation and discussion.

Effect is a term used in causal analysis (see Chapter 8, pp. 246–248) to describe the outcome or expected result of a chain of happenings. When dealing with the analysis of effects, writers should determine whether they want to work with immediate or final effects, or both. Thus, a writer analyzing the effects of an accidental nuclear explosion that happened in 1956 might choose to analyze effects immediately after the blast, as well as effects that still linger.

Emphasis suggests the placement of the most important ideas in key positions in the essay. Writers can emphasize ideas simply by placing important ones at the beginning or at the end of the paragraph or essay. But several other techniques help writers to emphasize important ideas: (1) key words and ideas can be stressed by repetition; (2) ideas can be presented in climactic order, by building from lesser ideas at the beginning to the main idea at the end; (3) figurative language (for instance, a vivid simile) can call attention to a main idea; (4) the relative proportion of detail offered to support an idea can emphasize its importance; (5) comparison and contrast of an idea with other ideas can emphasize its importance; and (6) mechanical devices like underlining, capitalizing, or using exclamation points (all of which should be used sparingly) can stress significance.

Essay is the name given to a short prose work on a limited topic. Essays take many forms, ranging from a familiar narrative account of an event in your life, to explanatory, argumentative, or critical investigations of a subject. Normally, in one way or the other, an essay will convey the writer's personal ideas about the subject.

Euphemism is the use of a word or phrase simply because it seems less distasteful or less offensive than another word. For instance, "mortician" is a euphemism for "undertaker"; "sanitation worker" for "garbage collector."

Fable is a narrative with a moral (see Chapter 4, p. 107). The story from which the writer draws the moral can be either true or imaginary. When writing a fable, it is important that a writer clearly presents the moral to be derived from the narrative, as Rachel Carson does in "A Fable for Tomorrow."

Figurative language, as opposed to *literal,* is a special approach to writing that departs from what is typically a concrete, straightforward style. It involves a vivid, imaginative comparison that goes beyond plain or ordinary statements. For instance, instead of saying that "Joan is wonderful," you could write that "Joan is like a summer's rose" (a *simile*); "Joan's hair is wheat, pale and soft and yellow" (a *metaphor*); "Joan is my Helen of Troy" (an *allusion*); or a number of other comparative approaches. Note that Joan is not a rose, her hair is not wheat, nor is she some other person named Helen. Figurative language is not logical; instead, it requires an ability on the part of the writer to create an imaginative comparison in order to make an idea more striking.

Flashback is a narrative technique in which the writer begins at some point in the action and then moves into the past in order to provide necessary background information. Flashback adds variety to the narrative method, enabling writers to approach a story not only in terms of straight chronology, but in terms of a back-and-forth movement. However, it is at best a very difficult technique and should be used with great care.

General/specific words are necessary in writing, although it is wise to keep your vocabulary as specific as possible. General words refer to broad categories and groups, while specific words capture with more force and clarity the nature of a term. The distinction between general and specific language is always a matter of degree. "A woman walked down the street" is more general than "Mrs. Walker walked down Fifth Avenue," while "Mrs. Webster, elegantly dressed in a muslin suit, strolled down Fifth Avenue" is more specific than the first two examples. Our ability to use specific language depends on the extent of our vocabulary. The more words we know, the more specific we can be in choosing words.

Illustration is the use of several examples to support our idea (see Chapter 4, p. 10).

Imagery is clear, vivid description that appeals to our sense of sight, smell, touch, sound, or taste. Much imagery exists for its own sake, adding descriptive flavor to an essay, as when Richard Selzer in "The Discus Thrower" writes, "I unwrap the bandages from the stumps, and begin to cut away the black scabs and the dead, glazed fat with scissors and forceps. A shard of white bone comes loose." However, imagery can also add meaning to an essay. For example, in Francke's essay, the pattern of imagery connected with the setting and procedure of her abortion alerts the reader to the importance of that event in the author's life. Again, when Orwell writes at the start of "A Hanging," "It was in Burma, a sodden morning of the rains. A sickly light, like yellow tinfoil, was slanting over the high walls into the jail yard," we see that the author uses imagery to prepare us for the sombre and terrifying event to follow. Writers can use imagery to contribute to any type of wording, or they can rely on it to structure an entire essay. It is always difficult to invent fresh, vivid description, but it is an effort that writers should make if they wish to improve the quality of their prose.

Introductions are the beginning or openings of essays. Introductions should perform a number of functions. They should alert the reader to the subject, set the limits of the essay, and indicate what the thesis (or main idea) will be. Moreover, they should arouse the reader's interest in the subject, so that the reader will want to continue reading into the essay. There are several devices available to writers that will aid in the development of sound introductions.

1. Simply state the subject and establish the thesis. See the Jade Snow Wong essay (p. 3), and "The Three New Yorks" (p. 186).

2. Open with a clear, vivid description of a setting that will become important as your essay advances. Save your thesis for a later stage, but indicate what your subject is. See the essay by Patricia Cayo Sexton (p. 9).

3. Ask a question or a series of questions, which you

might answer in the introduction or in another part of the essay. See the Jordan essay (p. 149).

4. Tell an anecdote (a short, self-contained story of an entertaining nature) that serves to illuminate your subject. See the Jacoby essay (p. 281).

5. Use comparison or contrast to frame your subject and to present the thesis. See the Russell Baker essay (p. 114).

6. Use several examples to reinforce your statement of the subject. See the Rensberger essay (p. 260).

7. Begin by stating your personal attitude toward a controversial issue. See the James Baker essay (p. 358).

These are only some of the devices that appear in the introductions to essays in this text. Writers can also ask questions, give definitions, or provide personal accounts—there are many techniques that can be used to develop introductions. The important thing to remember is that you *need* an introduction to an essay. It can be a single sentence or a much longer paragraph, but it must accomplish its purpose—to introduce readers to the subject, and to engage them so that they want to explore the essay further.

Irony is the use of language to suggest the opposite of what is stated. Writers use irony to reveal unpleasant or troublesome realities that exist in life, or to poke fun at human weaknesses and foolish attitudes. For instance, in "A Hanging," the men who are in charge of the execution engage in laughter and lighthearted conversation after the event. There is irony in the situation and in their speech because we sense that they are actually very tense—almost unnerved—by the hanging; their laughter is the opposite of what their true emotional state actually is. Many situations and conditions lend themselves to ironic treatment.

Jargon is the use of special words associated with a specific area of knowledge or a specific profession. It is similar to "shop talk" that members of a certain trade might know, but not necessarily people outside it. For example, in Bettleheim's essay there are several terms or applications of jargon relating to psychology. Use jargon sparingly in your writing, and be certain to define all specialized terms that you think your readers might not know.

Journalese is a level of writing associated with prose types normally found in newspapers and popular magazines. A typical newspaper article tends to present information factually or objectively; to use simple language and simple sentence structure; and to rely on relatively short paragraphs. It also stays close to the level of conversational English without becoming chatty or colloquial.

Metaphor is a type of figurative language in which an item from one category is compared briefly and imaginatively with an item from another area. Writers create metaphors to assign meaning to a word in an original way.

Narration is telling a story in order to illustrate an important idea (see Chapter 2, pp. 30–31).

Objective/subjective writing refers to the attitude that writers take toward their subject. When writers are objective, they try not to report their own personal feelings about their subject. They attempt to control, if not eliminate, their own attitude toward the topic. Thus in the essay by Rensberger (see pp. 260–265), we learn about how different food tastes are formed or acquired, but we don't learn about the writer's own tastes in food. Many essays, on the other hand, reveal the authors' personal attitudes and emotions. In Bradbury's essay (see pp. 85–90) the author's personal excitement over Halloween seems clear. He takes a highly subjective approach to the topic. For some kinds of college writing, such as business or laboratory reports, research papers, or literary analyses, it is best to be as objective as possible. But for many of the essays in composition courses, the subjective touch is fine.

Order is the manner in which you arrange information or materials in an essay. The most common ordering techniques are *chronological order* (involving time sequence); *spatial order* (involving the arrangement of descriptive details); *process order* (involving a step-by-step approach to an activity); *deductive order* (in which you offer a thesis and then the evidence to support it); and *inductive order* (in which you present evidence first and build toward the thesis). Some rhetorical patterns such as comparison and contrast, classification, and argumentation require other ordering techniques. Writers should select those ordering principles that permit them to present materials clearly.

Paradox is a statement that *seems* to be contradictory but actually contains an element of truth. Writers use it in order to call attention to their subject.

Parallelism is a variety of sentence structure in which there is "balance" or coordination in the presentation of elements. "I came, I saw, I conquered" is a good example of parallelism, presenting both pronouns and verbs in a coordinated manner. Parallelism can also be applied to several sentences and to entire paragraphs (see the Syfers' essay, pages 310–313). It can be an effective way to emphasize ideas.

Personification is giving an object, thing, or idea lifelike or human qualities. For instance, Ray Bradbury personifies Halloween when he writes that it "didn't just stroll into our yards" (see p. 87). Like all forms of figurative writing, personification adds freshness to description, and makes ideas vivid by setting up striking comparisons.

Point of view is the angle from which a writer tells a story. Many personal or informal essays take the *first-person* (or "I") point of view, as the essays by Wong, Moon, Lee, Francke, Hughes, Orwell, Williams, Bradbury, and others reveal. The first-person "I" point of view is natural and fitting for essays when the writer wants to speak in a familiar and intimate way to the reader. On the other hand, the *third-person* point of view ("he," "she," "it," "they") distances the reader somewhat from the writer. The third-person point of view is useful in essays where writers are not talking exclusively about themselves, but about other people, things, and events, as in the essays by Rensberger, Carson, and White. Occasionally, the second-person ("you") point of view will appear in essays, notably in essays involving process analysis where the writer directs the reader to do something; part of Ernest Hemingway's essay (which also utilizes third-person point of view) uses this strategy. The position that you take as a writer depends largely on the type of essay you write.

Prefix is one or more syllables attached to the front of another word in order to influence its meaning or to create a new word. A knowledge of prefixes and their meanings aids in establishing the meanings of words and in increasing the vocabulary that we use in writing. Common prefixes and their meanings include *bi-*(two), *ex-*(out, out of), *per-*(through), *pre-*(before), re-(back), *tele-*(distant), and *trans-*(across, beyond).

Process analysis is a pattern of writing that explains in a step-by-step way the methods for doing something or reaching a desired end (see Chapter 7, pp. 214–215).

Proposition is the main point in an argumentative essay. It is like a *thesis* except that it usually presents an idea that is debatable or can be disputed.

Refutation is a technique in argumentative writing where you recognize and deal effectively with the arguments of your opponents. Your own argument will be stronger if you can refute—prove false or wrong—all opposing arguments.

Root is the basic part of a word. It sometimes aids us in knowing what the larger word means. Thus if we know that the root *doc*-means "teach" we might be able to figure out a word like "doctrine." *Prefixes* and *suffixes* are attached to roots to create words.

Sarcasm is a sneering or taunting attitude in writing. It is designed to hurt by ridiculing or criticizing. Basically, sarcasm is a heavy-handed form of irony, as when an individual says, "Well, you're exactly on time, aren't you" to someone who is an hour late, and says it with a sharpness in the voice, a sharpness designed to hurt. Writers should try to avoid sarcastic writing and to use more acceptable varieties of irony and satire to criticize their subject.

Satire is the humorous or critical treatment of a subject in order to expose the subject's vices, follies, stupidities, and so forth. Syfers, for instance, satirizes stereotyped notions of wives, hoping to change these attitudes by revealing them as foolish. Satire is a better weapon than sarcasm in the hands of the writer because satire is used to correct, whereas sarcasm merely hurts.

Sentimentality is the excessive display of emotion in writing, whether it is intended or unintended. Because sentimentality can distort the true nature of a situation, writers should use it cautiously, or not at all. They should be especially careful when dealing with certain subjects, for example the death of a loved one, remembrance of a mother or father, a ruined romance, the loss of something valued, that lend themselves to sentimental treatment. Only the best writers—Thomas, Francke, Hughes, and others in this text—can avoid the sentimental traps rooted in their subjects.

Simile is an imaginative comparison using "like" or "as." When Orwell writes, "A sickly light, like yellow tinfoil, was slanting over the high walls into the jail yard," he uses a vivid simile in order to reinforce the dull description of the scene.

Slang is a level of language that uses racy and colorful expressions associated more often with speech than with writing. Slang expressions like "Gerald's my boss man" or "That chick is groovy" should not be used in essay writing, except when the writer is reproducing dialogue or striving for a special effect. Hughes is one writer in this collection who uses slang effectively to convey his message to the reader.

Suffix is a syllable or syllables appearing at the end of a word and influencing its meaning. As with prefixes and roots, you can build vocabulary and establish meanings by knowing about suffixes. Some typical suffixes are *-able* (capable of), *-al* (relating to), *-ic* (characteristic of), *-ion* (state of), *-er* (one who) appear often in standard writing.

Symbol is something that exists in itself but also stands for something else. Thus the "stumps" in paragraph 20 of Selzer's essay "The Discus Thrower" are not just the patient's amputated legs, but they serve as symbols of the man's helplessness and immobility. As a type of figurative language, the symbol can be a strong feature in an essay, operating to add depth of meaning, and even to unify entire essays.

Synonym is a word that means roughly the same as another word. In practice, few words are exactly alike in meaning. Careful writers use synonyms to vary word choice, without ever moving too far from the shade of meaning intended.

Theme is the central idea in an essay; it is also often termed the *thesis.* Everything in an essay should support the theme in one way or another.

Thesis is the main idea in an essay. The *thesis sentence,* appearing early in the essay, and normally somewhere in the first paragraph, serves to convey the main idea to the reader in a clear way. It is always useful to state your central idea as soon as possible, and before you introduce other supporting ideas.

Title for an essay should be a short, simple indication of the contents of your essay. Titles like "Backdrop of Poverty," "Death in the Open," "The Ambivalence of Abortion," and

"Why Marriages Fail" are the sorts of titles that convey the central subjects of these essays in brief, effective ways. Always provide titles for your essays.

Tone is the writer's attitude toward his or her subject or material. An essay writer's tone may be objective ("Arizona 87"), ironic ("I Want A Wife"), comic ("Salvation"), nostalgic ("Tricks! Treats! Gangway!"), or a reflection of numerous other attitudes. Tone is the "voice" that you give to an essay; every writer should strive to create a "personal voice" or tone that will be distinctive throughout any type of essay under development.

Transition is the linking of one idea to the next in order to achieve essay coherence (See *Coherence*). Transitions are words that connect these ideas. Among the most common techniques to achieve smooth transition are: (1) repeating a key word or phrase; (2) using a pronoun to refer back to a key word or phrase; (3) relying on traditional connectives like "thus," "for example," "moreover," "therefore," "however," "finally," "likewise," "afterwards," and "in conclusion"; (4) using parallel structure (see *Parallelism*); and (5) creating a sentence or an entire paragraph that serves as a bridge from one part of your essay to the next. Transition is best achieved when the writer presents ideas and details carefully and in logical order. Try not to lose the reader by failing to provide for adequate transition from idea to idea.

Unity is that feature in an essay where all material relates to a central concept and contributes to the meaning of the whole. To achieve a unified effect in an essay, the writer must design an introduction and conclusion, maintain a consistent tone and point of view, develop middle paragraphs in a coherent manner, and always stick to the subject, never permitting unimportant elements to enter. Thus, unity involves a successful blending of all elements that go into the creation of a sound essay.

Vulgarisms are words that exist below conventional vocabulary, and which are not accepted in polite conversation. Berlitz lists many vulgarisms in his essay. Always avoid vulgarisms in your own writing.

Acknowledgments

Maya Angelou, "The Flight," from *I Know Why the Caged Bird Sings* by Maya Angelou. Copyright © 1968 by Maya Angelou. Reprinted by permission of Random House, Inc.

James T. Baker, "How Do We Find the Students in a World of Academic Gymnasts and Worker Ants?" from *The Chronicle of Higher Education*. Copyright © 1982 by The Chronicle of Higher Education. Reprinted with permission.

Russell Baker, "The Two Ismo's," from *The New York Times*, 1982. Copyright © 1982 by The New York Times Company. Reprinted by permission.

Charles F. Berlitz, "The Etymology of the International Insult," from *Penthouse Magazine*. Copyright © 1970 by Charles F. Berlitz and reprinted with permission of Penthouse International, Ltd.

Bruno Bettelheim, "Fairy Tales and Modern Stories," from *The Uses of Enchantment: The Meaning and Importance of Fairy Tales*, by Bruno Bettelheim. Copyright © 1976 by Bruno Bettelheim. Reprinted by permission of Alfred A. Knopf, Inc.

Ray Bradbury, "Tricks! Treats! Gangway!" from *Reader's Digest*, October 1975. Copyright © 1975 by Ray Bradbury. Reprinted by permission of Don Congdon Associates, Inc.

Jane E. Brody, "The Evidence Builds Against Marijuana," from *The New York Times*, May 21, 1980. Copyright © 1980 by The New York Times Company. Reprinted by permission.

Rachel Carson, "A Fable for Tomorrow," from *Silent Spring* by Rachel Carson. Copyright © 1962 by Rachel Carson. Reprinted by permission of Houghton Mifflin Company.

Norman Cousins, "Back to Hippocrates," from *Saturday Review*, February, 1982. Copyright © 1982 Saturday Review Magazine. Reprinted by permission.

Jane Doe, "I Wish They'd Do It Right," from *The New York Times*, September 23, 1977. Copyright © 1977 by The New York Times Company. Reprinted by permission.

Annette Dula, "No Home in Africa," from *The New York Times*, July 27, 1975. Copyright © 1975 by The New York Times Company. Reprinted by permission.

Dr. Wayne W. Dyer, "Avoiding Immobilization," from *Your Er-*

Janet Selzer, Trustees. Reprinted by permission of Simon & Schuster, Inc.

Patricia Cayo Sexton, "Backdrop of Poverty," from pages 1–2 in *Spanish Harlem: Anatomy of Poverty* by Patricia Cayo Sexton. Reprinted by permission of Harper & Row, Publishers, Inc.

John Slote, "The Social Sport," from *Esquire*, July 1982: "Sports Clinic." Copyright © 1982 by John Slote. Reprinted by permission of John Slote.

Adam Smith, "A Very Short History of Some American Drugs Familiar to Everybody," from *Powers of Mind* by Adam Smith. Copyright © 1975 by Adam Smith. Reprinted by permission of Random House, Inc.

Judy Syfers, "I Want a Wife," from *The First Ms. Reader*. Copyright © 1970 by Judy Syfers.

Lewis Thomas, "Death in the Open," from *The Lives of a Cell* by Lewis Thomas. Copyright © 1973 by The Massachusetts Medical Society. Originally published in the *New England Journal of Medicine*. Reprinted by permission of Viking Penguin, Inc.

Judith Viorst, "Friends, Good Friends—and Such Good Friends." Copyright © 1977 by Judith Viorst. Originally appeared in *Redbook*.

E. B. White, "The Three New Yorks," from pages 121–122 in "Here Is New York," in *Essays of E. B. White*. Copyright © 1949 by E. B. White. Reprinted by permission of Harper & Row, Publishers, Inc.

Randall Williams, "Daddy Tucked the Blanket," from *The New York Times*, July 10, 1975. Copyright © 1975 by The New York Times Company. Reprinted by permission.

Elizabeth Wong, "The Struggle to Be an All-American Girl." Originally appeared in the *Los Angeles Times*. Reprinted by permission of Elizabeth Wong.

Jade Snow Wong, "Uncle Kwok," from pages 44–45 in *Fifth Chinese Daughter* by Jade Snow Wong. Copyright 1950 by Jade Snow Wong. Reprinted by permission of Harper & Row, Publishers, Inc.

Ben Yagoda, "What Every Man Should Know: How to Keep Your Place Nice," from *Esquire*, August 1983. Copyright © 1983 by Ben Yagoda. Reprinted by permission of Ben Yagoda.